**Designed for Delight** Alternative aspects of twentieth-century decorative arts

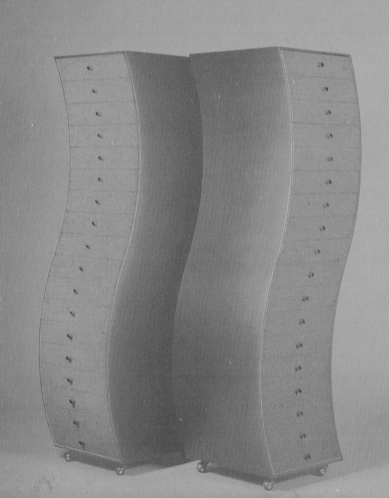

# Designed for Delight

## Alternative aspects of twentieth-century decorative arts

Edited by Martin Eidelberg

Essays by Steven C. Dubin, Martin Filler, Lenore Newman, Witold Rybczynski, and Jan L. Spak

Montreal Museum of Decorative Arts

Flammarion

Paris–New York

Participating Institutions
Canadian Museum of Civilization, Hull, Quebec
Cincinnati Art Museum, Cincinnati, Ohio
Montreal Museum of Decorative Arts, Montreal, Quebec
Musée des Arts Décoratifs, Paris
Muzeum Narodowe w Krakowie, Krakow
Die Neue Sammlung, Munich
J. B. Speed Art Museum, Louisville, Kentucky
Virginia Museum of Fine Arts, Richmond, Virginia

Exhibition Committee
Yvonne Brunhammer, Diane Charbonneau, Martin Eidelberg, Martin Filler, Marilyn Fish,
Louise Giroux, Toni Greenbaum, David A. Hanks, Michael McTwigan, Luc d'Iberville-Moreau,
Lenore Newman, Jan L. Spak, Alice Zrebiec

Designed for Delight: Alternative Aspects of Twentieth-Century Decorative Arts
This exhibition and its international tour are sponsored by Philip Morris Companies Inc.

Additional funding has been provided by the Ministry of Canadian Heritage, The Canada Council,
The W. Garfield Weston Foundation, and two anonymous Canadian foundations.

Montreal Museum of Decorative Arts
in association with
Flammarion
26, rue Racine, 75006 Paris
200 Park Avenue South, Suite 1406, New York, NY  10003

Library of Congress Cataloging-in-Publication Data

Musée des arts décoratifs de Montréal.
    Designed for Delight : alternative aspects of twentieth-century decorative arts / edited by Martin
Eidelberg.
        p.     cm.
    Exhibition catalog.
    Includes bibliographical references and index.
    ISBN 2-08-013595-3
    1. Decorative arts – History – 20th century – Exhibitions.
2. Modernism (Art) – Influence – Exhibitions.     I. Eidelberg, Martin
P.      II. Title
NK789.M87      1997
745'.074714'28 – dc21                                    96-52180

ISBN: 2-08013-595-3 (HB); ISBN: 2-08013-594-5 (PB)
Numéro d'édition: 1306 (HB); 1307 (PB)
Dépôt légal: May 1997

Designed by Hahn Smith Design, Toronto
Origination by Welcrome, Paris
Printed by Milanostampa, Italy

# Contents

# Sponsor's Statement

This pioneering exhibition presents a fascinating new view of design during the past hundred years. *Designed for Delight: Alternative Aspects of Twentieth-Century Decorative Arts* shows how the century's most respected designers and craftspeople looked beyond prevailing trends to create unprecedented works imbued with intelligence and humor. By presenting handcrafted works within the context of international design, the exhibition offers a fresh perspective on everyday objects that are part of our lives.

We applaud the Montreal Museum of Decorative Arts for its leadership in building the remarkable and comprehensive collection that forms the basis of this exhibition. In light of our commitment to promoting cultural exchange, we are delighted that this exhibition will be shown in major cultural centers of both Europe and North America, bringing highlights of an extraordinary collection to a diverse audience.

At Philip Morris, we have been active in the arts for nearly forty years. Our support of *Designed for Delight* reflects our long-standing involvement with craft and our interest in encouraging education and creativity in the arts. It is our hope that the relationships we have built with communities around the world will continue to grow and flourish through our participation in this exhibition.

*Geoffrey C. Bible*
Chairman and Chief Executive Officer
Philip Morris Companies Inc.

# Foreword

Since the Montreal Museum of Decorative Arts opened its doors to the public on 14 June 1979 as Canada's first museum devoted exclusively to the decorative arts, our focus has been to collect objects of international scope from the post-World War II period. Today our collection has earned recognition as one of the most comprehensive in North America, embracing all media — furniture, glass, ceramics, jewelry, metalware, and textiles — and representing a full range of mass-produced design and contemporary crafts. Through the publication of catalogues devoted to interpreting its permanent collection and through an active program of traveling exhibitions, the museum has made its collection available to an increasingly interested public, and has made a significant contribution to scholarship on twentieth-century design. *Eva Zeisel: Designer for Industry* (1984), *Design 1935–1965: What Modern Was* (1991), and *Frank Gehry: New Bentwood Furniture Designs* (1992) are but several of the museum's traveling exhibitions to have received critical acclaim. The survey exhibition *What Modern Was* marked the culmination of ten years of acquisitions and showcased the breadth of the museum's collection up to that point. Its accompanying catalogue was recognized by the Art Libraries Association of North America as one of the five best art books produced that year and it has since become a standard reference for the period.

We are now in the closing years of the twentieth century, an era that has wrought irreversible changes in the way we think and live. *Designed for Delight: Alternative Aspects of Twentieth-Century Decorative Arts* takes advantage of this rare opportunity to reconsider the progressive theories that have helped shape modern life. For the present exhibition, we have chosen to turn our attention to the entire century and reexamine commonly held beliefs about design. *Designed for Delight* maintains that despite exhortations to the contrary, important twentieth-century decorative arts have displayed those very qualities of individualization and personal expression that Modernist dictums sought to suppress. We believe it affirms the human capacity for *joie de vivre*, even in, or perhaps due to, the most turbulent of times.

In the belief that a museum's excellence should be judged by the quality of its collections, and with the immeasurable support of generous donors and advisors, we have devoted considerable energy to acquiring significant objects of quality and sharing them with an appreciative public. Our firm intent is to render masterpieces of twentieth-century decorative arts accessible to as broad an audience as possible. We hope that *Designed for Delight* will testify to this commitment and allow more people to partake of the pleasure we derive from these works.

*Mrs. David M. Stewart*
President, Montreal Museum of Decorative Arts

# Preface

In contemplating the museum's second major survey exhibition, we were excited by several prospects. The most obvious, of course, was to present a chronological sequel to *Design 1935–1965: What Modern Was*, highlighting our notable collection of more recent design and crafts, to which we have devoted considerable attention in the past ten years. However, a more intriguing possibility was to revisit the whole of twentieth-century decorative arts from our *fin de siècle* position, reevaluating through the museum's collection the most staunchly held beliefs of Modernism — fitness to purpose, lack of ornamentation, truth to materials, universality of expression, all factors that intentionally led to the standardization and sanitization of design. We wanted to present a more encompassing overview of the century's production, which in reality points to a broader interpretation of modern design. This interpretation proposes that there was a parallel path within Modernism that did not adhere to a rigid program of austerity, but rather succumbed to the intervention of such human qualities as humor and delight. Indeed, designers throughout the twentieth century created a vast array of significant objects that fell outside the narrow scope of traditional Modernist thought, objects that demonstrate quite forcefully that functionalism has not been the sole guide of Modernism.

Immediately, we embarked upon an exhibition scheme. The result is *Designed for Delight: Alternative Aspects of Twentieth-Century Decorative Arts*, which is demarcated by the turns of two centuries. The scope of this exhibition necessitated that we go beyond our original collecting mandate and procure representative objects from the early part of the century, as well as augment our already notable collection of late-century objects. It was recognized from the beginning that the examples of early twentieth-century design we obtained could not possibly rival in number those of the latter years, but they should both complement our present collection and reveal the unity of twentieth-century design for the purpose of the exhibition. The objects selected from all periods corroborate the underlying theme of the exhibition: that antirationalist and antifunctionalist forces played a major role in twentieth-century decorative arts. Of course, many of the Postmodern objects already in our collection, especially those from the 1980s, clearly embodied these forces. But it was only when we looked beyond that inventive decade that we saw just how pervasive those forces were throughout the entire century. Although almost all objects in the exhibition are from the museum's own collection, additional pieces have been borrowed from several private collections and from the Montreal Museum of Fine Arts, with whom we have established a new association.

*Designed for Delight* covers many major stylistic movements, from Art Nouveau and Art Deco to Postwar and Postmodern, and includes a full range of media, attesting to the creativity and energy of this century's most respected designers and craftspeople. The four themes of the exhibition explore aspects of twentieth-century decorative arts — ornament; the use of the body as an element of design; the unexpected or surprising inversion of standard design elements; and that rich mine of inspiration, fantasy — that hitherto fell outside the purview of traditional scholarship on modern design. And because the objects are organized thematically rather than chronologically, the resulting juxtapositions from different parts of this century illustrate the unsuspected unity of twentieth-century design.

This exhibition catalogue also represents a departure from standard practice. Instead of providing critical commentary for each object, as was done for *What Modern Was*, we have chosen to present the artist's own words, where possible, to accompany his or her work. The artist's voice, we feel, allows each object to speak for itself and permits the viewer to penetrate the creative process. In the case of deceased artists who left insufficient written legacy, we have turned to then-contemporary critics or modern historians for pertinent commentary. In the catalogue, we are delighted to feature several essays by scholars of international stature. These essays help place the exhibition in a proper historical perspective as well as provide provocative analysis of the subject.

This exhibition and the accompanying publication are the result of a long collaboration between members of the museum's staff and a team of consulting scholars. The idea was first conceived in 1991 by Martin Eidelberg, advisor to the museum's previous traveling exhibition, *Design 1935–1965: What Modern Was*, and skilled editor of its accompanying catalogue. Instead of organizing a chronological sequel to this exhibition, the team proposed an exhibition that would explore a new direction for scholarship in twentieth-century design. This path would reveal aspects of this century's aesthetic beyond the strictly Modernist tenets of functionalism and rationalism. In addition, it would present, ideally, the artists' own voices. We are immeasurably indebted to the consulting scholars for their contributions, and particularly to Dr. Eidelberg, editor of this catalogue, for his keen intellect, extensive knowledge, and judicious guidance.

The coordination of the exhibition and catalogue was implemented with profound dedication and proficiency by the museum's staff in Montreal and New York. Diane Charbonneau, Head, Collections Management, smoothed the way through this exhibition's many challenges with her usual resourcefulness, enthusiasm, and careful determination. The job of verifying registrarial information fell to Anne-Marie Chevrier, who accomplished this task with unswerving perseverence. Object verification was scrupulously accomplished by Beth Morgan and Elizabeth Lewis. Annick Houle, Estelle Thibodeau, Suzanne Taylor, Jacques Suprenant, and Cheryl François each made particular contributions. We are indebted to Marcel Marcotte for his discerning design for the installation of this exhibition. Beth Morgan and staff photographer Giles Rivest are responsible for the striking images in the catalogue, with additional photography skillfully carried out by Richard P. Goodbody, New York. Photography permissions and additional archival photographs were painstakingly researched by Linda-Anne D'Anjou with the able assistance of Anne-Marie Chevrier.

For his constant encouragement and commitment to the museum, we owe special thanks to David A. Hanks, an invaluable collaborator since the museum's inception. As project coordinator, Jan L. Spak has been responsible for numerous aspects of the exhibition, including overseeing the publication, coordinating curatorial decisions, and co-authoring the thematic essays of the catalogue; throughout, her dedication and attention to detail have been admirable. Lenore Newman has contributed to many phases of the project, including cataloguing the objects, supervising the research, and co-authoring the thematic essays. Eldon Wong ably helped with acquisitions and administrative details at the beginning of the project, and with great efficiency Dorys Codina provided managerial assistance towards the end. Special thanks go to Cynthia Brown for her skill and constant good cheer.

The research for the project presented special challenges. We extend our utmost appreciation to Louise Giroux and Marilyn Fish, who pursued this challenge so zealously. In addition, Toni Greenbaum and Michael McTwigan assisted in their respective specialties, jewelry and ceramics, with both research and advice on acquisitions. We are especially indebted to Yvonne Brunhammer, whose close relationship with the museum has brought increasingly rewarding results. Martin Filler's writing skills and knowledge of twentieth-century design added considerably to the concepts of this exhibition. In his engaging essay, Witold Rybczynski has once again demonstrated his capacity to integrate the arts with cultural phenomena. Finally, Steven C. Dubin has provided provocative sociological insights in his essay. For their invaluable work in translating texts, we are indebted to Jacques Bédard, Christina di Stefano, David Radzinowicz Howell, Philippa Hurd, Paul Jackson, Toshiko Mori, Joan Rosasco, Frederik Takkenberg, and Suzanne Tise.

Such an ambitious exhibition could only be achieved through the unstinting cooperation of many participants. Above all, we owe our deepest gratitude to the artists and designers included in this exhibition for the illuminating words that make their objects come alive. The contribution of the following has greatly enlivened this exhibition: Ron Arad, Junichi Arai, Sergio Asti, Rudy Autio, Ralph Bacerra, Alfredo Barbini, Flavio Barbini, Mario Botta, Andrea Branzi, Wendell Castle, Peter Chang, Dale Chihuly, Tony Costanzo, Ramón Puig Cuyás, Gunnar Cyrén, Riccardo Dalisi, Roseline Delisle, Tom Dixon, Guido Drocco, Donato D'Urbino, Robert Ebendorf, Ken Ferguson, Arline M. Fisch, Gianfranco Frattini, Pedro Friedeberg, Stephen Frykholm, Frank Gehry, Massimo Iosa Ghini, Piero Gilardi, Mieczyslaw Górowski, Red Grooms, Dorothy Hafner, Alfred Hofkunst, Fujiwo Ishimoto, Elizabeth Browning Jackson, Kiyoshi Kanai, Eleanor and Henry Kluck, Jack Lenor Larsen, Beth Levine, Ross Littell, Oliver Lundquist, Lysiane Luong, Adelle Lutz, Peter Macchiarini, Enzo Mari, Ingo Maurer, Peter Max, Franco Mello, Alessandro Mendini, Bruce Metcalf, Floris Meydam, Olivier Mourgue, Enrico de Munari, Richard Notkin, Sue Palmer, David Palterer, Nathalie Du Pasquier, Gaetano Pesce, Giò Pomodoro, Gerd Rothmann, Niki de Saint-Phalle, Astrid Sampe, Ruth Adler Schnee, Joyce Scott, Ettore Sottsass, the late Eddie Squires, Philippe Starck, Reiko Sudo, Janna Syvänoja, Toshiko Takaezu, Matteo Thun, Shigeru Uchida, Masanori Umeda, Maciej Urbaniec, Massimo Vignelli, Peter Voulkos, Hans Wegner, and Arnold Zimmerman.

Without the generosity of the following, we would not have achieved the research goals of our exhibition. Many scholars, archivists, and family members and friends of the designers have willingly and generously shared information, especially concerning the deceased artists included in the exhibition. Those who aided with information about the artists and their specific works include: Laurens d'Albis; Peter Anker, former Director, Vestlandske Kunstindustrimuseum, Bergen; Cesare Birignani and Pola Cecchi, Studio Most; Whitney Blousen; Geneviève Bonté, Bibliothèque des Arts Décoratifs, Paris; Dr. Marjan Boot, Curator, Haags Gemeentemuseum, The Hague; Bruno Busetti, Istituto Italiano di Cultura, Montreal; Anne Chafe, the Seagram Museum, Waterloo, Ontario; Paul Chénier, Librarian, Canadian Centre for Architecture, Montreal; Anita Colpron; Priscilla Cunningham; J. D. van Dam, Curator of Ceramics, Rijksmuseum, Amsterdam; Erica Davies, Freud Museum, London; Franco Deboni; Ulysses G. Dietz, Curator, Decorative Arts, and Library, The Newark Museum, Newark, New Jersey; Norbert Drey; T. G. te Duits, Curator, Stichting Nationaal Glasmuseum Leerdam, Leerdam; J. Alastair Duncan; Claudine Dupré and Jean-René Lasonde, Bibliothèque Nationale du Québec; Elisabetta Epifori, Museo di Doccia, Doccia; Antoinette Faÿ-Hallé, Chief Curator, Musée National de Céramique, Sèvres; Jane Fisher, Photographic Equipment Museum, Eastman Kodak Company, Rochester, New York; Barnaba Fornasetti; the Frelinghuysen Arboretum Library, Morristown, New Jersey; Maria Galetta, Italian Cultural Institute, New York; Philippe Garner, Sotheby's, London; Todd

Gustavson and Becky Simmons, George Eastman House, Rochester, New York; Widar Halén, Curator, Kunstindustrimuseet i Oslo, Oslo; Bodil Hartman, Royal Danish Consulate General, New York; Amy Hau, The Isamu Noguchi Garden Museum, New York; Hedvig Hedqvist; Italian Trade Commission, New York and Atlanta; Barbro Hovstadius, Nationalmuseum, Stockholm; Mary Dodge Hujsak, Librarian, American Craft Council, New York; Madeleine Jenewein, assistant to Hans Hollein; Charlotte Hüni-Rondeau, Musée Municipal de Longwy, Longwy; Sam Jornlin, assistant to Peter Voulkos; The Juliette K. and Leonard S. Rakow Research Library, The Corning Museum of Glass, Corning, New York; Kaj Ove Jørgensen, Sct. Peders Kirke, Slagelse; Dan Klein; John and Kieron Kramer; Anne Lajoix; Barbara Lynn; Gérard Malabre; Félix Marcilhac; Nicole Maritch-Haviland; Richard McBride, Meriden Public Library, Meriden, Connecticut; Connie McNally, Silver Magazine; Susan Mellor, Design Library, New York; The Museum of Modern Art, New York; Milena Mussi; Marie Norberg, Swedish Information Service, Consulate General of Sweden, New York; Bengt Nyström, Nordiska Museet, Stockholm; Guido Niest, assistant to Lino Sabattini; Eunice Pardon; Janice Parente and Valérie Villeglé, Archives Niki de Saint-Phalle, Paris; Evelyne Possémé, Curator, Musée des Arts Décoratifs, Paris; Dr. Benton Seymour Rabinovitch; Madame Michel Renson, Curator, Archives Municipales, Nancy; Marie-Claude Saia, Montreal Museum of Fine Arts; Laurence Shukor, assistant to Philippe Starck; Kristian Rafn Sørensen; Monica Steger, Assistant to Mario Botta; Stephen Van Dyk, Librarian, and Joanne Warner, Assistant Curator, Wallcoverings, Cooper-Hewitt, National Design Museum, New York; Dr. Angela Völker, Curator, Österreichisches Museum für angewandte Kunst, Vienna; The Thomas J. Watson Library, The Metropolitan Museum of Art, New York.

For important information about the objects, many manufacturers, studios, and retailers have offered invaluable assistance. Among them are Reinhard Backhausen, Joh. Backhausen & Söhne; Jörg Brinkmann, H. Bahlsens Keksfabrik KG; Karen S. Chambers and Joanna Sikes, Chihuly Studio; George DeSotle, Springs Industries; Flavia Destefanis, Director of Communications and Development, Vignelli & Associates; Hélène Dulude, Bauer Inc.; Joël Feigly, Puiforcat Orfèvre; The Fabric Workshop; Roberto Gasparotto, Archivist, Venini S.p.A.; Anne Gros, Christofle; Nina Aase Hestness, Theodor Olsens Eftf.; Paul Jackson; Peter A. Jeffs; Ingegerd Johansson, Kosta Boda; Sue Kerry, Warner Fabrics; Anne Lacroix and Tamara Préaud, Manufacture Nationale de Sèvres; François Le Ciclé, Haviland; Christian Leclercq, Société des Céramiques d'Art de Longwy; Claus Lorenz, Friedrich Otto Schmidt; Matteo Mattioli, Artemide S.p.A; Jan van der Meer, Alterego; Tim Nix, Time Inc.; Inger Nordgren, Curator, Keramiskt Centrum, Gustavsberg Porslin; Birgitta Nordmark, Hackman Rörstrand AB; Shima Pezeu, Kuramata Design Office; Leonard J. Rawson, Kurz-Kasch, Inc.; Beatrice Riesenfelder, Wiener Porzellanmanufaktur Augarten; Chantal Roos, Beauté Prestige International; Royal Leerdam Glassworks; Cynthia L. Shulga, The Napier Co.; John I. Taylor, Zenith Electronics Corporation; Miki Uono, Nuno Corporation; Petra Werner, Archivist, Rosenthal AG; Carol Whitehouse, Pozzi-Ginori Co. of America.

An active acquisition program mounted over the past few years has yielded excellent results. Acquisitions were directed toward completing the themes of the exhibition, while giving focus to the museum's growing collection of twentieth-century objects. To our advisory committee — George Beylerian, Helen Williams Drutt English, Jack Lenor Larsen, Toshiko Mori — we are indebted for their knowledge and vision, and to our many donors we cannot adequately express our gratitude. Among the numerous collectors and dealers who have been instrumental in accomplishing our acquisition policy, we would like to acknowledge

Mr. and Mrs. Jean-Jacques Boucher, Vivian and David M. Campbell, Garth Clark, Dr. René Crépeau, Samuel Esses, Paul Leblanc, Mark and Esperanza Schwartz, and Mr. and Mrs. Charles Stendig.

As with any collection of historical objects, those presented in this exhibition were often in need of expert conservation. The skilled conservators in Canada and the United States to whom we owe our sincere gratitude are: Michel Cauchon, Director, and Sharon Little and Suzanne Holme, Conservators, Centre de Conservation du Québec, Quebec; Marlene Eidelheit, Conservator, The Cathedral Church of St. John the Divine, New York; Mary Clerkin Higgins; and Hermes Knauer, Conservator, and Chris Paulocik, Conservator, Costume Institute, The Metropolitan Museum of Art, New York. For assistance in obtaining photographs, we would like to thank Pauline Cadieux, Canadian Embassy, Rome, and Caroline Hancock, Director of Communications, Michael Graves, Architect.

The comprehensive educational component of this exhibition has been developed jointly with several of the participating venues. We wish to thank the following for their significant contributions: Anita J. Ellis, Curator of Decorative Arts, Cincinnati Art Museum, Cincinnati; Ronald Epps, Assistant Special Programs Coordinator, Virginia Museum of Fine Arts, Richmond; Sandra Lorimer, Director, Exhibitions and Design, Canadian Museum of Civilization, Hull; and especially Cynthia Moreno, Director of Education, J. B. Speed Art Museum, who was instrumental in developing the family guide, and also the website with Sharon Colton and Ron Schildknecht, University of Louisville. Public relations has been ably handled by Claire Thériault, Public Relations Officer, Montreal Museum of Decorative Arts, and by Frederick C. Schroeder, Sophie Henderson, and Sascha D. Freudenheim of Resnicow Schroeder, New York.

The task of producing a publication of this nature can be daunting. Flammarion has lent a great deal of support to the project and proved the perfect partner for a joint English-French publication. Suzanne Tise, Director of Flammarion's English Language Publications, has been involved in the project from the beginning and has provided considerable expertise in facilitating the production of the catalogue, as has Philippa Hurd, Editor. Sheila Schwartz adroitly copyedited the manuscript in the early stages, Christa Weil applied her consummate skills to this task as the catalogue neared production, and Sheila O'Leary was an expert proof-reader. We are extremely grateful to Hahn Smith Design for the masterful design and layout of the book.

We are beholden to the staff of the Macdonald Stewart Foundation, which has been a steady source of support. To James Carroll, Director of the foundation, we owe a special debt. He has magnanimously overseen the exhibition and catalogue from inception to fruition, and has patiently advised on all aspects of its execution. We would also like to offer our special thanks to Lucille Riley for her indefatigable efficiency. To the American Friends of Canada, in particular Stanley M. Ackert III, we are exceedingly grateful for expediting the acquisition of numerous objects that appear in the exhibition.

In these difficult economic times, an ambitious exhibition such as this would not be possible without substantial support from funding partners. We gratefully acknowledge the beneficence of Philip Morris Companies Inc., sponsor of this exhibition, long known for its generous support of the arts. Karen Brosius, Director, Corporate Contributions, along with Stephanie French, Vice President of Corporate Contributions and Cultural Programs, offered unflagging enthusiasm for the exhibition's objectives; Marilynn Donini, Jennifer Goodale, and Kaiko Hayes, Cultural Programs, diligently oversaw the many details of the project; and Douglas Wink was responsible for the engaging designs of the brochure, poster, and other printed materials accompanying the exhibition. The publication has been subsidized by a generous grant from The Canada Council and the Ministry of Canadian Heritage, and we would particularly like to thank Doug Sigurdson for recognizing the significance of this project. Board member Marian Bradshaw was instrumental in helping to secure key grants from Canadian foundations. We acknowledge the generosity of The W. Garfield Weston Foundation and two anonymous Canadian foundations for their continued support.

Without doubt, we owe our sincerest thanks to Mrs. David M. Stewart and the late David M. Stewart for their initial commitment to promoting scholarship and appreciation of twentieth-century crafts and design. Mrs. Stewart has continued to provide the support that makes this exhibition possible.

*Luc d'Iberville-Moreau*
Director, Montreal Museum of Decorative Arts

**Note on the Use of the Catalogue**

Dimensions are in centimeters, followed by inches in parentheses, taken to the nearest sixteenth of an inch. Height precedes width precedes depth. In measurements of textiles, warp precedes weft. Jewelry is measured across, in closed position.

Marks in script or printed in italics are rendered here in italics.

An asterisk following a donor's name indicates an object given to the American Friends of Canada and placed on permanent loan to the museum from the American Friends of Canada.

After its initial reference in the endnotes, the Montreal Museum of Decorative Arts will be abbreviated as MMDA.

**Designed for Delight**  Alternative aspects of twentieth-century decorative arts

# Modernism's Alter Ego

*by Martin Filler*

If there is one popular perception of the modern movement in architecture and design, it is that of severity: an aesthetic devoid of the decorative intricacy and pictorial charm that most people associate with the Western art tradition before the twentieth century. To a certain extent that misapprehension is justified, for mainstream histories of the innovative art and design of this century have more often than not excluded those tendencies that do not fit into the formative image of Modernism as it was promulgated in the 1920s and 1930s. The vision of Modernism put forth in the United States by Henry-Russell Hitchcock, Philip Johnson, and Alfred H. Barr, Jr., in their epochal 1932 show at the Museum of Modern Art, *Modern Architecture: International Exhibition*, and Johnson's 1934 MoMA survey, *Machine Art*, was paralleled by the polemical writings in Britain of Nikolaus Pevsner (whose *Pioneers of the Modern Movement* first appeared in 1936) and in Switzerland by those of Siegfried Giedion (whose *Space, Time and Architecture: The Growth of a New Tradition* was initially published in 1941). Together, those highly persuasive advocates of the machine aesthetic in Modernism succeeded in making theirs the dominant point of view in the years after World War II, when modern architecture and design for the first time became internationally accepted by developers and manufacturers.

But the triumph of the International Style was also a victory of suppression. Those offshoots of Modernism that did not fit neatly into the Procrustean bed built by its establishment leaders were lopped off, as it were, consigned to a historical limbo curiously at odds with the supposed objectivity of the ascendant aesthetic. There were selective exceptions, to be sure. The immensely influential Design Collection of New York's Museum of Modern Art, founded in 1935, included several examples of anti-rationalist Art Nouveau design, although those objects were placed in a linear historical development that paradoxically excluded the Art Deco period that was its direct successor. By the late 1920s, the machine aesthetic had fixed itself so firmly in the minds of MoMA's founders as the true faith of architecture and design that Art Deco was rejected out of hand as a mere commercial bastardization of Modernism.

The revisionist attitudes that have reshaped our understanding of modern architecture and design since the decline in the 1970s of the International Style's hegemony have also prompted a more thoroughgoing reevaluation of the long-forgotten aspects of Modernism that fall outside the realm of reductivism, utilitarianism, and rationalism. This, which might be called the secret history of Modernism, is only now beginning to come to full light. In the process, the selective bias that was an essential component of the International Style program is being exposed as an exercise in aesthetic sanitization. Our sense of innovative twentieth-century design can no longer be what the polemicists of sixty years ago wished it to appear to be. Though it now seems highly doubtful that the age of Modernism is over, as a new generation of polemicists proposed in the late 1970s, it certainly does seem as though our interpretation of what Modernism was and continues to be has irrevocably changed.

*Designed for Delight: Alternative Aspects of Twentieth-Century Decorative Arts* is an investigation of those aspects of Modernism that had been conveniently excluded from the received establishment canon. The inclusive historical, geographical, and categorical range of the objects chosen to illustrate tendencies contrary to canonical Modernist beliefs is indication enough that such work was not some sporadic aberration but in fact constitutes an entirely parallel, alternative development. If one needs,

Fig. 1. Marcel Breuer, living room,
Piscator apartment, Berlin, 1927.

Fig. 2. English, living room, London, 1969.

Fig. 3. Mario Buatta, living room,
Kips Bay Decorator Show House, New York, 1987.

as the proposition goes, an exception to prove the rule, these exceptional designs taken as a whole indicate that only at the end of the century of Modernism are we able to formulate a truly representative perspective on the movement as a whole as well as on some of its most intriguing individual manifestations.

This exhibition affirms that Modernism was no monolith and that, for all the movement's high moral purpose and urgent social program, the pleasure principle also played an important role in the applied arts. "The practical object," the German architect and designer Peter Behrens was quoted as decreeing in 1901, "does not seem any longer entirely subservient to mere utility, but combines therewith a certain degree of pleasure."[1] Admittedly, there are those who find undeniable pleasure in the conventional image of Modernist design — chaste, unadorned, and therefore seemingly functional — but the works included in this exhibition demonstrate that those very restrictions fed countercurrents of creativity among those who believed that a contemporary aesthetic need not be ascetic. As Irene Sargent wrote in her defense of Art Nouveau published in 1902, "Decorative or domestic art has assumed an importance which even a century ago it could not have been believed to possess. Through it the personality of the present age expresses itself as strongly as through more practical mediums, and our generation, like those which have preceded it, sees itself mirrored in works of the imagination."[2]

And what imagination the creators of these unexpected objects have had! Transformations worthy of Ovid's *Metamorphoses* break forth at every turn, changing mundane furnishings of everyday life into magical presences charged with a vitality that forces us to reconsider the often unchallenged premises of useful design. If, as Sigmund Freud proposed, "We are so made that we can derive intense enjoyment only from a contrast, ..."[3] then the quite startling nature of these maverick objects offers a wonderful antidote to the supposed truths of mainstream Modernism. In fact, it is only in architecture and design that such a narrow outlook prevailed. It would be as if the history of twentieth-century painting focused on Purism and the New Objectivity, but ignored Expressionism and Surrealism. The correspondences between many of the objects in this exhibition and contemporaneous movements in the fine arts is case enough for a closer look at these once-forbidden products of what might be considered the alter ego of Modernism.

The long denial of the irrepressible instincts expressed in different ways in each of the objects on view here recalls the observation that the Swedish designer Stig Lindberg made in 1952: "Beauty without pleasure is sterile in the same way that intelligence without humor often means a genuine stupidity."[4] Similarly, at the end of a century marked by such surpassing sadness, it would be tragic indeed if we did not better inform ourselves of the life-enhancing impulses celebrated in objects, life-enhancing impulses that speak directly to human concerns as old as design itself and as new as today.

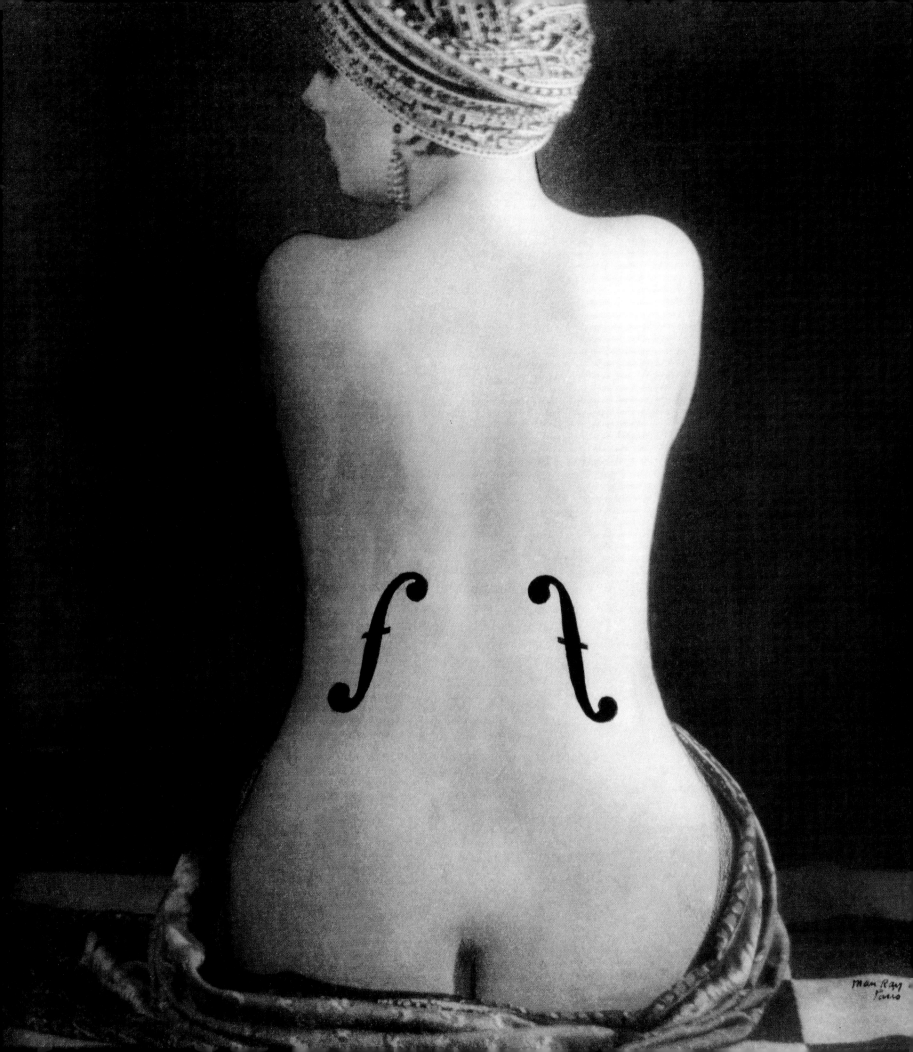

# Bodies of Thought, Bodies of Evidence

*by Steven C. Dubin*

*Nothing human is alien to me.*
—Terence, *The Self-Tormentor*[1]

The human body is undoubtedly the most fundamental template for aesthetic expression and design. In most cultures, both fine artists and artisans have modeled some of their creations upon the human form (save certain notable instances where religious taboos expressly impeded such endeavors). The body is ubiquitous: it can be a source of inspiration, a compelling metaphor, and an indispensable building block for cultural creations, both high and low. It serves as the basis for a broad variety of representations that traverse historical era, geography, ideology, and artistic style and medium.

Who can imagine artists without the human form, especially the female form? As John Berger argues in his enormously popular *Ways of Seeing*, ever since the Renaissance, wealthy male patrons have commissioned paintings that either venerated their material accomplishments, or allowed them to gaze upon a seemingly endless supply of sexually available women, passively waiting to be taken.[2] Whether these prizes were inanimate or animate, they were commodities to be displayed and savored. For Berger, oil paintings from about 1500 to 1900 primarily recorded the man's place within the world.

Even when, by the late nineteenth century, significant shifts in patronage (and society as a whole) engendered a series of stylistic movements that broke the chokehold of academic styles and subjects, the body in general, and the female body in particular, remained central to the artistic enterprise. As Berger argues, this is as true of a French nineteenth-century Salon painting as it is of today's advertising campaigns, many of which incorporate or mirror older works.

Modernism, in other words, has not significantly altered the traditional depiction of women as the submissive, attainable object of male desire. Such images serve to objectify the female, just as they help ratify male power, enabling men symbolically to capture and control women.

At the same time, the relative paucity of nude male images in the cultural archive signals our greater discomfort with looking at, and thereby objectifying, male bodies. This disparity is now more obvious than ever, and is being increasingly challenged. The Guerrilla Girls, that cheeky band of anonymous women who puncture the sanctity of the New York art world, put it this way in a pithy 1989 broadside: "Do women have to be naked to get into the Met. Museum? Less than 5% of the artists in the Modern Art Sections are women, but 85% of the nudes are female."[3] Although we are still a long way from gender parity in the cultural sphere, certain people are now closely monitoring the matter.

Make a pilgrimage some time to the Freud Museum in the Hampstead district of London. This was the home where Freud died in 1939, having been driven from his native Vienna by the Nazis the year before. Here he recreated his study and famous consulting room, surrounding himself with thousands of books and ancient artifacts, the accumulation of a lifetime. The master's intense presence can still be felt: here is the original psychoanalytic couch; there is the desk where he wrote his acclaimed books. His patients poured out their neuroses in this

Fig. 4. The study of Sigmund Freud, London, the Freud Museum.

Fig. 5. Salvador Dalí, *Venus de Milo with Drawers*,
1936. Bronze with white patina,
ermine buttons, cast iron.
98 x 32.5 x 34 cm (38⁹⁄₁₆ x 12¹³⁄₁₆ x 13⅜ in.).
Brussels, Galerie Patrick Derom.

Fig. 6. Marcel Duchamp, *Please Touch*,
cover for deluxe edition of catalogue, 1947.
Velvet and foam rubber; glass display case.
41.8 x 34.7 x 7.1 cm (16⁷⁄₁₆ x 13⅝ x 2¾ in.).
Paris, Musée National d'Art Moderne, Centre Georges
Pompidou, gift of Daniel Cordier, 1989.

setting, and Freud shaped this raw material into a theory which helps define the twentieth century.

One of the most distinctive features in these chambers is the chair at Freud's desk (fig. 4). Its shape closely models the human body, with arms and a headrest that envelop the sitter. It is not crucial for our purposes to pinpoint the chair's exact date and place of origin. What is important is that you might not want accidentally to stumble upon this chair in the dark. It bears an uncanny resemblance to B-movie space aliens, with its gangly arms and bulbous headrest. It looks as though it could almost stand up and skulk about of its own volition. Being enfolded in its embrace, however, must feel extremely comforting, even womblike.

If we honor Freud's own insights, his choice of furnishings cannot have been accidental. Why did he not buy some sleek model from a modern workshop, like the Wiener Werkstätte, an object more representative of the Modernist triumph of "form follows function"? Rationality may have trumped the irrational when Freud wrote his methodical case studies, but rationality does not seem to have determined his selection of furniture. There is something of a primitive residue in his aesthetic preferences, betraying a stratum of id similar to what primeval sorcerers tapped into, the supernatural *mana* or life force. And that is also why you will spot hundreds of antiquities scattered throughout his office, not the more cerebral nor technologically sophisticated works of artists who were his contemporaries.

Freud's chair reflects a tradition that spans thousands of years wherein the body was adapted as an element of design. For example, sculpted women were recruited to carry the weight of the entablatures of Greek temples upon their stone heads as caryatids (fig. 28). Their male counterpart was the atlas, employed most especially from the Renaissance onward and named after the giant in Greek mythology. Significantly, both caryatids and atlantes stood erect; they bore their burden with dignity, disclosing no signs of strain. The titan Atlas stooped under the weight he supported, however. On the one hand, this may suggest an important counterbalance to the generally unflattering depictions of women as "the weak sex"; on the other, we may be comparing apples and oranges: caryatids and atlantes supported buildings, while Atlas shouldered the entire world.

In the twentieth century, the female body continued to be adapted to the design of furniture and buildings, by avant-garde artists as well as by anonymous roadside architects. For example, Salvador Dalí produced female figures as chiffoniers: in the 1936 drawing *City of Drawers*, a woman's breasts are open drawers with knobs where the nipples should be, and her groin is fitted with a keyhole; in *Venus de Milo with Drawers* (fig. 5), the torso of the renowned statue is the housing for three open drawers with ermine-wrapped handles. The message here is ready sexual access. And Marcel Duchamp playfully designed the catalogue of an exhibition on Surrealism with a three-dimensional foam rubber breast bursting through the cover, and the impudent title *Please Touch* (fig. 6). Duchamp is like a schoolboy, intentionally acting out in public.

On Route 61 in Natchez, Mississippi, stands Mammy's Cupboard, a gas station and rest stop, taking the form of a gigantic Aunt Jemima (fig. 7).[4] She first opened for business in 1939. To convey an idea of the scale, her earrings are horseshoes! Comfort is offered beneath her massive skirt, a sly allusion to the complex sexual and racial hierarchy of the pre-civil rights American South.[5] Duchamp voyeuristically placed the body of a nude woman spread-eagled in the grass behind a wooden door in his *Given That (Étant Donné)* of 1946–66. She can be seen only by peering through a peephole, as in a sleazy movie arcade. As much as Duchamp engaged in dialogue with the most avant-garde movements of his time—Cubism, Dada, Surrealism, and even anticipated Conceptualism—his interest in the female

Fig. 7. Mammy's Cupboard on Route 61, Natchez, Mississippi, c. 1939.

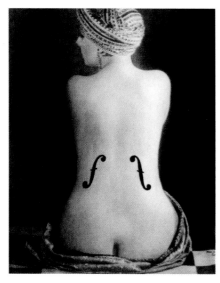

Fig. 8. Man Ray, *Ingres's Violin*, 1924. Silver print, heightened with pencil and india ink. 28.2 x 22.5 cm (11⅛ x 8⅞ in.). Paris, Musée National d'Art Moderne, Centre Georges Pompidou.

body demonstrates some continuity with more traditional artistic practices such as those highlighted by Berger.

Duchamp's fellow modernists likewise explored and built upon the human form. Man Ray used his companion Kiki (née Alice Prin) as the model in his famous photograph *Ingres's Violin* (fig. 8) to draw a parallel between God's creation and human handiwork. In this case he makes a double reference to the painter Ingres, creator of sensuous nudes and also an avid violinist. The same sense of jest is incorporated into Man Ray's *Priapus Paperweight* (fig. 9), an object as streamlined as any factory-designed, machine-age implement but an obvious homage to an eternal design, the male member. It is like a trace of graffiti cast in metal, forthrightly and robustly declaring its presence.

Surrealist René Magritte returned again and again to the female form, with visual equivalents of the literary device of magic realism. The bottles he conceived accommodate the female form to the natural shape of the vessel, as seen in *Lady* (fig. 10), which transubstantiates the human body into something that either serves or is consumed. In his painting *The Rape* (fig. 11), Magritte conflates a woman's torso with her face, creating a startling visual pun: the breasts become eyes, the navel a nose, and the delta of pubic hair a sly grin. While not a literal object in the manner of *Lady*, it objectifies the female physique nevertheless. And his painting of 1947, *Philosophy in the Boudoir*, has an eerie, hallucinatory quality, with a gown sprouting breasts and a pair of shoes with miraculously grown toes. The human essence somehow has been scraped out, leaving only the shell of a person. An alternative interpretation may relate to the amorphousness of identity, which we slip into as easily as a trip to the armoire for an outfit. Both these interpretations, however, take the subject's perspective. It is equally clear in each of Magritte's three works that the woman's body has once again been placed on display for the male's pleasure. From this viewpoint, the woman's body is a receptacle, waiting for the male's desire to fill it up, make it complete; it has been separated from personality and reduced to its sexual parts, no more and no less.

When creations are taken from their original contexts and presented in a fresh setting, they can sometimes activate controversy. For example, when Chicago's Halsted Theatre Center used Magritte's *The Rape* to advertise its production of Franca Rame and Dario Fo's play *Female Parts*, the *Chicago Tribune* rejected the ad, citing its "no nudity" policy. The paper later compromised by covering up the "eyes" and the "mouth."[6] And when rock singer David Bowie used four kouroi (Archaic Greek male statues) on the cover of his *Tin Machine II* album in 1991, Gannett Outdoor of Southern California refused to present the nude images on a Sunset Boulevard billboard, and many record retailers balked at handling the record. Company executives feared that hulking male bodies were simply not acceptable to large segments of the populace—even coated with the patina of legitimacy that history can supply—and the design was subsequently changed.[7] Beauty as well as obscenity, it seems, perpetually remain in the eye of the beholder.

Prehistory had the *Venus of Willendorf* (fig. 35). The Classical era boasted the *Venus de Milo*. But nineteenth-century Londoners and Parisians glimpsed their Venus in the flesh: Saartjie Baartman, also known as "the Hottentot Venus." Baartman, a native of what is now South Africa, was put on public display in 1810 because of her steatopygia, a condition where fatty deposits greatly enlarge the hips and buttocks. She was widely renowned as a "heavy-arsed heathen," and is still not spared cheap shots from present-day commentators: "Inevitably she became the butt of many asinine jokes...," we are informed.[8] After she died of smallpox in 1815, a plaster cast was taken of her body. It is exhibited to this day in the Musée de l'Homme, Paris.

Fig. 9. Man Ray, *Priapus Paperweight*,
1920 (1966 edition). Silver.
12.5 x 9.5 x 9.5 cm (4⅞ x 3¾ x 3¾ in.).
Paris, Lucien Treillard collection.

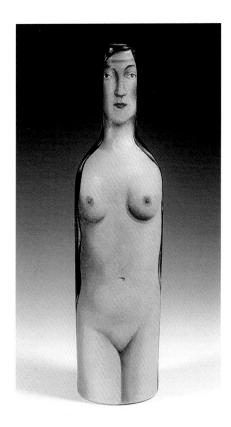

Fig. 10. René Magritte, *Lady*, 1945.
Oil on glass bottle.
Height: 31 cm (12³⁄₁₆ in.).
Belgium, private collection.

Fig. 11. René Magritte, *The Rape*, 1945.
Oil on canvas.
65.3 x 50.4 cm (25¹¹⁄₁₆ x 19⅞ in.).
Paris, Musée National d'Art Moderne,
Centre Georges Pompidou,
bequest of Madame Georgette Magritte, 1987.

Throughout the nineteenth century, the issue of what was suitable for display—and for whom—was hotly contested. According to historian Lawrence Levine, our contemporary notions of high and low, elite and popular culture, did not solidify until late in the last century. Before that hundred-year benchmark, all sorts of cultural expressions were presented simultaneously: Shakespeare along with elephant acts, fine paintings with jugglers. Levine compellingly dissects Chicago's 1893 World Columbian Exposition as an example of this nascent cultural segregation: the White City of classical buildings and serious, informational displays set against the pandemonium of the neighboring Midway Plaisance, with hucksters, the world's first Ferris wheel, and "native villages" populated by ersatz residents.[9]

*The Greek Slave*, a Neoclassical statue by Hiram Powers, a celebrated nineteenth-century American sculptor who worked in Italy, triggered controversy on both sides of the Atlantic. When it was exhibited at London's Crystal Palace in 1851, critics blasted the fact that the nude figure was handcuffed (she represents a Greek Christian captured by the Turks). The sculpture subsequently toured the United States, rousing the concern of certain clergymen in Cincinnati who wished to block its display. After some deliberation they concluded that "since her hands were chained, her undraped condition was beyond her control, and she would not endanger public virtue."[10]

"Public virtue" was the credo of the zealot Anthony Comstock, leader of the New York Society for the Suppression of Vice. He spearheaded a movement to remove all sorts of material, including birth control information, from the public domain. To his censorial mind, the average citizen was simply not equipped to handle certain things. In a celebrated case in 1887, Comstock raided the eminent New York City gallery of M. Knoedler & Co. and arrested the proprietor. It was one thing to sell paintings of nudes, Comstock reasoned; they were collected by the wealthy and cultured, people who would not be adversely affected by them. But Knoedler was also selling photographic reproductions of works of art, some of them with nude figures. To Comstock, this practice was incendiary. Made more accessible and affordable through the new technology of photography, such images could fall into the wrong hands, i.e., the masses, most particularly lower-class men. Comstock believed that if the nude was "kept in its proper place, and out of the reach of the rabble...[then] its power for evil will be far less."[11]

The arena which was (and still is) most prone to spark controversy was art set in a public place. Sure enough, when Jean-Baptiste Carpeaux designed the sculpture *Dance* for the Opéra Garnier in Paris, some people decried it. The work depicts a genie of the dance, encircled by frolicking figures. The genie touched a nerve: the face appears to be female, while the trunk is that of a slender young male. Its unorthodox blending of masculine and feminine features led Napoleon III to order it removed, although the banishment was never carried out.[12]

Vigorous public debate also arose over *Diana*, a statue by Augustus Saint-Gaudens that topped Stanford White's Beaux-Arts masterpiece, Madison Square Garden, in New York in 1891. The nude huntress, nineteen feet tall, disturbed the public's peace of mind, causing male spectators to linger about and prompting a policeman to remark, "People as has kids...says as how she is immoralizing [*sic*], and so they won't let their young ones come here no more. Not as I blames them. I don't think no such statue should be allowed myself, not in a public place."[13] The sculpture was removed after it was deemed too large for the site. It was then relocated to Chicago to adorn a structure at the 1893 World's Columbian Exposition. Not without reservations, however. As the local *Herald* harrumphed, "why invite Diana the huntress to tiptoe...above a building dedicated to agriculture? Is that the proper caper?"[14] The monumental Diana later mysteriously disappeared, but a smaller, thirteen-foot version had been put on the original pedestal in 1892. She reigned there in relative serenity until Madison Square Garden was demolished in 1925. When she was liberated from storage seven years later to be installed in Philadelphia's Fairmont Park, she had not lost her knack to push people's buttons: a local antipornography crusader raised the banner against her, but the campaign quickly fizzled.[15]

At the same time Diana made her first appearance, a similar controversy began to brew with the design of a monumental sculpture for Manhattan's City Hall Park. Frederick MacMonnies conceived the design in 1891, and received his commission for the project in 1909. It was not until 1922 that *Civic Virtue* was actually erected, however, and by then it ran headlong into trouble. The sculptural group consists of a fig-leafed, sword-bearing male figure (Civic Virtue) vanquishing two females, Vice and Corruption, who wriggle beneath him. Between its genesis and actual birth, the world had changed considerably: for instance, the American suffrage movement successfully pressured Congress and a majority of states to ratify the Nineteenth Amendment in 1919–1920, guaranteeing American women the right to vote. Thus by the 1920s, the concept of women solely as dangerous diversions to the manly art of politics seemed outmoded.

The negative response eventually led to the work's banishment to the new Queens Borough Hall in 1941. There it rusticated in peaceful obscurity until 1987, when Queens acquired its first female borough president, Claire Shulman, who attempted to have it exiled once again. This move was stymied primarily by fiscal considerations.[16]

This narrative demonstrates that works of art are *never* completed, but experience cycles of reception: succeeding generations project their own distinctive concerns onto them, complementing or contradicting the original intentions of the artist. For example, the *Venus de Milo*, among the pantheon of great artworks of the Western world, once appeared on a poster advertising Palmolive soap. Despite her seemingly sacrosanct status, local censorship regulations dictated that a white patch obscure her breasts when the poster was displayed in Montreal in 1927.[17] And, lest we sit back and smugly feel that we are far superior to this, note that similar incidents — the controversy over Robert Mapplethorpe's photographs, for instance — have proliferated in the past few years, signaling our continued uneasiness with depictions of the body.

Cultural critic Richard Goldstein once observed in the liberal New York City weekly *The Village Voice*, "In America today, the most popular entertainment reinforces orthodoxies, while the most powerful art is a weapon of dissent."[18] Although it would not be difficult to amass a list of counterexamples to such a sweeping generalization, Goldstein does have a point. Popular culture aims to please — as vast an audience, as frequently as possible. That means its creators must keep their fingers on the social pulse, must fathom and savor the assumptions of their era. In bowing to the Zeitgeist, they also fortify it. Someone working within the industry of popular culture is more likely to uphold, rather than challenge, dogma; the person is more likely to pander to time-worn prejudices than put them up to the harsh light of analysis. An examination of popular culture can expose the dark underside, the shadows of a community, and reveal how standard beliefs subordinate certain groups of individuals, freeze them into a particular social location, and help solidify established sites of power.

Such uncritical incorporation of dominant ideologies is now being exposed. Prominent feminist art historian Linda Nochlin published an anonymous nineteenth-century photograph entitled *Buy My Apples* (fig. 12).[19] A young woman —

nude except for black boots, thigh-length hosiery, and a multistrand necklace — invites the viewer to sample the ripe pleasures on her tray, which holds apples as well as her ample bosom. Everything about the image is a come-on, including her stance: one leg is placed before the other, and she has cocked her upper body ever so slightly, like the eager barmaid in a beer logo. Nochlin draws a significant parallel with Gauguin's *Tahitian Women with Mango Blossoms*, where a young maiden's breasts also rest upon a platter brimming with fecund offerings. Nochlin concludes, "There is obviously a time-honored connection, dignified by the sanction of high culture, between fruit and women's inviting nudity: apples and breasts have been associated from the time of Theocritus's pastoral verse down to Zola's eroticized paean to fruit in *Le Ventre de Paris*." However, she finds no such "association of fruit with male sexuality,"[20] thus acknowledging the general lack of objectified depictions of men.

Many examples from contemporary popular culture extend Nochlin's conclusions. Popular culture may sometimes be crude, but it often dilutes its potency with humor to disguise the level of virulence it actually contains. Humor can serve a number of purposes. For one thing, it can be a "safety valve" when used between equals of inferior status. The dynamic is different between people of different status, however, especially when someone in a dominant position uses humor as a weapon to keep an inferior in place. As Freud argued, "the humorist acquires his superiority by assuming the role of the grown-up ... while he reduces the other people to the position of children."[21] Wit has this dual nature, therefore: it can be funny to one party and simultaneously demeaning to another.

The groups most likely to be the butt of jokes are those who already have less status and respectability in a community, generally because of some inborn characteristics. Recall the beleaguered Hottentot Venus. She was a woman who belonged to an exotic race, and her physique was virtually a self-caricature. She became a prime target for wisecracks: clichéd views about race and gender are the two ingredients which most commonly leaven this sort of denigrating humor.

The vast pool of items from popular culture that reproduce the female figure is fed by the spring of gender stereotypes, thus adding an important dimension to Freud's notion of reducing other people to a subordinate status. These items diminish the woman to a character who can be easily manipulated, somewhat like children's playthings. A central characteristic of this material is that the women are commonly depicted as waiting to serve. They are available, willing, and capable. But, like Sleeping Beauty, they need someone outside themselves to make them come alive, to fulfill their potential. Furthermore, an additional pernicious element resides in many of these pieces: when the intended functions of the objects are carried out, symbolic gestures of violence may also be activated.

An ingenuous young maid cheerily anticipates your beck and call in a salt and pepper set, probably of German origin, from the 1920s (fig. 13). Like the examples Nochlin cites, immense eggs replace her bosom, conflating the upper and lower portions of her reproductive system. The woman is virtually equated with her exaggerated procreative capacity; outsized ova/breasts render her a totem of tableside fertility. But never mind routine rules of decency and propriety; she is readily available, and you can grab her whenever you wish.

A ceramic toast rack made by the English firm Wiltshaw and Robinson in the 1980s consists of a symmetrical row of five female legs (fig. 14). The legs, bare except for their seductively decorated toenails, are bent in frankly suggestive sexual positions. Place your toast between the openings in this queue, and you have accomplished a small act of penetration.

Fig. 12. French, *Buy My Apples*, nineteenth century.
Photograph.

Fig. 13. German, salt and pepper set,
c. 1920–30. Ceramic.

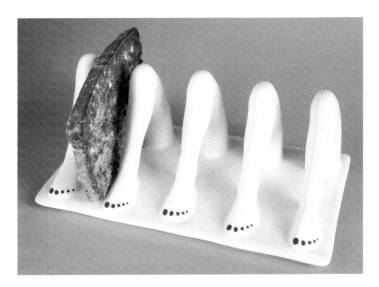

Fig. 14. English, toast rack, c. 1980. Ceramic.
Produced by Wiltshaw and Robinson.

In 1969, English designer Allen Jones upped the metaphorical ante a notch. His table rests its weight on the back of a sculpted kneeling woman. Her hip boots, long gloves, and corset signal a sado-masochistic scene, and she is in a slave position. It is not necessary that her master be present: the woman is completely controlled, her humiliation visible through the glass tabletop.[22]

A golf tee from St. Andrew's, Scotland (an acclaimed site for the sport), takes the shape of a nude, decapitated woman's body (fig. 15). Even more drastically than Magritte's *The Rape*, her face is obliterated and she has been reduced to her sexual characteristics. Like the salt and pepper set, toast rack, and glass-topped table, she too is absurdly pressed into service, the golf ball resting upon her truncated torso. The figure stands motionless as the player rears back and powerfully swings right above it. Like a comely knife-thrower's assistant, she is expected not to flinch.[23] And there are ashtrays which likewise feature female images. Crush your cigarette out in one, and you have performed another small act of degradation.

Finally, consider *Naughty Nellie*, a Victorian-era bootjack (fig. 16). She lies on the ground, bedecked in sexy undergarments, hands behind her head, her legs hoisted and spread. She is a male fantasy set in the classic missionary position, awaiting the man's entry. The device assists a gentleman in removing his boots. To accomplish the task, he jams his foot directly into her crotch. This merger of sex, humor, and aggression once again produces an object of dubious social worth.

In many of these cases, the objects were probably rather unselfconsciously used, their messages overlooked and unchallenged. They are such little things, after all, barely worth noticing or contesting. Besides, until the modern feminist movement gained momentum in the 1960s, who would have raised a ruckus? These images confirmed a male view of the world, and many women probably also found them to be "cute." But they undeniably hold a deeper significance. The pervasiveness of such characters helped lock women into a symbolic subordination and servitude which molded public opinion—until recently neither men nor women could have easily envisioned different roles—and partially neutralized any real-world advances for gender equality. Try a simple test: in your mind's eye, substitute the body of an adult male into any of these items. The debasement and preposterousness at their core will surface immediately.

Fig. 15. Scottish, golf tee from St. Andrew's, twentieth century. Plastic.

Fig. 16. American, *Naughty Nellie* bootjack, nineteenth century. Iron.

Intellectually speaking, Postmodernism is today's most fashionable academic style of thinking. It reigns on many campuses and in numerous museums and galleries as well. Yet it is one of those vast, slippery terms like pornography: no one can precisely define it, but you may swear you know it when you see it. Broadly defined, Postmodernism examines the world from multiple perspectives, particularly in terms of class, race, and gender. It contends that knowledge and power derive from various "discourses" or ways of conceptualizing and speaking about experience.

Postmodernists not only analyze the world immediately surrounding them, but also use prisms of group affiliation (e.g., feminist, gay) to cast a revisionist glance upon the canon of received wisdom and creation. Postmodernists thumb their noses at eternal categories; they reject the notion of thinking in black and white and want to increase the amount of gray area we perceive.

Contemporary artists use these same lenses to observe their own worlds and to explore subjects which may have been taboo in the past. To invoke Freud once again, Postmodernism represents "the return of the repressed": thoughts which were denied in the past and suppressed from public sight have come back. Many formerly forbidden topics are now bubbling up with the energy of a long-dormant volcano.

Fig. 17. Judy Chicago, *Emily Dickinson Place Setting* from *The Dinner Party*, 1979.
Mixed media. Diameter of plate: 35.5 cm (14 in.).
Belen, New Mexico, *The Dinner Party* Trust.

Fig. 18. Édouard Manet, *Luncheon on the Grass*, 1863.
Oil on canvas. 208 x 264.5 cm (81⅞ x 104⅛ in.).
Paris, Musée d'Orsay.

Feminism is a prime example of an approach that has sensitized Postmodernist art critics and artists alike. For example, Judy Chicago spearheaded a large collaborative project, called *The Dinner Party*, from 1974 to 1980. The result was a gallery-sized, mixed-media installation featuring a triangular table prepared for a ceremonial banquet. Thirty-nine different place settings appear, each representing a notable female figure (fig. 17). Each woman's life is compacted into the unique design of her setting. The plates progress from flat to high relief, symbolizing the gradual emergence of women from past social constraints. Each simulates female genitalia to one degree or another, in some instances explicitly showing the labia and vagina.

*The Dinner Party* celebrates women's accomplishments and sexuality; embraces a cooperative model of creation, contradicting the image of artists as rugged (and typically male) individualists; and promotes the practice of traditionally female crafts, such as embroidery and pottery. Women's minds and their bodies are equally its subjects, in contrast to Magritte's earlier, more objectified depiction (fig. 10), with which *The Dinner Party* settings share a superficial resemblance.

Other feminists have also repositioned how we now view the body. In 1983, artist Cath Tate reenacted Édouard Manet's *Luncheon on the Grass* (fig. 18), a work that some critics have argued helped signal the demise of the classic nude. In Manet's painting, two fully suited men appear in the foreground. They lounge on the grass and engage in animated talk. Next to them is a nude woman. This scene shocked Manet's contemporaries, especially its absurd mixture of clothed and unclothed, and the model's forthright stare out at the audience. It hardly mattered that this was a product of Manet's imagination rather than an actual scene, or that it quoted a configuration in *The Judgment of Paris*, an engraving by Marcantonio Raimondi after Raphael. Even bearing such an art historical pedigree, Manet's canvas broke the conventions of his time, pointedly demonstrating how women were generally considered peripheral, mere accessories to the realm of real, male action.

Tate's photomontage presents a remedial gender reversal (fig. 19). Here clothed women take over the places formerly occupied by the men, and a nude, bearded male is shoved into the exposed position. It is merely one twentieth-century update of the protracted battle between the sexes. In the same spirit, Linda Nochlin revised *Buy My Apples* with her own photographic creation, *Buy My Bananas* (fig. 21).[24] Here a bearded and bushy-haired man—nude, save shoes and socks—leans over slightly and dreamily holds a tray. On it are five bananas, framing (and mirroring) his own genitalia.

Still others have recast yet another controversial Manet painting, *Olympia*. In the 1960s, body/performance artist Carolee Schneemann performed a collaborative piece with Robert Morris entitled *Site*. Schneemann installed herself as a live incarnation of Manet's prostitute who unabashedly stares back at her viewers; she honored Olympia by becoming her. *Site* celebrated Olympia as a woman before her time: yesterday's provocateur becomes tomorrow's role model.

Art historian Eunice Lipton undertook an unusual research project by giving center stage to Victorine Meurent, the model for both of Manet's aforementioned paintings, further shaking the foundations of the artistic pantheon.[25] Lipton discovered that Meurent was also an artist, a lesbian, and a participant in the lively late nineteenth-century demimonde of Paris. She was thus a dynamic presence, not just a body. Lipton theorizes that instead of Meurent being a passive model processed through the genius of the artist, Manet's paintings may more accurately represent a creative collusion between the two: Meurent's irrepressible spirit could be what drives these works as much as Manet's talent and imagination.[26]

Fig. 19. Cath Tate, *Picnic on the Grass*, 1983. Photomontage. 19.3 x 24 cm (7⅝ x 9⁷⁄₁₆ in.).

Fig. 20. Yasumasa Morimura, *Portrait (Twin)*, 1988. Colored photograph, transparent medium. 210 x 300 cm (82¹¹⁄₁₆ x 118⅛ in.). Pittsburgh, Carnegie Museum of Art.

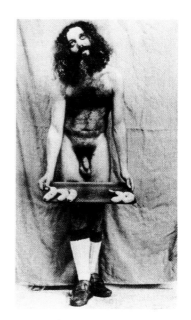

Fig. 21. Linda Nochlin, *Buy My Bananas*,
c. 1970. Photograph.

Yasumasa Morimura pushes this one step further in *Portrait (Twin)* of 1988 (fig. 20). The male artist casts himself as Olympia, nude except for a blond wig, earrings, a choker, and mules. He relocates the nude male body from a formerly invisible zone foursquare into female territory. Or, more accurately, he challenges our basic notions of masculine and feminine, and demonstrates that the body is no longer as stable an entity as it once was. As a Postmodernist, Morimura is certainly smudging the line between traditional gender categories that most people hold very dear.[27]

The French performance artist Orlan brings us full circle: she uses her own body as raw material, objectifying herself. In 1993, the forty-six-year-old went under the knife in the seventh of her series of surgeries to become the quintessential woman. Her artistic medium? Skin, muscle, cartilage, and bone. Her ultimate product? Herself, transformed. Her models? Not the femmes fatales of the big screen but the glamour girls of art history: the mythological goddesses Venus and Diana, and the *Mona Lisa*. Orlan directs her doctors to recreate on her face features borrowed from these other women's faces. Is this the ultimate feminist statement, a display that retards women's social progress, or simply the work of a deranged mind? Each interpretation has been suggested.

Orlan's archetypes may be timeless, but her working style is high-tech and media-savvy. In one episode, she and the surgical staff all wore matching designer outfits. Of course, the operations were videotaped and broadcast to a gallery audience, and her recovery process was fully documented. And Orlan sells what she calls "reliquaries": petri dishes containing fat removed from her body, with accompanying text.[28]

So the human body—its various shapes and sizes, its sensuality, its social significance—continues to be a powerful influence on artists. Although few ever take the idea of the body as a template to its outer limits, as Orlan does, the body remains basic, surviving whatever new sorts of technology artists subject it to, whatever esoteric theories they project onto it, and whatever schemes they devise to use, abuse, or honor it.

# Homo Ornarens
*by Witold Rybczynski*

Ornament is as old as human history. The desire to embellish began with the body itself, which, over the centuries, has been dyed, smeared, and painted. The chronicle of the treatment of hair alone is an encyclopedia of braiding, coloring, curling, flouncing, greasing, powdering, shaving, teasing, and wigging. Perukes have been out of fashion since the eighteenth century, but the appetite for personal adornment continues. We may eschew tattoos—an ancient form of decoration that is experiencing a modest revival—but we wear jewelry, patterned ties, colorful scarves; even a sober-suited banker cannot resist the urge to decorate, adding a pocket handkerchief or a boutonniere. Accessories, we call them, as if they were merely afterthoughts, but they are much more fundamental than that.

We likewise adorn everyday objects. Engraved utensils and painted bowls are found in all preindustrial cultures. The decoration of utilitarian objects both humanizes them and makes them more enjoyable to use. An engraved knife cuts no more effectively than a plain one, but embellishment adds significance to the act of cutting. It is easy to forget in our functionalistic age that, until recently, most machinery was decorated, locomotives as well as lathes. Expensive shotguns are still ornamented, as are some musical instruments such as harpsichords; but, on the whole, modern tools are distressingly plain. Automotive designers have opted for a bare and unadorned style, although this has not stopped people from adding body stripes, decals, and bumper stickers. The computer with which I am writing is a wondrous machine but an uninspired, utilitarian object. On the other hand, the old silver snuffbox that holds my paper clips is a constant source of pleasure. The only modern ornamented tool that I own is a fountain pen.

We may be content with artless tools, but we still decorate our surroundings. We "dress up" our houses with flower boxes, shutters, and door ornaments on the exterior, and wallpaper and window treatments on the interior. It does not sound like much, but remove these embellishments and a house looks bare, unlived-in, abandoned. All in all, our home decorating is relatively conservative; other societies have been more exuberant. Certain North American Indians, for example, covered the buffalo hide and canvas covers of their tepees with decorations (fig. 22), and the Haida and Kwakiutl people of the Northwest coast elaborately carved and painted the entire fronts of their plank houses (fig. 23). The desire to ornament emerges in the least auspicious circumstances. I have seen houses in New Delhi slums that were little more than shacks, but whose entrances were carefully outlined with colored paint. Here, modest decoration made the difference between misery and self-respect. Like body painting, domestic ornament has an ancient lineage. The existence of prehistoric cave paintings, probably the earliest example of interior decoration as well as art, suggests that we may be genetically programmed to ornament the places in which we live. Not just *Homo sapiens*, then, but *Homo ornarens*.

The delight that almost all peoples have found in decorating buildings is striking. Why ornament? The eminent British art historian Sir John Summerson once wrote that architectural ornament has two distinct roles. The first is the modulation of surfaces by patterns and other decorative means. The purpose here is simple enough: to break up blank wall surfaces, or to give large rooms scale. This is what

Fig. 22. Sarcee, tepee with painted decoration, British Columbia, 1885.

Fig. 23. Kwakiutl, house front with "devouring mouth," Tsadsisnukwomi, British Columbia, c. 1900.

Fig. 24. Diagram of frieze with buchrania and guttae
(from John Summerson,
*The Classical Language of Architecture*).

Fig. 25. William Van Alen, gargoyle, Chrysler Building,
New York, 1930.

happens when a chair rail or molding is carried around a wall, or when wainscoting or paneling is introduced into a room. At other times, decoration is there merely to give pleasure to the eye — a floor enlivened by an ornamental pattern of tiles, or a ceiling animated by coffering. It just looks nice that way, we say.

The second role of ornament is more complicated. Summerson gave it the unwieldy name of subjunctive architecture. "The original incentive has about it the desire to act *as if* something were otherwise than it is," he wrote.[1] A wrought-iron gate, shaped in a floral motif, turns inert metal into something organic and alive; it also makes the gate look "as if" it were leafy and insubstantial. In Roman architecture, the stone capital of a Corinthian column is a stylized acanthus plant, and the delicate leaves and tendrils make the heavy entablature above look "as if" it were nearly floating in the air. The facades of Kwakiutl plank houses, to pick a different example, sometimes are painted to resemble the faces of mythological animals, with the mouth acting as a door (fig. 23). The so-called devouring mouth motif is said to be a warning that only worthy persons may enter without harm.[2] The conical top of a Blackfoot tepee was stained a dark color to represent the sky, including depictions of stars and entire constellations. Thus, the peak of the tent and the sky were one.

Ornament is often about the transmission of symbolic information regarding culture in general or the building and its occupants in particular. On a tepee, a zigzag line depicts lightning, and figure paintings represent the hunting or martial exploits of the owner or his ancestors. The structural supports of a Haida dwelling are carved in animal shapes — they are at once posts and totems. The language of Classical architecture is replete with meaning. In the Doric order, the triglyphs on the architrave surmount little ornamental pieces called guttae. Guttae means "drops" in Latin, and these ornaments represent drops of blood flowing from the sacrificial altar, recalling that Greek temples were places of religious sacrifice.[3] Sometimes, relief sculptures of animal skulls were placed between the triglyphs to further underline the grisly metaphor (fig. 24). Such symbolism is lost on most modern viewers, however, so when William Van Alen designed the Chrysler Building in 1930, he dispensed with Classical language and adopted a different vocabulary to suit his automotive client. The scalloped top of the skyscraper is made up of shapes that recall hubcaps, and the four giant chrome eagles on the sixty-first floor are overscale versions of the Chrysler hood ornament (fig. 25). A more literal, or rather literary, example of the communicative role of ornament is the incorporation of writing into the facade of a building. Milton's "Beholding the bright countenance of truth in the quiet and still air of delightful studies" adorns the main library at McGill University in Montreal; the frieze of the United States Post Office in New York City, designed by Charles McKim in 1913, contains the now-famous inscription (adapted from Herodotus), "Neither snow nor rain nor heat nor gloom of night stays these couriers from the swift completion of their appointed rounds." Not only civic buildings are graced by literary quotations; Arts and Crafts architects frequently used proverbs as interior decoration. A young Frank Lloyd Wright inscribed the portentous "Truth is life" over his mantle in his first home. At about the time Wright was building his house and studio in Oak Park, the Swedish painter Carl Larsson was constructing his famous home, Lilla Hyttnäs. Larsson also incorporated proverbs into the decor, although they tended to be more homely: "Love one another, children, as love is all," and "I tell you what: Be glad and good."

Summerson called the urge to act as if something were otherwise than it is "subjunctive," but it equally well could be called play-acting. Play is never far beneath the surface of ornament. Because we have learned to treat Classical architecture with a respect that often borders on reverence, it is easy to miss how joyous and even prankish Classical ornament can be. This is particularly so in the case of decoration derived from plant life. Plants carried serious symbolic meanings: the evergreen, eternity; the vine, fertility; the oak, wisdom; and the laurel wreath, victory. At the same time, the rotund fruits, curling leaves, and sinuous stalks undermine the solid, architectural order and introduce a frolicsome element to the building.

The flutes on Classical columns are said to recall the folds of draped clothing, which reminds us that the columns, in turn, represent the human figure: the Doric is male, the Ionic, female. Thus, the regularly spaced columns of a Doric temple could be seen as rows of soldiers. But when this conceit is carried to its logical extreme, as it is in caryatids (columns carved in the shape of human figures), the result can be distinctly odd. The porch of the Erechtheion on the Acropolis has caryatids instead of columns (fig. 28). Are we really meant to take those young women balancing the heavy roof on their heads altogether seriously? At least in the case of Michael Graves's Team Disney office building in Burbank we know the joke is on us — the caryatids on the main facade are the Seven Dwarfs (fig. 29)!

Grotesque figures are greatly in evidence in the ornamentation of Gothic cathedrals, which are otherwise far from playful places. But in its rich, revival mode, the Gothic style proved extremely playful indeed. The Woolworth Building in New York City was dubbed the "Cathedral of Commerce." The lobby resembles a vaulted nave and its first impression is of a baptistry or lady chapel — with elevator doors. But if you look carefully near the ceiling you can see cheery little corbels representing the builder Louis J. Horowitz, the architect Cass Gilbert, and the client Frank Woolworth himself (fig. 26). The founder of the national chain of five-and-ten-cent stores is represented holding — what else? — a nickel. Equally playful are the gargoyles of the Memorial Gymnasium at the University of Idaho, a collegiate Gothic structure, designed in 1929 by David Lange. The exterior of the gym has gargoyles in the form of little squatting, helmeted football players.

This brings us to an aspect of decoration that accounts in large part, I think, for its continuing fascination. Decoration is often fun. Whatever its serious underlying iconographic or symbolic content, it inevitably deals with illusion. It blurs the distinction between what we perceive and what we know to be real. That is why architectural ornament has always consisted not only of abstract geometric shapes but also of garlands, wreaths, and swags; ropes, knots, and tassels; as well as human and animal figures. Such decoration starts by catching the eye, and finishes by engaging the mind. This is something that pure abstraction cannot accomplish. Imagine, for example, the entrance to the New York Public Library flanked by two steel Alexander Calder constructions. Most people would find them a distinctly poor substitute for the stately lions. We call them "lions," but they are really solid carved stone. Yet to say they are bogus misses the point — it is precisely because they are *not* real that they are fascinating. They are like an illusionist's levitation or a conjurer's card trick.

*Trompe l'oeil* is the ultimate architectural illusion. The ceiling between the rafters of the garden house where I am writing is painted blue with puffy clouds. Looking up, it is easy to imagine that the roof has been removed and one is seeing the actual sky. The practice of painting a ceiling to resemble the sky is one of the oldest decorative illusions and dates back at least to the Renaissance; it was also fashionable in domestic decorating in France during the second half of the eighteenth century. The ballroom of Rosecliff, a Newport mansion designed by Stanford White in 1902, has a beautiful sky-ceiling which gives the impression that one really is outside (fig. 27).

Fig. 26. Cass Gilbert, corbel sculpted with portrait of Frank Woolworth, lobby of Woolworth Building, New York, 1913.

Fig. 27. Stanford White and Jules Allard et fils, ballroom, Rosecliff, Newport, Rhode Island, 1902.

Fig. 28. Alkamenes, caryatids, Porch of the Maidens, Erechtheion, Athens, c. 420–405 B.C.

Fig. 29. Michael Graves, Team Disney office building at the Disney Studios in Burbank, California, 1991.

Fig. 30. Paolo Veronese and Andrea Palladio, mural in the Villa Barbaro, Maser, 1557.

Painted ornament has been used in a variety of ways, for instance to simulate materials (especially marble and stone), or to create counterfeit architectural elements like panels, coffers, moldings, and even niches with statuary. Of course, painting is cheaper than the real thing, but there is more to *trompe l'oeil* than economics. It has to do with that *frisson* of delight when we discover that what looks like veined marble is really oil paint — the realization that the world is not what it appears to be. Ambiguity and illusion can also produce other reactions. In Palladio's Villa Barbaro, built in 1557, there is a room in which symmetry demanded that a door be located where none was required (fig. 30). Palladio solved the problem by designing a fake doorway, complete with carved frame and pediment. He then had his collaborator, Paolo Veronese, paint a false door, to match the real one on the opposite wall. But Veronese went a step further, painting one leaf of the door slightly ajar, and adding the figure of a young girl peering out. There are several such personages in the villa, many of them representing members of the original Barbaro household. The effect is spooky. As Mary McCarthy wrote, "It is a stage house inside a real house — an idea that sounds sportive and playful, a mirror trick, but that is too well executed to be amusing, like the sort of game where the children playing it work themselves up till they begin to cry."[4]

It should be evident by now that ornament is not a frill or a superfluous trifle. It is integral to the human experience. It provides an opportunity to introduce not merely detail but meaning into our surroundings. That is why, in one way or another, it has survived all attempts to banish it from architecture and design. Seventy-five years of Modernism have taught us that the plain unvarnished truth is often, well, boring. It lacks the nuanced richness, both intellectual and visual, that had always been an integral part of the man-made environment. Without ornament there is no meaning, without meaning, buildings and objects become, quite literally, meaningless. And without decoration there is no play, and without play our world is impoverished indeed.

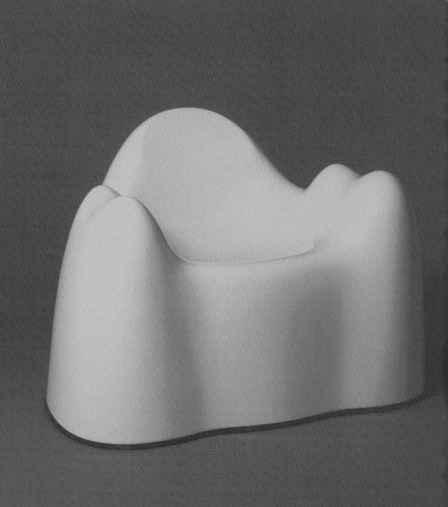

# Body Language

# Body Language

*by Lenore Newman and Jan L. Spak*

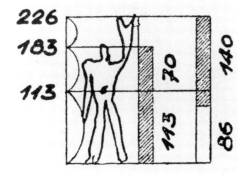

Fig. 31. Le Corbusier, *Modulor Man*, 1946.
(From Willy Boesiger, *Le Corbusier*).

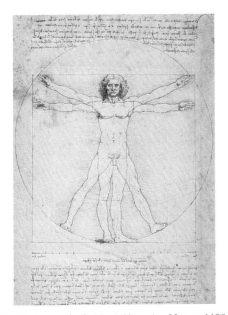

Fig. 32. Leonardo da Vinci, *Vitruvian Man*, c. 1490.
Ink on paper. 34.3 x 24.5 cm (13½ x 9⅝ in.).
Venice, Galleria dell'Accademia.

One of the most famous symbols of Modernism is Le Corbusier's *Modulor Man* (fig. 31), a stylized figure with one hand raised overhead, intended as a standard of proportion for buildings. It is not only an evocative reminder of the early Modernists' desire to remake the world in concert with healthful human habitation, but also a reminder of the attempt to regulate measurement in relation to human scale. It is not unlike Leonardo's celebrated drawing of the *Vitruvian Man*, a heroic male nude constructed within a square and circle (fig. 32). While Le Corbusier's and Leonardo's schemes may embody different mathematical relationships (as does their architecture), both images forcefully remind us of the central place of the human figure within Western thought. We might recall the adage (however politically incorrect its phrasing), "Man is the measure of all things."

Paradoxically, though, the *Modulor Man* was one of the few representations of the body in avant-garde twentieth-century architecture. Innovative architects tended toward abstract ordering systems rather than those based on anthropomorphic allusions. The *Modulor Man* occasionally has been an influential image, especially in recent decades. The Swiss architect and designer Mario Botta, for example, modeled his *Shogun Terra* lamp (cat. no. 136) on it: "The central hole that goes through the stand is 1.13 meters from the floor, like the navel of Le Corbusier's *Modulor*. It is meant to be a strong and hieratic figure, like a warrior in the domestic landscape."[1] Likewise, Olivier Mourgue's *Bouloum* chaise longue (cat. no. 3) was conceived as "the scale man" on architectural drawings. However, for the greater part of this century, the human figure was displaced from the standard canon of Modernist design.

That notwithstanding, an older tradition of referring to the body has persisted in the world of design, and if we consider the history of twentieth-century design without prejudice, we will find that in the main currents (and through various subterfuges as well) the human body has continued to play a central role in forming the language of modern decorative arts. This should not be surprising. Historically, the human figure has always been a primary source for creative endeavors. It is revealing to consider the terminology traditionally assigned to elements of utilitarian objects, for the words are both explicit and symbolic. One has only to think of the most common metaphoric terminology—the arms and legs of a favorite chair, the neck and lip of a bottle—to realize that we think anthropomorphically. Among the most familiar and clever plays on this mode of thought are those of the Surrealists, whose transformations remain among the most haunting appropriations of the body in modern art and design. For example, Kurt Seligmann used female mannequin legs to support his disquieting *Ultrameuble* table (fig. 46), and Salvador Dalí transformed Mae West's moist red lips into, appropriately enough, a love seat (fig. 41). Only recently, however, has attention been drawn to examples from throughout the century, spurred in part by the challenges made in the past two decades to the dominance of the International Style.

The human form, presented in its entirety or in its component parts, has been an underlying theme not only throughout the entire century but, in fact, it has been a universal focus of cultures in all periods. From the very start, sculptural objects both large and small were created in imitation of the human form. Figurines such as the amply rounded *Venus of Willendorf* (fig. 35) and the group

Fig. 33. Albert-Ernest Carrier-Belleuse, Taxile Doat,
and Claudius Marioton, coupe, 1886.
Porphyry, silver, porcelain, obsidian, brass.
44 x 28.8 x 27.6 cm (17⁵⁄₁₆ x 11⅝ x 10⅞ in.).
Paris, Musée d'Orsay.

Fig. 34. Michael Powolny, centerpiece, 1910.
Glazed ceramic. Height: 23.5 cm (9¼ in.).
Produced by Wiener Keramik. Vienna, Österreichisches
Museum für angewandte Kunst.

of wide-eyed figures from Sumer (fig. 36) are vivid reminders from the beginnings of Western culture, but almost every society can point to comparable imagery, and often these objects serve similar ritualistic and mystical purposes. Both ancient and modern cultures have used the body metaphorically for functional and ornamental purposes. Weight-bearing caryatids such as the Mayan ones at Chichén-Itzá are a universal phenomenon. The more famous Greek maidens that grace the Erechtheion (fig. 28) and innumerable buildings since the Baroque period demonstrate just how basic this symbolic representation of support has become. We might think of the countless small objects in the last five hundred years that have also used this device. Carrier-Belleuse's coupe (fig. 33) continues this classical tradition in a resplendent, decorative way, but examples are not restricted to the Belle Epoque. A ceramic centerpiece with highly stylized caryatid figures designed by Michael Powolny for the Wiener Werkstätte (fig. 34) reminds us that such ideas carried over into the modern era as well.

Given our sense of familiarity with our own bodies, it is little wonder that a number of modern designs for chairs actually depict sitting bodies. Sculptor Niki de Saint-Phalle's spirited *Charly* and *Clarice* armchairs (cat. nos. 1, 2) are straightforwardly representational, unlike Mourgue's *Bouloum* (cat. no. 3), which is a transfiguration of the graphic symbol for man. Whether abstract or representational, however, these three chairs have been given definite personas by the artists, a notion totally antithetical to Modernism's dictates; they even spoof the charming convention of assigning names to inanimate objects. Saint-Phalle's comments on the accessibility of the human figure are germane: "I like the fact that I am able to say something on a very immediate level. So much of art today has become tied up with ideas, with philosophy, with the abstracts, and a lot of people feel excluded from it because of the impoverishment of the image. Nobody is excluded from my work."[2]

More bizarre than amusing, Mieczyslaw Górowski's Kafkaesque theater poster (cat. no. 4) reflects the satirical aspects of interpersonal relationships explored in the represented drama. Here, as in its Surrealist literary counterpart, metamorphosis bridges two worlds: a couch metamorphoses into a man, complete with arm and leg supports and upholstery pulled aside to reveal a hairy back, a reminder that we view furniture anthropomorphically. Clearly parodic as well is Red Grooms and Lysiane Luong's garment bag in the cartoonish form of an Egyptian mummy case (cat. no. 5), a whimsical sarcophagus to hold human clothing rather than human remains. More abstract is the *Up 5* and *Up 6* chair and footrest (cat. no. 7) by Gaetano Pesce, who typically infuses his designs with social commentary and technological innovation. The *Up 5* chair is ingeniously packed flat in a mundane cardboard box but, when released, inflates spontaneously into a comfortably rounded doll. It is an accretion of swelling protuberances irreverently nicknamed *La Mamma*, which is perhaps appropriate since the chair explores stereotypical ideas of woman's inferior status in society; the female form is chained irrevocably to a ball that serves as the footrest, indicative of the baggage with which woman trudges through life.

As has been suggested, there is a tendency to anthropomorphize common household objects, much like the animate tea set seen in the staging of Maurice Ravel's opera *The Child and the Magic Spells (L'Enfant et les sortilèges)* (fig. 37) and in the more recent Disney adaptation of *Beauty and the Beast*. Riccardo Dalisi's trio of figurative coffeemakers for Alessi (cat. nos. 8–10) is the result of his long-term research project on classic Neapolitan coffeemakers; Dalisi has likened their folkloric spirit to Punchinello, a masked character in the *commedia dell'arte*: "For me, he represents a love of life, ironic, sympathetic, witty and

Fig. 35. *Venus of Willendorf*, c. 15,000–10,000 B.C.
Stone. Height: 11 cm (4⁵⁄₁₆ in.).
Vienna, Naturhistorisches Museum,
Prähistorische Abteilung.

Fig. 36. Sumerian, votive statuettes from Tell Asmar, c. 2900–2600 B.C. Limestone, alabaster, gypsum.
Height of tallest: 72 cm (28⅜ in.). Chicago, The Oriental Institute Museum of The University of Chicago.

Fig. 37. Scene from Maurice Ravel, *The Child and the Magic Spells*. Costume and set design by John MacFarlane.
Performance by the Netherlands Dance Theater, 7 June 1984, at the Circustheater, Scheveningen.

Fig. 38. Madonna in performance, Worcester, Massachusetts, 1990.

Fig. 39. Mochican, stirrup vase, A.D. 800–1200. Ceramic. 24.5 x 13.5 x 19 cm (9⅝ x 5⁵⁄₁₆ x 7½ in.). London, The British Museum.

non-conformist as he is."[3] Dalisi's animate objects, although never put into production, recall the charm of the beloved Tin Man from *The Wizard of Oz*.

The world of design has traditionally been dominated by men, and perhaps this helps explain why the seductive female has remained such an appealing constant. At the turn of the century, when electricity was inevitably personified as a woman, many lamps were in the form of women bearing the sparkling new jewels of light. Perhaps no figure was more objectified than the early modern dance sensation Loïe Fuller. Frozen in motion in Raoul Larche's Art Nouveau table lamp (cat. no. 11), she is performing one of her famous veil dances, the striking effect heightened by the electric light shining through her voluminous veils. In sharp contrast to the graceful imagery of the early century is the equally expressive *Dancers* brooch by Sam and Carol Kramer (cat. no. 12), Greenwich Village bohemians whose work evokes the spiritual excitement of a Freudian world.

Since time immemorial woman has been a metaphor for the very concept of the vessel—the body of a vase, the waist and neck of a bottle. The Surrealists toyed with this idea, as in Magritte's *Lady* bottle (fig. 10). The svelte curvature of the female torso is represented abstractly in Fulvio Bianconi's glass bottle for Venini (cat. no. 13). In this object, one of Murano's master craftsmen has further enlivened the allusion through the use of a pale, flesh-toned glass. Similar in color but more explicitly erotic through the addition of provocative undergarments, Jean-Paul Gaultier's perfume bottles (cat. nos. 14, 15) go to a brash extreme of representation. The fashion designer's racy scheme was first seen in his couture collections which proposed the use of undergarments as outerwear, a trend that was popularized by performing artist Madonna (fig. 38).

The face and its expressive features have offered designers opportunities to be both decorative and symbolic. At the turn of the century and under the potent influence of the Symbolist painters, Art Nouveau designers were especially preoccupied with the female face. René Lalique was the first to apply this Symbolist convention to jewelry, as seen in a pendant (cat. no. 19) that is one of the few early pieces that this gifted artist produced in multiples. The image of a luxuriously coiffed female head emerging from a poetic framework of leaves and flowers then became a ubiquitous decorative device in two- and three-dimensional art. The dissemination of this imagery is registered in the cigarette case designed by the artist Hans Christiansen (cat. no. 20), who worked in Paris during the 1890s before returning to his native Germany. The idea was transmitted across the Atlantic to North America, where objects such as William Kerr and Co.'s brooch (cat. no. 21) and the Unger Brothers's bonbon dish (cat. no. 22) became immensely popular.

The head has been the basis for a variety of three-dimensional object types. An early example is a pre-Columbian container (fig. 39) that was used to store and pour liquids. Certainly no twentieth-century artist was more inspired to see the human form in the age-old contours of pottery than Pablo Picasso. His imaginative work for the Madoura pottery at Vallauris is epitomized by his *Tripod* vase (cat. no. 23), which takes the traditional head vase one step further by the addition of arms that serve to support the vessel. Another popular variant of this ancient form is the vase by Vally Wieselthier (cat. no. 24), the ceramist who had made such lighthearted sculpture for the Wiener Werkstätte before emigrating to the United States. The vase truly reveals its whimsical character when it is filled with flowers and the ceramic hat, in effect, is adorned with a gay bouquet. Ena Rottenberg, another Wiener Werkstätte designer, used heads as finials for her mocha service (cat. no. 27), appropriating an older convention in which native figures adorned objects and announced the exotic ingredients within, a Turkish or Javanese person for coffee, a Chinese person for tea, etc.

Fig. 40. Greek, pair of earrings, c. 350 B.C.
Gold. Height: 4 cm (1⁹⁄₁₆ in.).
St. Petersburg, The Hermitage.

Fig. 41. Salvadór Dalí, sofa, *Mae West's Lips*, 1936.
Felt. 92 x 213 x 80 cm (36¼ x 83⅞ x 31½ in.).
Brighton, The Royal Pavilion,
Art Gallery and Museums.

In Isamu Noguchi's *Radio Nurse* (cat. no. 28), the abstracted form (as might be expected from a student of Brancusi) served as a radio monitor for safeguarding children, and its allusion to human presence was meant to provide comfort. In contrast, George Lynn's hockey mask (cat. no. 29) employed an equally abstract language of form for an opposite end: to frighten the opponent. Similarly expressive, the universally recognized facial pictograms on the handles of the *Tatzine* coffee cups (cat. no. 30) communicate the conviction of Milanese designer Andrea Branzi that objects do indeed have souls. Extreme stylization is also seen in Ed Wiener's highly schematic but readily identifiable head-shaped earrings (cat. no. 31), an interesting contrast to ancient or Renaissance examples with more realistically rendered faces (fig. 40).

Through nuances of individual facial features — shifty eyes, smiling lips, flaring nostrils — we commonly read a person's character traits. Since facial features possess such inherent power, it is not surprising that among the oldest forms of talismans are charms formed as eyes to ward off evil. They are still made and used in regions throughout the world, such as the Mediterranean. The brooch by Sam Kramer and his assistant, Charles Wendell (cat. no. 32), though more abstract in style and shocking in its use of a glass taxidermy eye, recalls those charms, as well as the oversize eyes seen in Sumerian statues (fig. 36) which were meant to suggest the communication of the spirit. Andrea Branzi's ear vase (cat. no. 33), intended to be hung on a wall, brings to mind Surrealist imagery of the 1930s in which disembodied eyes, ears, and mouths acted as metaphors for unconscious desires. Indeed, his drawings (cat. no. 34) reveal his indebtedness to Surrealist painting and sculpture of those years. Branzi's use of the ear as a container is unsettling, especially when it is planted with the cactus it was meant to contain and whose white fuzz suggests a growth of hair.

Stanley Tigerman's coffeepot (cat. no. 35) is similarly surrealistic, its pouring lip fashioned like lips and its braided-hair handle giving it a disconcertingly animate presence. In its play on the human lip as the literal lip of the coffeepot, the object exploits the common tendency to anthropomorphize the components of a vessel. It is only one of the latest in a memorable line of objects paying homage to this sensuous feature of our anatomy; it is perhaps not surprising that during the Pop-dominated 1960s, Studio 65 updated Dalí's earlier Mae West love seat (fig. 41) when it created *Marilyn*, another lip-shaped sofa that paid homage to a voluptuous femme fatale of the cinema. One more classic example of Pop imagery is Wendell Castle's *Molar* chair (cat. no. 37), an exaggerated tooth worthy of Pop culture, and a witty transformation of a body part not usually exposed for public contemplation. The chair, one of three designs mass-produced in plastic by this renowned woodworker, reveals Castle's quirky sense of humor and his preference for things organic.

Far more common as a metaphoric reference is the hand, a popular talisman (much like the eye) signifying protection when the palm is open and thrust forward, and signifying friendship or fidelity when clasped (fig. 42). During past centuries, hands holding illuminating objects such as candelabra alluded to the close affinity between the light and the torch bearer (fig. 43). Modern designers have also found the hand an appealing metaphor; sometimes, as in a Venini vase of 1956 (fig. 44), we find a direct revival of the Victorian concept of a hand holding the vessel. In Bruno Martinazzi's jewelry designs, such as a bracelet whose golden fingers grip the wearer's wrist (cat. no. 38), the designer capitalizes on the bonding symbolism of the gripping hand. In a different way, the impression left by a gripping hand in a supposedly malleable surface is suggested in the irregular metal shaft of a champagne glass by David Palterer and Borek Sípek (cat. no. 39), two contemporary

Fig. 42. French or German, fidelity ring, c. 1550.
Gold. Paris, Musée des Arts Décoratifs.

Fig. 43. Dutch, wall sconce, c. 1650–1700.
Silver. 40 x 33.5 x 49 cm (15¾ x 13³⁄₁₆ x 19¼ in.). Amsterdam,
Amsterdams Historisch Museum.

Fig. 44. Fulvio Bianconi, vase, 1956.
Glass. Produced by Venini S.p.A.

Fig. 45. Max Ernst, *Oedipus 25* (from *Une Semaine de Bonté*), 1934.
19.3 x 14 cm (7⅝ x 5½ in.).

designers as interested in the ritual meaning of objects as in their utilitarian function. In the work of Mexican Surrealist Pedro Friedeberg, whose paintings and furniture utilize the hand and other symbols derived from mysticism and folklore, the giant cupped hand becomes a chair and the outstretched hand a table supported by human legs and feet (cat. nos. 40, 41). The table is curiously reminiscent of Seligmann's *Ultrameuble* (fig. 46), which was a shocking but amusing contribution to the 1938 Surrealist exhibition in Paris. In an umbrella stand by the century's most successful Surrealist industrial designer, Piero Fornasetti (cat. no. 42), the dismembered, sandal-clad foot is like a fragment of classical sculpture, but mystically invested with umbrellas and walking sticks.

Because internal organs are not readily visible, they rarely are appropriated by the world of design. The one exception, but a ubiquitous one, is the stylized human heart—as in the motto "I ♡ New York," where the heart symbolizes the word "love." In stark contrast, Richard Notkin's shockingly realistic teapot in the form of an ironclad heart (cat. no. 43) is the very antithesis of the ideas we normally associate with hearts because of its startling realism and the trepidation we feel at seeing, much more at touching, such vital organs. Notkin's teapot is both a descendant of traditional Yixing teapots, which are favored by Chinese literati and play on the idea of imitative facsimiles, and an affirmation of the heart as the center of human emotions, sometimes vulnerable and in need of a defensive mechanism. "Hearts," Notkin remarked, "encased in armor or camouflaged for battle, become hardened visually as well as literally."[4]

Among the more provocative images in the decorative and graphic arts are representations of the female breast, prime (and primal) symbol of sexual innuendo as well as of nurturing and fertility. In his poster *Obsession and Fantasy* (cat. no. 44), graphic artist Robert Brownjohn projects circular shapes—here the "O" of the first word of his title—on bare breasts, cleverly correlating the visual image with the psychological component. Fornasetti's porcelain plate (cat. no. 45) contains a sly mixture of sexual allusion and startling physical juxtapositions, the provocative nature of the breastlike balloons providing an ironic contrast to the innocent demeanor of the woman's face. Fornasetti employed a nineteenth-century engraving style similar to that seen in Max Ernst's Dada collages (fig. 45). Compared to these blatant references to female sexuality, Bianconi's female-form bottle (cat. no. 13) seems a subtle image indeed. But everyone's notion of what constitutes eroticism is determined by their own time and place. Certainly Giò Pomodoro's necklace (cat. no. 46), in which male and female genitalia are formed from precious metals and gemstones, is explicit and perhaps more provocative than decorative. Contemporary German jeweler Gerd Rothmann actually molds his jewelry forms on selected parts of the client's body such as underarms, earlobes, and breasts, thereby achieving the ultimate personal connection between creator and consumer. Yet, ironically, what one might naturally think would be the most flagrant of these objects, a necklace Rothmann cast from a female nipple (cat. no. 47), is more abstract and less evocative, unless one knows the history of its creation.

However it is used—literally or metaphorically, representationally or abstracted—the body communicates on a very immediate level. Regardless of stylistic period or medium, and despite Modernist doctrines that have scorned figural imagery, many prominent artists and designers throughout the century have delighted in exploiting the body as a whole and in its many provocative parts, and clearly this will continue.

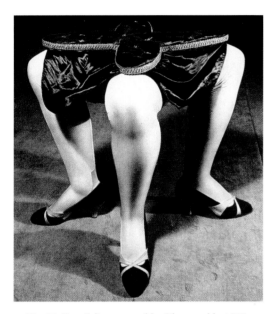

Fig. 46. Kurt Seligmann, table, *Ultrameuble*, 1938.

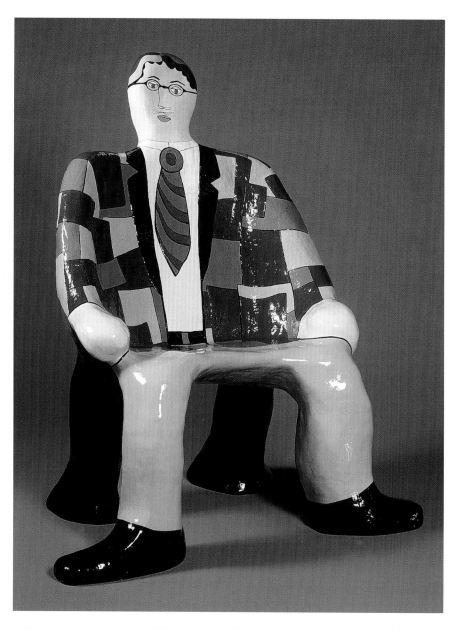

**1. Catherine-Marie-Agnès Fal (Niki) de Saint-Phalle**
(born 1930, Neuilly-sur-Seine, France)
Armchair, *Charly*
Designed 1981–82. Painted polyester
134 x 119 x 84.8 cm (52 # / 4 x 46 & / 8 x 33 # / 8 in.)
Produced by Plastiques d'art R. Haligon (Périgny), 1981–82
Impressed on underside, within oval: PLASTIQUES/R.HALIGON/D'ART;
within smaller oval: *Niki*/5/20
D91.420.1, gift of Esperanza and Mark Schwartz

**2. Catherine-Marie-Agnès Fal (Niki) de Saint-Phalle**
Armchair, *Clarice*
Designed 1981–82. Painted polyester
120 x 112.5 x 88.9 cm (47 ! /4 x 44 # / 16 x 35 in.)
Produced by Plastiques d'art R. Haligon (Périgny), 1981–82
Impressed on underside, within oval: PLASTIQUES/R.HALIGON/D'ART;
within smaller oval: *Niki*/2/20
D91.420.2, gift of Esperanza and Mark Schwartz

*"Throughout my life, I have had a deep love and respect for the ancient civilizations of Egypt, Mexico and India. In the artistic traditions of these cultures, I found human figures and those of animals and fabulous creatures used for all kinds of functional and ritualistic objects. In the themes of my own work, the forms of woman or animal or man or monster recur again and again, and have been adapted for everything from architectural spaces to the design of flower vases.*

*I have always enjoyed juxtapositions which create a visually ambiguous situation or psychological provocation. Chairs are simply expected to be nondescript in look and form. By fashioning them as human figures, the chairs* Clarice *and* Charly, *named for two of my friends, become 'unexpected guests,' assuming a presence of their own. They confuse the seat with the sitter, merging the identities of the two. I also like the idea that* Clarice *and* Charly *bring to mind childhood memories of comfort or awkwardness when sitting in the lap of an adult."*
Niki de Saint-Phalle, 1996[5]

**3. Olivier Mourgue**
(born 1939, Paris, France)
Chaise longue, *Bouloum*
Designed 1968. Fiberglass, urethane foam,
steel, nylon jersey
66.1 x 76.2 x 142.9 cm (26 x 30 x 56 !/4 in.)
Produced by Airborne (Montreuil), 1968-74;
produced by Arconas Corporation (Mississauga,
Ontario, Canada), 1975 to the present
Unmarked
D93.257.1, gift of William Prévost

*"Once upon a time there was Bouloum, a name given to a small child who was to become a large adult. For a long time he was 'the scale man' on architectural drawings. Due to his normal size he clearly indicated the proportions of a building.*

*One day, under the pretext of going out to buy matches, he left without telling anyone. He fled the enormous dark city, the factories, and the ever-present crowd. He left in search of friends resembling himself. They ran through ploughed fields, through water, through forests full of ivy, and fields of flowers. From time to time they played rugby and shoved each other. When they felt tired they would change into chairs, alone or cuddling one another."*
Olivier Mourgue, 1971[6]

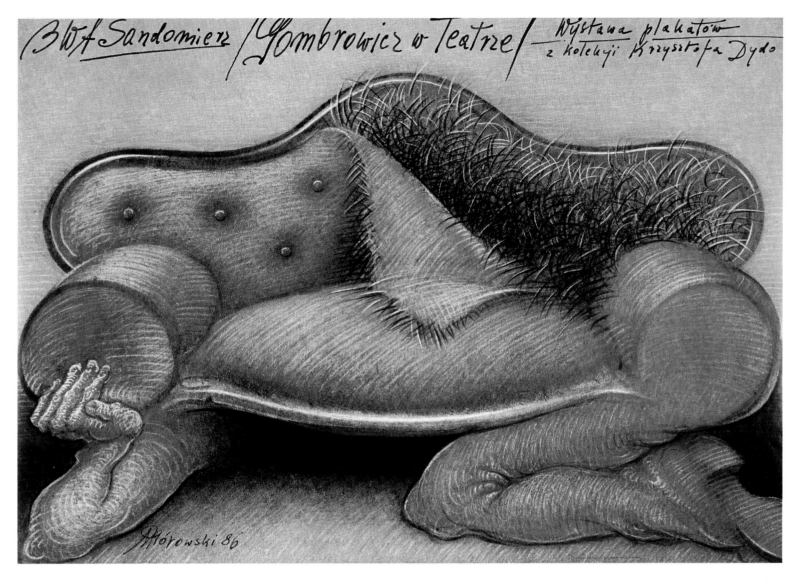

**4. Mieczyslaw Górowski**
(born 1941, Milkowa, Poland)
Poster, *Playwright Gombrowicz*
*(Gombrowicz w Teatrze)*
Designed 1986. Offset lithograph
67.9 x 97.7 cm (26¾ x 38⁷⁄₁₆ in.)
Printed by Drukarnia Narodowa (Warsaw) for BWA
(Sandomierz), 1986
Printed in black on lower left: *M Górowski 86*; on
lower right: Drukarnia Narodowa Z-2. Zam. 5856/86.
500szt. A-18/2862
D90.177.1, The Liliane and David M. Stewart Collection

*"My image represents a human being (incomplete, but
discernible by the presence of an arm and a leg) incorporated
into the volume of the sofa. It is the man-servant, the human
being degraded, and physically destroyed.... One could consider
the title of the poster as representing the specific nature of
Gombrowicz's theater. The most typical features of this theater
are interhuman relationships presented in a manner that is
satirical, ludicrous, as well as parodical and often absurd."*
Mieczyslaw Górowski, 1994[7]

**5. Red Grooms**
(born 1937, Nashville, TN, USA)
**Lysiane Luong**
(born 1951, Paris, France)
Garment bag, *Mummy Bag*
Designed 1985. Printed cotton
116.9 x 66.5 x 10.8 cm (46 x 26³/₁₆ x 4½ in.)
Produced by The Fabric Workshop (Philadelphia, PA),
1985 to the present
Printed in black ink on cotton label inside: *Lysiane
Luong & Red Grooms/for Pixie* [i's dotted with x's]
*Productions*/HANDPRINTED AT THE FABRIC WORKSHOP ©1985
D92.165.1, gift of Mrs. Stanley Hanks and Norbert
Schoenauer, by exchange

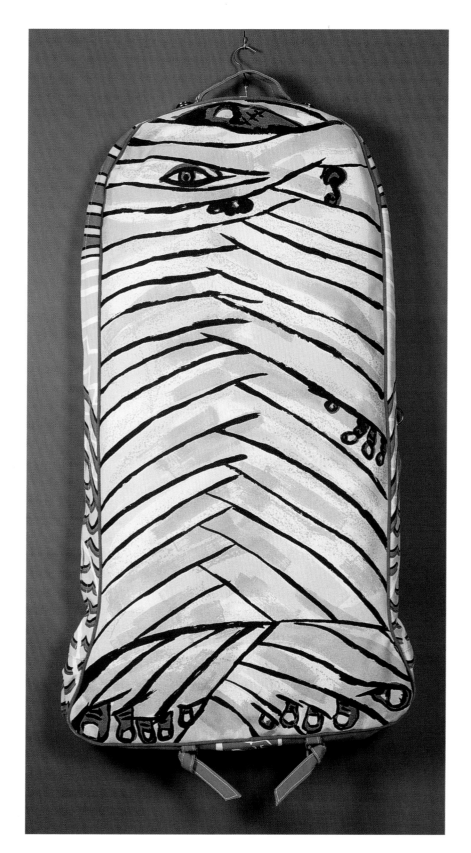

"We were trying to do a spin-off from the 'Tut's Fever Theater,' so that's the imagery. To personalize the bag ... [we made] the joke of a mummy being outside the bag on the back side and then the very nice sarcophagus on the front. One of the reasons I didn't think I'd be good at fabric design is that I focus on the human figure and it's not very decorative."
Red Grooms, 1994[8]

**6. Gaetano Pesce**
(born 1939, La Spezia, Italy)
Armchair, *Delilah III (Dalila III)*
Designed 1980. Rigid polyurethane foam, epoxy resin
83 x 71 x 61 cm (32¹¹⁄₁₆ x 27¹⁵⁄₁₆ x 24 in.)
Produced by Cassina S.p.A. (Meda Milano), 1980
Unmarked
D92.188.1, The Liliane and David M. Stewart Collection,
by exchange

*"I thought there should be different chairs, just as there are
different people, sitting around a table. This is based on the
concept of friends sitting around, talking at the end of a meal.
We are all different. The chairs should be individual too, not a
matched set as we used to have.... And so, looking at the three
Dalila chairs, we have more of the idea of a society composed
of different people. One is fat and old, another is young and thin;
one is blond, the other is black. That is the best society, and
I really believe that."*
Gaetano Pesce, 1993[9]

**7. Gaetano Pesce**
Chair and footrest, *Up 5* and *Up 6*
Designed 1969. Polyurethane foam,
viscose/nylon/Lycra fabric
Chair: 100 x 113.7 x 125.1 cm (39³⁄₈ x 44¾ x 49¼ in.)
Footrest: 59.1 x 59.1 x 59.1 cm (23¼ x 23¼ x 23¼ in.)
Produced by C&B Italia S.p.A. (Novedrate), 1970-72;
produced by B&B Italia (Novedrate), 1973-81, 1984,
1994 to the present
Unmarked
D84.179.1-2, gift of B&B Italia

*"When people try to understand a concept that is not evident,
each one makes his own interpretation. In the case of the Up 5,
some interpreted the chair as the body of the mother who
always receives us with a lot of love, who cradles us in her arms.
Others said it was a symbol of sex. Still others said different
things. That was good for me — to see that the object was open
to different interpretations. Mine was that it represented
someone who had no freedom, a prisoner walking with a ball
attached to their leg. It is a female body with a ball. It is true
that throughout history women were always sacrificed because
of men's prejudices. It is like being in jail, like walking around
with a weight on your leg all the time. The only way to express
this concept was to display the ottoman or ball related to the
female body with a chain."*
Gaetano Pesce, 1993[10]

*"If Walt Disney (and he's not been the first) has 'humanized' animals as beings between man and animal, why not humanize objects as beings between man and things? Certainly, an object can remain unanimated before me; but if I grow fond of it, then it grows animated because it takes its soul from me, from my passion.... My coffeemakers entered into the imaginary world and invaded it as in a peaceful conquest. My first characters have been the most popular* maschera *('fancy mask'): Pulcinella and the Neapolitan comedy theater. It was as though their goblin wit entered the coffeemaker, animating it."*
Riccardo Dalisi, 1994[11]

**8. Riccardo Dalisi**
(born 1931, Potenza, Italy)
Coffeemaker prototype, *Toto*
Designed 1987. Tin, brass, copper
32.4 x 21 x 12.1 cm (12¾ x 8¼ x 4¾ in.)
Executed by Don Vincenzo (Naples) for Alessi
S.p.A. (Crusinallo), 1987
Impressed on underside: OFFICINA/ALESSI/1987
D88.229.1, gift of Vivian and David Campbell

**9. Riccardo Dalisi**
Coffeemaker prototype, *The King (Il Re)*
Designed 1986. Tin, copper, brass, paint
33 x 24.2 x 12.7 cm (13 x 9½ x 5 in.)
Executed by Don Vincenzo (Naples) for Alessi
S.p.A. (Crusinallo), 1986
Impressed on underside: OFFICINA/ALESSI/1986
D88.236.1, gift of Vivian and David Campbell

**10. Riccardo Dalisi**
Coffeemaker prototype, *The Greeting Coffeemaker (Caffettiera che saluta)*
Designed 1988. Copper, tin, plastic
15.5 x 22.6 x 8.3 cm (6⅛ x 8⅞ x 3¼ in.)
Executed by Don Vincenzo (Naples) for Alessi
S.p.A. (Crusinallo), 1988
Impressed on underside: OFFICINA/ALESSI/1988
D88.244.1, gift of Vivian and David Campbell

*"Modelled in glowing embers, Loïe Fuller does not burn; she oozes brightness, she is flame itself. Standing in a fire of coals, she smiles and her smile is like a grinning mask under the red veil in which she wraps herself, the veil which she waves and causes to ripple like the smoke of a fire over her lava-like nudity: she is Herculaneum buried beneath ashes, she is the Styx and the shores of Hades, she is Vesuvius with its gaping jaws spitting the fire of the earth, and she is Lot's wife transfixed in a statue of salt amid the avenging conflagration of the five accursed cities, this motionless and yet smiling nakedness among the coals with the fire of heaven and hell for a veil."*

Jean Lorrain, 1900[12]

**11. François-Raoul Larche**
(born 1860, St. André-de-Cubzac, France; died 1912, Paris)
Table lamp, *Loïe Fuller*
Designed c. 1898. Gilt bronze
46 x 19.4 x 19.5 cm (18⅛ x 7⅝ x 7¹¹⁄₁₆ in.)
Produced by Siot-Decauville (Paris), c. 1898–1901
Impressed on lower right: Raoul Larche; on lower left:
SIOT-DECAUVILLE/FONDEUR/PARIS [within a circle];
on back: N573
D94.309.1, The Liliane and David M. Stewart Collection

**12. Sam Kramer**
(born 1913, Pittsburgh, PA, USA; died 1964, New York, NY)
**Carol Kramer**
(born 1918, New York; died 1986, New York)
Brooch, *Dancers*
Executed c. 1947. Silver, gold, peridot, garnet, tourmaline
13.3 x 6.4 x 2.5 cm (5¼ x 2½ x 1 in.)
Impressed on front: [device of a mushroom within a circle surmounted by two semicircles]; engraved on reverse: '47
D93.319.1, The Liliane and David M. Stewart Collection

*"Carol Kramer in New York works with a personal, sensitive kind of expressionism, so that many of her pieces suggest human figures, often whimsical. By using normal stones, carefully selected for some unusual or subtle quality ... and spotting them at different places, she frequently conveys in her pieces surprise, fascination, wit."*
Sam Kramer, 1952[13]

**13. Fulvio Bianconi**
(born 1915, Padua, Italy; died 1996, Milan)
Bottle
Designed c. 1950. Glass
31 x 13.8 x 11.2 cm (12³⁄₁₆ x 5⁷⁄₁₆ x 4⁷⁄₁₆ in.)
Produced by Venini S.p.A. (Murano), 1950-53
Acid-stamped on underside: venini/murano/MADE IN ITALY
D94.183.1, The Liliane and David M. Stewart Collection

*"Immediately after the Second World War, the Murano factories started reproductions of nineteenth-century glass, very commercial and without a real spirit of innovation. Bianconi's works ... present a kind of reaction against this production, they want to be a 'metaphysical' version of these objects.... The female body is used, in my opinion, as a consequence of this nineteenth-century revival. You just have to think about those mold-blown bottles in the 1800s with the shape of a woman's torso. Mr. Bianconi, in any case, always had a great interest in the female body, full of joy and happiness...."*
Franco Deboni, 1995[14]

**14. Jean-Paul Gaultier**
(born 1952, Arcueil, France)
Display bottle
Designed 1991. Glass, metal
31 x 13 x 10 cm (12³⁄₁₆ x 5⅛ x 3¹⁵⁄₁₆ in.)
Produced by Verreries Pochet Du Courval for Parfums
Jean-Paul Gaultier (Paris), 1993 to
the present
Printed in gray around perimeter of clear plastic oval
sticker on underside: PARFUMS JEAN-PAUL GAULTIER/BPI -
75008 PARIS - MADE IN FRANCE - 30% VOL.; within oval:
VENTE INTERDITE - NOT FOR SALE/e 1000 ml - 34 FL. OZ.;
on left side: U.T.I.F. N565 M1/IDR 1000ml/AN 298,4 ml; in
center: EMB 45155-REF. 0015750; on right side: NON
DISPERDERE/NELL'AMBIENTE/DOPO L'USO; printed in black
in center of oval: KGU09 X
D95.138.1, The Liliane and David M. Stewart Collection

*"In his return to the sources of perfumery and glassmaking, in his journey into the past, Gaultier has but one principle, one point of departure, one trigger of inspiration. For his women of glass, he wants flesh. Here she is: she has the forms and color of a creature that is at once mythical and real. Idealized, victorious, she is like an Eve of the future and a madonna of today. She is the color of flesh because she is warmth, light, sensuality. She is corseted because that is how it is. How 'He' has decided 'She' shall be."*
Jean-Paul Gaultier Haute Parfumerie, 1993[15]

**15. Jean-Paul Gaultier**
Perfume bottle
Designed 1991. Glass, metal
11.7 x 4.7 x 4.3 cm (4⅝ x 1⅞ x 1¹¹⁄₁₆ in.)
Produced by Verreries Pochet Du Courval for Parfums Jean-Paul Gaultier (Paris), 1993 to the present
Printed in gray around perimeter of clear plastic oval sticker on underside: PARFUMS JEAN-PAUL GAULTIER/BPI - 75008 PARIS - MADE IN FRANCE - 70% VOL.; within oval: PARFUM/e 30 ml - 1 FL. OZ.; on left side: U.T.I.F. N565 M1/IDR 30 ml/AN 21 ml; on right side: NON DISPERDERE/NELL'AMBIENTE/DOPO L'USO; printed in silver at bottom center of oval: XIU15x
D95.105.1, gift of Mode et Parfums

**16. Jean-Paul Gaultier**
After-shave lotion bottle, *Le Male*
Designed 1995. Glass, metal
15.5 x 7.5 x 4.5 cm (6⅛ x 2¹⁵⁄₁₆ x 1¾ in.)
Produced by Verreries Pochet Du Courval for Parfums Jean-Paul Gaultier (Paris), 1995 to the present
Printed in gray around perimeter of clear plastic oval sticker on underside: PARFUMS JEAN-PAUL GAULTIER/BPI - 75008 PARIS - MADE IN FRANCE - 60% VOL.; within oval: LOTION APRES RASAGE/AFTER SHAVE LOTION/e 125 ml - 4.2 FL. OZ./U.T.I.F. N565 MI/IDR 125 ml/AN 74,7 ml; NON DISPERDERE/NELL'AMBIENTE/DOPO L'USO; printed in silver in center of oval: EUY 19x
D96.140.1, gift of Beauté Prestige International

*"'The Valet chair,' as its title suggests, is a humoristic thing, a whimsical creation. Wegner thought to himself: there's never anywhere to hang one's jacket when one goes to bed ... all right then, I'll make a chair whose top rail is a clothes hanger. The next thought was the fact that one never has anywhere to hang one's pants either.... The chair is now a unique example of whimsicality and fun. There is something both Rococo and violin-like about the bold curves of the back and seat in contrast to the drooping horns of the hanger."*
Johan Møller Nielsen, 1965[16]

**17. Hans Wegner**
(born 1914, Tønder, Denmark)
Chair, *Valet*
Designed 1953. Teak, brass, leather
96.2 x 51.3 x 51.3 cm (37⁷⁄₈ x 20³⁄₁₆ x 20³⁄₁₆ in.)
Produced by Johannes Hansens Møbelsnedkeri
(Søborg), 1953-86; produced by P.P. Møbler (Allerød),
1987 to the present
Unmarked
D83.103.1, gift of Edward J. Wormley

**18. Sam Kramer**
(born 1913, Pittsburgh, PA, USA;
died 1964, New York, NY)
**Peggy Ackerly**
(born 1921, Cheyenne, WY)
Bracelet
Executed c. 1948. Silver, copper
3.6 x 7.5 x 4.6 cm (1⁷⁄₁₆ x 2¹⁵⁄₁₆ x 1¹³⁄₁₆ in.)
Impressed inside: [device of a mushroom within a
circle surmounted by two semicircles]/STERLING
D94.246.1, gift of Paul Leblanc


*"... I usually make a rough plan of the idea before I start. Then
I gather together fragments of silver (usually left-over scraps
of sheet and wire in many forms and sizes). These are piled next
to the work so they can be added in a flash as the piece starts
to grow. Some of the larger scraps are settled ... in a skeleton
pattern. This is somewhat like the rough sketch."*
Sam Kramer, 1952[17]

**19. René Lalique**
(born 1860, Ay, France; died 1945, Paris)
Pendant
Designed c. 1898. Gold, enamels
10 x 3 x 0.4 cm (3¹⁵/₁₆ x 1³/₁₆ x ³/₁₆ in.)
Impressed on lower right edge: LALIQUE
D94.299.1, The Liliane and David M. Stewart Collection


*"Perhaps the imagination of M. Lalique is even better revealed in the designs where the woman becomes an insect or fish, keeping only the face or the torso of her human appearance. It would be fitting to open a special chapter on the images of his woman-flowers, living incarnations of the dream that obsessed Walter Crane and Richard Wagner. Certain masks, haloed or framed by an undulating mass of disheveled hair, evoke the memory of Maurice Maeterlinck...."*
Roger Marx, 1901[18]

**20. Hans Christiansen**
(born 1866, Flensburg, Germany; died 1945, Wiesbaden)
Cigarette case, *The Night (Die Nacht)*
Designed 1898. Enameled and partially gilt silver
1 x 8.1 x 4.1 cm (³/₈ x 3¼ x 1⅝ in.)
Produced by Louis Kuppenheim (Pforzheim), c. 1898–1900
Impressed on underside of lid: LK [device of moon with crown] 800 95/19; stamped at ends of lid and box: P; enameled in black on lid: [monogram of CH]
D94.206.1, gift of Dr. René Crépeau

*"There is no question of that philosophical depth which, in so many of our contemporaries, reveals itself on close inspection as confusion or pretension, nor of the struggles of mystical expression, but rather the very joy in creating that allowed Master Böcklin to produce his worlds of wonders. Christiansen's work was fertilized by sheer joy in form and color."*
Hans Schliepmann, 1898[19]

**21. Unknown designer**
Brooch
Designed c. 1904-10. Silver
6.5 x 5.9 x 2 cm (2⁹/₁₆ x 2⁵/₁₆ x 1³/₁₆ in.)
Produced by William B. Kerr and Co.
(Newark, NJ, USA), c. 1904-10
Impressed on oval plaque affixed to underside:
[device of axe]/STERLING/1703
D94.190.1, The Liliane and David M. Stewart Collection

**22. Attributed to Philemon Dickinson**
(dates of birth and death unknown)
Bonbon dish
Designed c. 1900. Silver
1.9 x 16.2 x 18.6 cm (¾ x 6³/₈ x 7⁵/₁₆ in.)
Produced by Unger Brothers
(Newark, NJ, USA), c. 1900-10
Impressed on underside: [device of intertwined UB
encircled by STERLING/925 FINE] 0547
D94.191.1, The Liliane and David M. Stewart Collection

*"The symbolist head found its way into American jewelry factories both through German and French design books, and through the immigration of designers and metalworkers.... Industrial die-stamping techniques allowed for the mass production of relatively large-scale, stylish jewelry that could be sold at low cost to a wide consumer audience. The original poetic symbolism of the female head, with its swirling hair and langorous expression, had given way to a popular stylishness summed up in the advertising slogans of the period: 'If you love pretty things it will please you, and if you like to save a dollar it will interest you.'"*
Ulysses Dietz, 1996[20]

*"Almost to the exclusion of men, it is the woman who dominates the Art Nouveau world and the aspect of woman which preoccupies the artist is her hair — long, flowing hair which may merge with drapery or become part of a general wavy configuration."*
Peter Selz, 1960[21]

**23. Pablo Picasso**
(born 1885, Málaga, Spain; died 1973, Cannes, France)
Vase, *Tripod*
Designed 1951–52. Glazed earthenware
72.7 x 26.7 x 29.5 cm (28⅝ x 10½ x 11⅝ in.)
Produced by Poterie Madoura (Vallauris, France), c. 1952
Impressed on underside of two arms: EDITION/PICASSO;
impressed on underside of right arm: MADOURA/[encircling
device of a flame]/PLEIN FEU; painted in black near base of
rear support: 4/75
D96.109.1, The Liliane and David M. Stewart Collection

*"In a few strokes with the flat of the knife, he [Picasso] shapes
the fresh clay.... He presses three times with thumb and
forefinger, in the exact right spots, and the shape of a woman
emerges, perfect.... On the surface of clay, still damp, a few
passes bring out a face – hilarious and irresistible...."*
*Craft Horizons,* 1950[22]

**24. Valerie (Vally) Wieselthier**
(born 1895, Vienna, Austria; died 1945, New York, NY, USA)
Vase
Designed c. 1935. Glazed porcelain
24 x 18.2 x 11.9 cm (9 7/16 x 7 5/16 x 4 11/16 in.)
Produced by General Ceramics Co. (Keasby, NJ), c. 1935-40
Printed in blue on underside: v. [device of vase] w./U.S.A./
BY GENERAL CERAMICS
D94.192.1, The Liliane and David M. Stewart Collection


*"Ceramics are made ultimately with a purpose, whether religious or useful or decorative; they are always ... lived with.... They are to reflect the personality of the owner besides that of the maker, and the owner, when he looks at a genuinely-worked piece of pottery, should feel as happy as the artist when he made it: he should laugh with the artist."*
Vally Wieselthier, 1929[23]

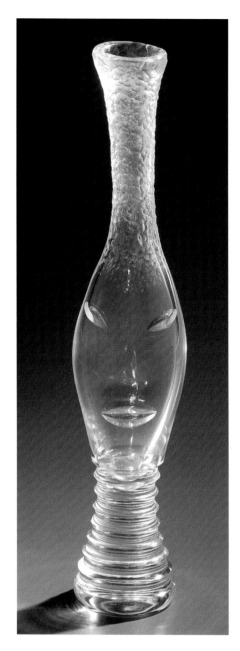

**25. Viktor (Vicke) Emanuel Lindstrand**
(born 1904, Göteborg, Sweden; died 1983, Åhus)
Vase, *Negress*
Designed 1953. Glass
40.4 x 8.6 x 8.6 cm (16 x 3½ x 3½ in.)
Produced by Kosta Glasbruk (Kosta), 1953–c. 1956
Acid-stamped on underside: LIND-/STRAND/KOSTA [within
a square]; engraved on underside: LS 580
D95.160.1, The Liliane and David M. Stewart Collection

*"In this vase, Vicke Lindstrand has transformed African totemic
art into a Western style anthropomorphic vase. As early as
1937, he had designed glass vases with African motifs, and his
fascination with this theme persisted throughout his career.
His awareness of Picasso, Matisse, Brancusi, as well as his own
training both in painting and sculpture, are evident here in his
skillful blend of African art with the stylistic innovations of the
Paris school."*
Dan Klein, 1995[24]

**26. Peter Voulkos**
(born 1924, Bozeman, MT, USA)
Vase
Executed 1955. Glazed and slip-painted stoneware
63.5 x 22.9 x 21.6 cm (25 x 9 x 8½ in.)
Painted in oxide on underside: *Voulkos*
D91.324.1, gift of Mr. and Mrs. Jean Boucher

*"His influences at that time were not Miró and Picasso; he didn't know much about their ceramics then. He was trying out all kinds of things that he liked to do. More specific influences were Chinese, Cypriot and Greek ware. He says the relationship between the figure and the surrounding decoration are for him 'one and the same; it speaks for itself.'"*
Sam Jornlin (assistant to Peter Voulkos), 1994[25]

"This mocha service was manufactured in two versions that suggest the dual, almost schizoid, nature of Viennese design in the years after World War I. The first was unadorned, and its austere, well-proportioned forms continued the purism of Hoffmann and the early Wiener Werkstätte. The second was decorative: it utilized the very same forms but replaced the plain knobs with charming, exotic heads — each national type suggesting the locale of the product contained within. Such figurative finials recall eighteenth-century usage and, like so many designs from the later Wiener Werkstätte and like the music of Richard Strauss, possess a sweet, elegiac neo-Rococo flavor."
Martin Eidelberg, 1995[26]

**27. Emma Helena (Ena) Rottenberg**
(born 1893, Oravica, Romania; died 1950, Vienna, Austria)
Mocha service, *Exotic*
Designed 1930. Glazed porcelain
Mocha pot: 16.4 x 19.5 x 11.5 cm (6⅞ x 7¹¹⁄₁₆ x 4½ in.)
Produced by Wiener Porzellanmanufaktur Augarten
(Vienna), 1930 to the present
Printed in blue on underside of each: [device of banded shield surmounted by a crown with a cross]/*Wien*
D95.108.1-3, The Liliane and David M. Stewart Collection

*"I was willing to do almost anything to get out of my rut – to find the means to practice an art I did not have to sell.... That year I did my only strictly industrial design called* **The Radio Nurse,** *a device for listening in to other rooms within a house, as a precaution against kidnapping (such as the Lindbergh case) made by the Zenith Radio Company."*
Isamu Noguchi, 1968[27]

**28. Isamu Noguchi**
(born 1904, Los Angeles, CA, USA; died 1988, New York, NY)
Shortwave radio transmitter, *Radio Nurse*
Designed c. 1937. Bakelite housing
21 x 16.5 x 16.5 cm (8¼ x 6½ x 6½ in.)
Produced by Zenith Radio Corporation (Chicago, IL), c. 1938–c. 1941; housing produced by Kurz-Kasch, Inc. (Dayton, OH) and Chicago Molded Products Corp. (Chicago)
Impressed on back: ZENITH RADIO CORPORATION [device with S.O.S. and figure in bed] NURSE/design by Noguchi/patent applied for/117 volts-50/60 cycle-25 watts/ZENITH RADIO CORP., CHICAGO
D90.101.1, The Liliane and David M. Stewart Collection

*"The design of the mask was supposed to inspire fear and intimidation in the opponent."*
Barbara Lynn, 1994[28]

**29. George A. Lynn**
(born 1941, Brampton, Ontario, Canada; died 1983, Ottawa)
Hockey Mask, *HM6 Goalie Face Guard*
Designed 1971. Polyethylene
23.5 x 19 x 13 cm (9¼ x 7½ x 5⅛ in.)
Produced by Cooper Canada Limited (Toronto), c. 1972–c. 1989
Unmarked
D85.165.1, gift of Cooper Canada Limited

**30. Andrea Branzi**
(born 1938, Florence, Italy)
Coffee cups and saucers, *Tatzine*
Designed 1986. Glazed porcelain
Cup: 7.4 x 9.9 x 8.2 cm (2¹⁵⁄₁₆ x 3⅞ x 3¼ in.)
Saucer: 3.2 x 11.8 x 8 cm (1¼ x 4⅝ x 3⅛ in.)
Produced by Alessi S.p.A. (Crusinallo), 1986
Cups: one printed in black within rectangular outline
on underside of handle: ᴛ; other unmarked
Saucer: one printed in black around underside:
ᴛᴇɴᴅᴇɴᴛsᴇ ɪᴛᴀʟʏ ᴅᴇsɪɢɴ ᴀɴᴅʀᴇᴀ ʙʀᴀɴᴢɪ; other unmarked
D91.388.1-4, gift of Andrea Branzi

*"The design of Tatzine refers to an animist idea, i.e., to the matter that objects have a soul, that they must be a friendly presence — somewhat domestic elves."*
Andrea Branzi, 1993[29]

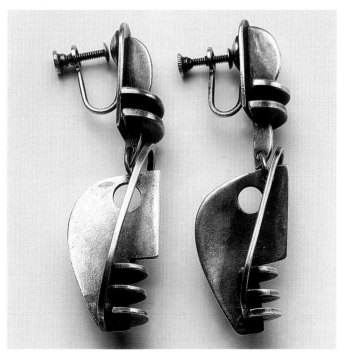

**31. Ed Wiener**
(born 1918, New York, NY, USA; died 1991, New York)
Pair of earrings
Executed c. 1949. Silver
6.7 x 1.7 x 1.8 cm (2⅝ x ¹¹⁄₁₆ x ¹¹⁄₁₆ in.)
Impressed on each screwback: STERLING
D94.275.1, gift of Paul Leblanc

*"What I responded to were forms that stimulated associations without being descriptive. Could it be a face, a figure, a motion, a remembered object? ... In paintings I saw myriad forms to be explored and ... translated into reflective silver ... negative space, volume, air, all had to be redefined in sheet and wire ..."*
Ed Wiener, 1988[30]

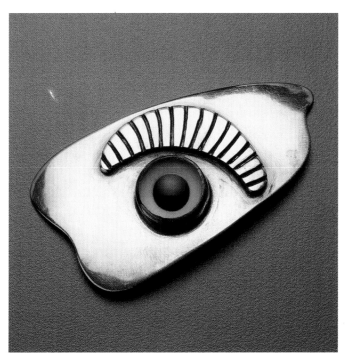

**32. Sam Kramer**
(born 1913, Pittsburgh, PA, USA; died 1964, New York, NY)
**Charles Wendell**
(born 1919, New York; died 1993, Santa Barbara, CA)
Brooch
Executed c. 1948. Silver, glass taxidermy eye
4.2 x 7.3 x 1.5 cm (1⅝ x 2⅞ x ⁹⁄₁₆ in.)
Impressed on underside: [device of a mushroom within a circle surmounted by two semicircles]/STERLING
D93.224.1, anonymous gift

*"An adventurous attitude leads to the use of many unexpected materials. In our jewelry workshop we use glass eyes from stuffed animals, ... teeth and tusks and bones ... chunks of meteorites, and pieces of colored glass.... Every conceivable material, often not ordinarily associated with jewelry, can be used. Each of these materials will provoke a certain feeling, and at the same time suggest a multitude of intriguing design possibilities."*
Sam Kramer, 1952[31]

*"The ear is the symbol of man inside the present Sensorial Revolution, which is a revolution produced by the great development of all ... superficial, electronic, symbolic communications. The ear is the human organ that links us constantly with the 'background noise' of the artificial universe, and that allows us to tune in the messages and the voices within the great gray sound around us."*
Andrea Branzi, 1993[32]

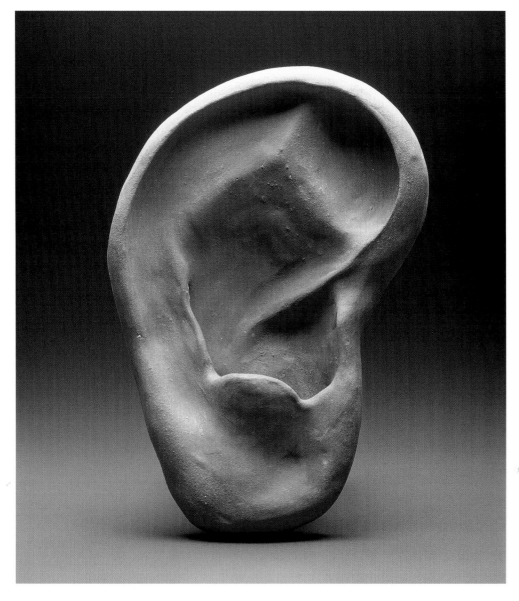

**33. Andrea Branzi**
(born 1938, Florence, Italy)
Vase, *Ear (Orecchio)*
Designed 1986. Unglazed earthenware
25.1 x 16 x 6.4 cm (9⅞ x 6⁵⁄₁₆ x 2½ in.)
Produced by Ceramiche di Capraia (Capraia), 1986
Unmarked
D91.398.1, gift of Paul Leblanc

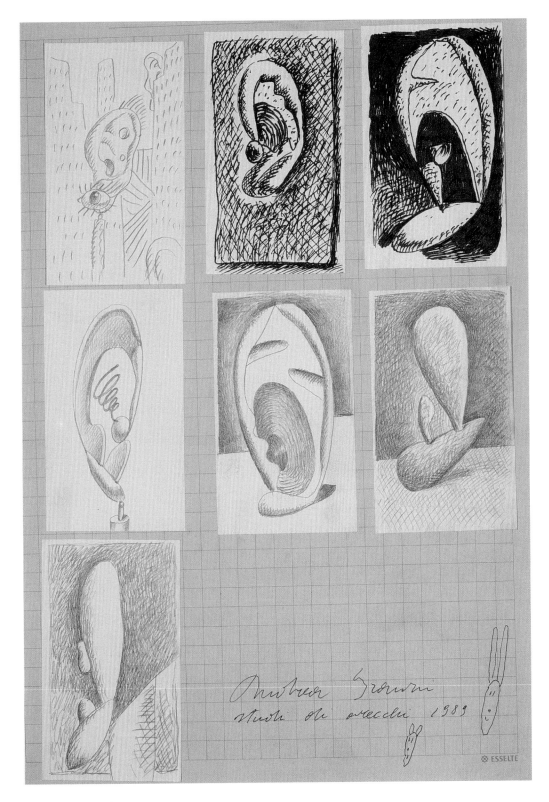

**34. Andrea Branzi**
Drawings, *Studies of Ears (Studi di Orecchi)*
Executed 1989. Pencil and ink on paper
41.9 x 29.6 cm (16½ x 11⅝ in.)
Signed in blue/black ink at bottom right: *Andrea Branzi/studi di orecchi 1989* [device of two repeated stylized rabbit heads]
D91.397.10, gift of Paul Leblanc

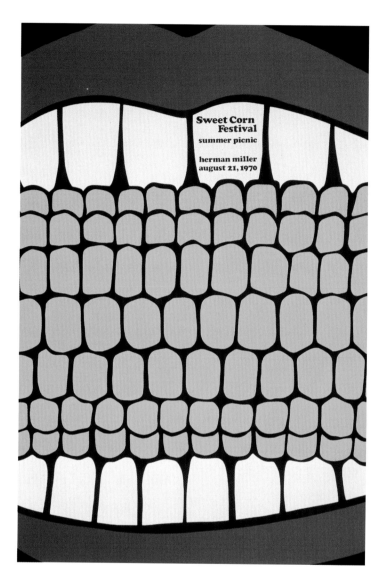

**35. Stanley Tigerman**
(born 1930, Chicago, IL, USA)
Coffeepot prototype
Designed 1979. Brass
20.7 x 15.3 x 9.2 cm (8⅛ x 6 x 3⅝ in.)
Produced by Alessi S.p.A. (Crusinallo, Italy), 1983
Impressed on underside: [device of an eagle
surmounting OFFICINA/ALESSI]/T/M/1982/1/1
D88.214.1, gift of Vivian and David Campbell

*"Stanley Tigerman is the only one to give tea and coffee a pointedly sexual flavor. Reminiscent of Goldfinger and Lolita at once, Tigerman's set is decidedly kinky to touch. Its tray handles are lifelike hands; its spouts are pouty lips that open and close; one picks up the sugar bowl by its ears, while the other containers are lifted by their ponytails."*
Brooks Adams, 1984[33]

**36. Stephen Frykholm**
(born 1942, Seattle, WA, USA)
Poster, *Sweet Corn Festival*
Designed 1970. Printed paper
100 x 63.5 cm (39⅜ x 25 in.)
Printed by Continental Identification Products
(Sparta, MI) for Herman Miller, Inc. (Zeeland, MI), 1970
Unmarked
D87.202.1, gift of Herman Miller, Inc.

*"When the picnic committee decided to call the annual picnic the 'sweet corn festival,' what else could I do besides corn on the cob?... I've always depicted food as seen from the point of view of the Lilliputians in Gulliver's Travels. This point of view adds to the enjoyment and surprise of looking at the posters."*
Stephen Frykholm, 1989[34]

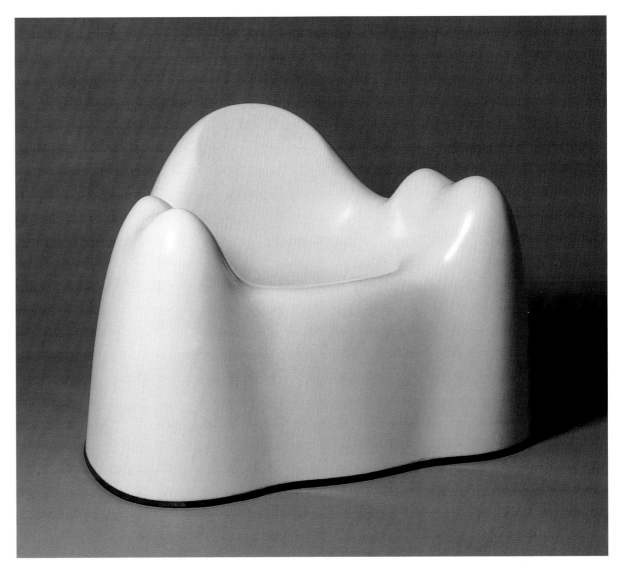

**37. Wendell Castle**
(born 1932, Emporia, KS, USA)
Armchair, *Molar*
Designed 1968. Fiberglass-reinforced polyester
86.4 x 71.1 x 61 cm (34 x 28 x 24 in.)
Produced by Northern Plastics Corporation (Syracuse, NY)
for Beylerian Limited (New York), 1969-70
Unmarked
D95.158.1, The Liliane and David M. Stewart Collection

*"What's important to me, not in as much as I think about playfulness, but what I think about all furniture — and that's as true today as it was with the molar — is that I like the idea that things are not exactly what they appear to be, that there's sort of a little bit of a deception going on.... And by that kind of thinking, sometimes, there's kind of the introduction of humor, and then the title sometimes also has some impact on the humor.... If you didn't call the molar chair the molar chair and called it something else, it might not have the same impact. So I think there is humor by virtue of its scale and that it is an abstraction of a tooth, and a material and everything that goes into it."*
Wendell Castle, 1996[35]

*"[I] presented reality in human body forms. The first series was the* MOUTH *– symbol of society's waste and greed that eventually devours itself. Next came the* FIST, *representing encounters between forces, not necessarily of violence. After that, the* HAND *– hand as creative, an instrument of knowledge and invention, meant to establish a relationship with others."*
Bruno Martinazzi, 1978[36]

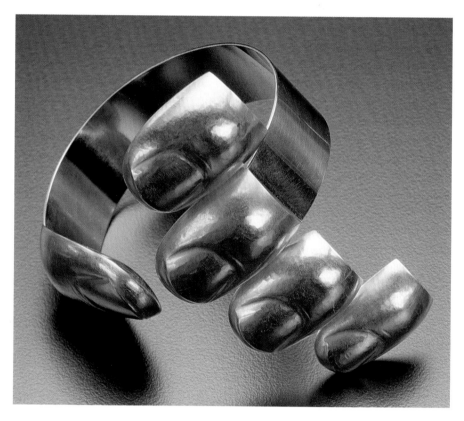

**38. Bruno Martinazzi**
(born 1923, Turin, Italy)
Bracelet, *Goldfinger*
Executed 1969. Yellow and white gold
7.6 x 6.4 x 5.7 cm (3 x 2½ x 2¼ in.)
Engraved behind thumb: MARTINAZZI;
on underside of thumb: III/XII
D93.203.1, The Liliane and David M. Stewart Collection

**39. Metal: David Palterer**
(born 1949, Haifa, Israel)
**Glass: Borek Sípek**
(born 1949, Prague, Czechoslovakia)
Champagne glass prototype, no. 106
Designed 1986. Silver-plated bronze,
silver-plated brass, glass
24.2 x 14.9 x 14.6 cm (9½ x 5⅞ x 5¾ in.)
Metal produced by Fonderia Metalli (Florence, Italy); glass
produced by Petr Novotny (Novy Bor, Czechoslovakia) for
Alterego (Amsterdam, The Netherlands), 1986-90
Unmarked
D90.145.1, The Liliane and David M. Stewart Collection

*"'Man is the measure of all things' (Protagoras).... In this
perspective, the hands with which human beings work and exert
their strength are not only a unit of measurement, but are also
the object of beliefs and cults.... The use I make of the grip
consciously appropriates the hand as a metaphor, not through
its image but through its imprint, its 'reflected image,' a negative that, in turn, is a handle par excellence, succeeding not only
in having a function but also in describing it."*
David Palterer, 1994[37]

**40. Pedro Friedeberg**
(born 1937, Florence, Italy)
Chair, *Baphomet's Handchair*
Designed 1961. Mahogany
87 x 61 x 51 cm (34¼ x 24 x 20⅛ in.)
Executed by Pedro Friedeberg
(San Miguel de Allende, Mexico), 1961-77
Incised on base: PEDRO FRIEDEBERG
D89.203.1, gift of Esperanza and Mark Schwartz

**41. Pedro Friedeberg**
Table, *Baphomet's Handtable*
Designed 1961. Mahogany
46 x 87 x 59 cm (18⅛ x 34¼ x 23¼ in.)
Executed by Pedro Friedeberg
(San Miguel de Allende), 1961-77
Painted in black on underside of one foot:
PEDRO FRIEDEBERG
D89.203.2, gift of Esperanza and Mark Schwartz

*"When it [Baphomet's Handchair] was first created it was mainly as a reaction against Mies van der Rohe's hideous Barcelona chair, which had already been around for over thirty years and which the public was just discovering as the latest in modern furniture! Many are still sitting in it.*

*Baphomet was a devil-like creature or idol supposedly worshiped by the Knights Templar in the thirteenth century and one of the reasons that this worthy secret society was abolished. Baphomet was described as having a bearded woman's head (or sometimes a pig's head with horns) and, usually, large hands and feet. He was invested with supernatural divine and diabolical powers. He sired 666 children, some of whom he ate for supper one moonless night. He had over five hundred credit cards that helped him conquer Jerusalem and Constantinople ... anybody who sits in Baphomet's Handchair for a period of 666 seconds is automatically invested with intensely obsolete diabolical and angelic powers."*
Pedro Friedeberg, 1994[38]

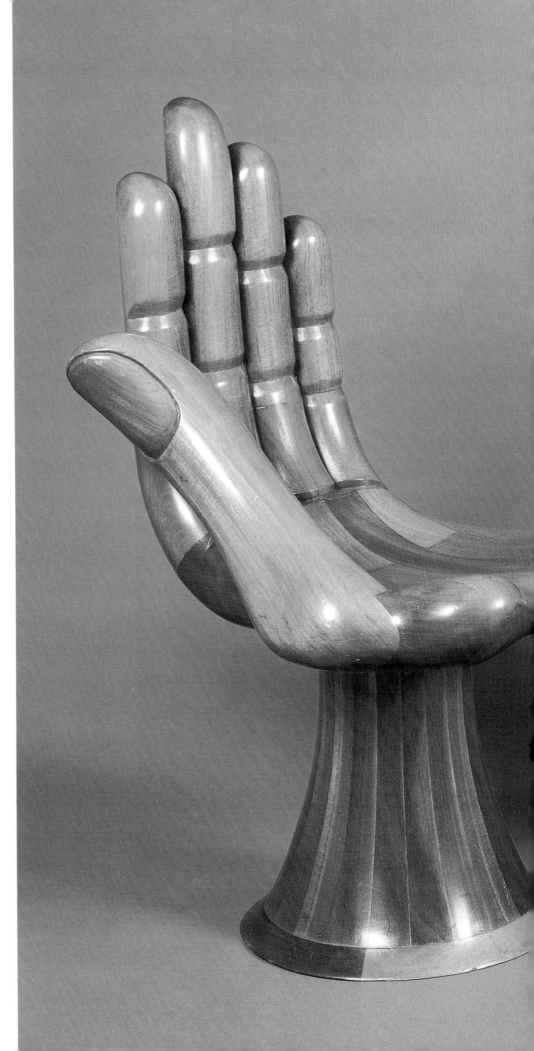

**42. Piero Fornasetti**
(born 1913, Milan, Italy; died 1988, Milan)
Umbrella stand, *Roman Foot*
Designed 1953. Glazed porcelain
60 x 17 x 44 cm (23⅝ x 6¹¹⁄₁₆ x 17⁵⁄₁₆ in.)
Produced by Piero Fornasetti (Milan), 1953-70
Printed in black on gold paper sticker affixed to heel:
FORNASETTI MILANO MADE IN ITALY/[device of hand
holding a paint brush]
D95.146.1, The Liliane and David M. Stewart Collection

*"What a delight to sit with one's back to the
smiling face of the sun, or the capital of a
Corinthian column; to eat grapes from a plate
engraved with Eve's foot, filet mignon from
Adam's ribs ... take freshly starched shirts
from a Palladian villa; place a dripping umbrella
in a Roman sandal...."*
Stephen Neil Greengard, 1989[39]

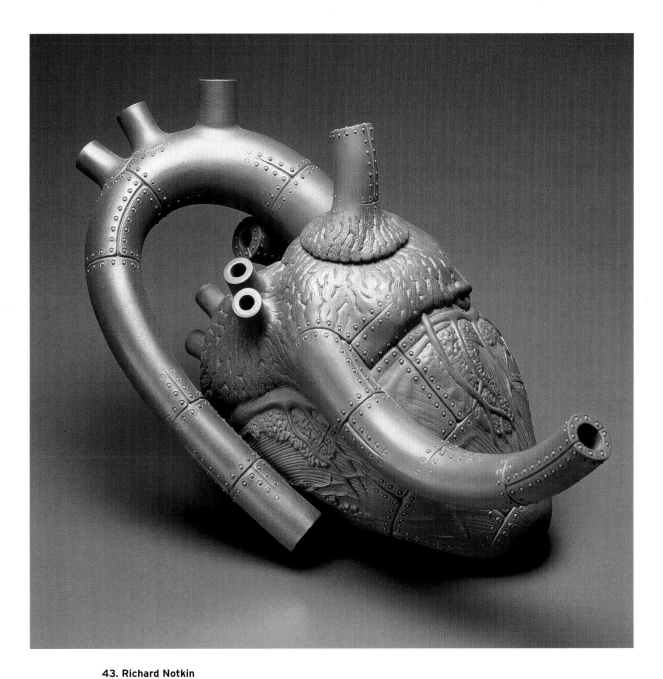

**43. Richard Notkin**
(born 1948, Chicago, IL, USA)
Teapot, *Heart Teapot: Metamorphosis II*
Executed 1989, Unglazed stoneware
15.2 x 27 x 13.4 cm (6 x 10⅝ x 5¼ in.)
Incised on underside: *Notkin/1989*
D94.205.1, gift of Dr. René Crépeau

*"The teapot, as a domestic, universally acceptable and unthreatening object, provides a bridge to 'everyperson' and draws unsuspecting viewers into the deeper, initially hidden meanings. At first, recognition that the teapot is also a heart provides the viewer with a sense of amusement, one that soon transforms into the discovery of more unsettling concepts. The metamorphosis of the visual narrative of the object, from teapot to heart and then to heart of armor – or thorns, or stone, or charred flesh, or ice – requires a metamorphosis of thought process in the viewer. It's a bit of a dirty trick, the old 'bait and switch,' but it works. The teapot is the hook."*
Richard Notkin, 1994[40]

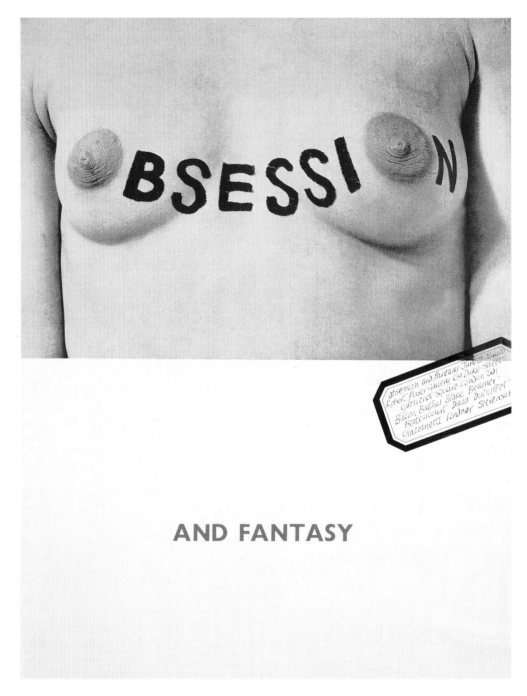

**44. Robert Brownjohn**
(born 1925, Newark, NJ, USA; died 1970, London, England)
Poster, *Obsession and Fantasy*
Designed 1963. Offset lithograph
61.1 x 45.8 cm (24 1/16 x 18 1/16 in.)
Printed by Graphis Press Ltd (London) for
Robert Fraser Gallery (London), 1963
Printed in black along lower left edge: DESIGNED BY ROBERT
BROWNJOHN/PRINTED BY GRAPHIS PRESS LTD
D95.102.1, gift of Luc d'Iberville-Moreau

**45. Piero Fornasetti**
(born 1913, Milan, Italy; died 1988, Milan)
Dinner plate
Designed c. 1960. Glazed porcelain, transfer printed
26.4 x 26.4 x 2.5 cm (10⅜ x 10⅜ x 1 in.)
Produced by Piero Fornasetti (Milan, Italy),
c. 1960-64
Printed in black on underside of plate: [device of eye
within rectangle]/TEMA E/VARIAZIONI/182 [device of
hand holding a paint brush]/FORNASETTI · MILANO/
MADE IN ITALY
D88.157.1, The Liliane and David M. Stewart Collection

*"[When I see Fornasetti] it seems I am looking at a very dear, very sophisticated child, a magic child with charms that can transform the world into a place of fantastic memories, into a supermarket of postcards, stickers, games, puzzles, writings, photographs that come from far-away lands where everything is beautiful, silent, pleasant, noble and even a bit comic, a bit ridiculous, a bit erotic, a bit beguiling. Far-off lands where we all, as good children and as no-good children, would like to go."*
Ettore Sottsass, 1991[42]

**46. Giorgio (Giò) Pomodoro**
(born 1930, Orciano di Pesaro, Italy)
Necklace, *Comrade in Hermes! (Koinos Hermes!)*
Executed 1963, Pink and white gold, rubies, emeralds,
chalcedony concretion (agate)
Extended: 41.9 cm (16½ in.); pendant: 7.6 x 5.4 x 1.9 cm
(3 x 2⅛ x ¾ in.)
Etched on reverse of shaft: *Giò Pomodoro*
D88.124.1, The Liliane and David M. Stewart Collection

*"This necklace ... is an object for personal use invested
with symbolic meanings derived from the Hermetic
tradition. The ithyphallic emblem of Hermes (the erect
phallus) and the Moon emblem (embodied in the chalcedony concretion) are the most obvious aspects.*

*The piece is not intended to be provocative; on the
contrary, it refers to the mythological traditions of the
Greek Olympian religion, in which the myth of Hermes
numbered among the most important. Far removed from
the ideology of contemporary 'design,' this object has
a practical value that refers to the sphere of the sacred
and it is therefore not merely a decorative object.*

*The title I propose for the necklace are the words of
exhortation exclaimed by the followers of Hermes before
embarking on their adventures: 'Koinos Hermes!'"*
Giò Pomodoro, 1995[43]

**47. Gerd Rothmann**
(born 1941, Frankfurt, Germany)
Necklace, *Jewelry for a Dancer (Schmuck einer Tänzerin)*
Executed 1986, Silver
4.7 x 64.3 x 0.4 cm (1⅞ x 25⁵⁄₁₆ x ³⁄₁₆ in.)
Written in pencil on underside of accompanying box:
*Schmuck einer Tänzerin/1986/Rothmann*
D93.220.1, The Liliane and David M. Stewart Collection

*"The necklace was an exchange. I wanted an abstract
picture from a friend, a well-known painter. He had a
beautiful, proud, wonderful friend, a dancer from
Argentina.... She knew of our [planned] trade and
I wanted to speak to her about how and what I could
make.... The dance or the ballet, this kind of world has
a sensual-erotic emanation. I had already molded many
forms based on bodies and had them cast in metal.
It remained to find the appropriate body-form which
touched on or better still was associated with this
sensual eroticism.... At first one sees the discs with an
emphasis on the central point – attractive as jewelry,
not exceptional or classical. On second glance, one
discovers [that] the origin of this delicate modeling
[is the nipple]."*
Gerd Rothmann, 1993[44]

*"Many cultures made udder-shaped clay pots which grew from earlier vessels.... The model was animal or human, actually a breast form – a container. My triple udder pots start from these vessels.... The handle has a mermaid head – the face cannot be pretty, or it could look like a 1937 Pontiac hood ornament.... The breasts are in the pot. The handle has a fishlike tail termination as it tucks in between the udder forms."*
Ken Ferguson, 1995[45]

**48. Ken Ferguson**
(born 1928, Elwood, IN, USA)
Pitcher, *Mermaid Triple Udder Pitcher*
Executed 1994, Glazed stoneware
46.5 x 25.4 x 35 cm (18⁵⁄₁₆ x 10 x 13¾ in.)
Unmarked
D95.144.1, The Liliane and David M. Stewart Collection
and gift of Geoffrey N. Bradfield, by exchange*

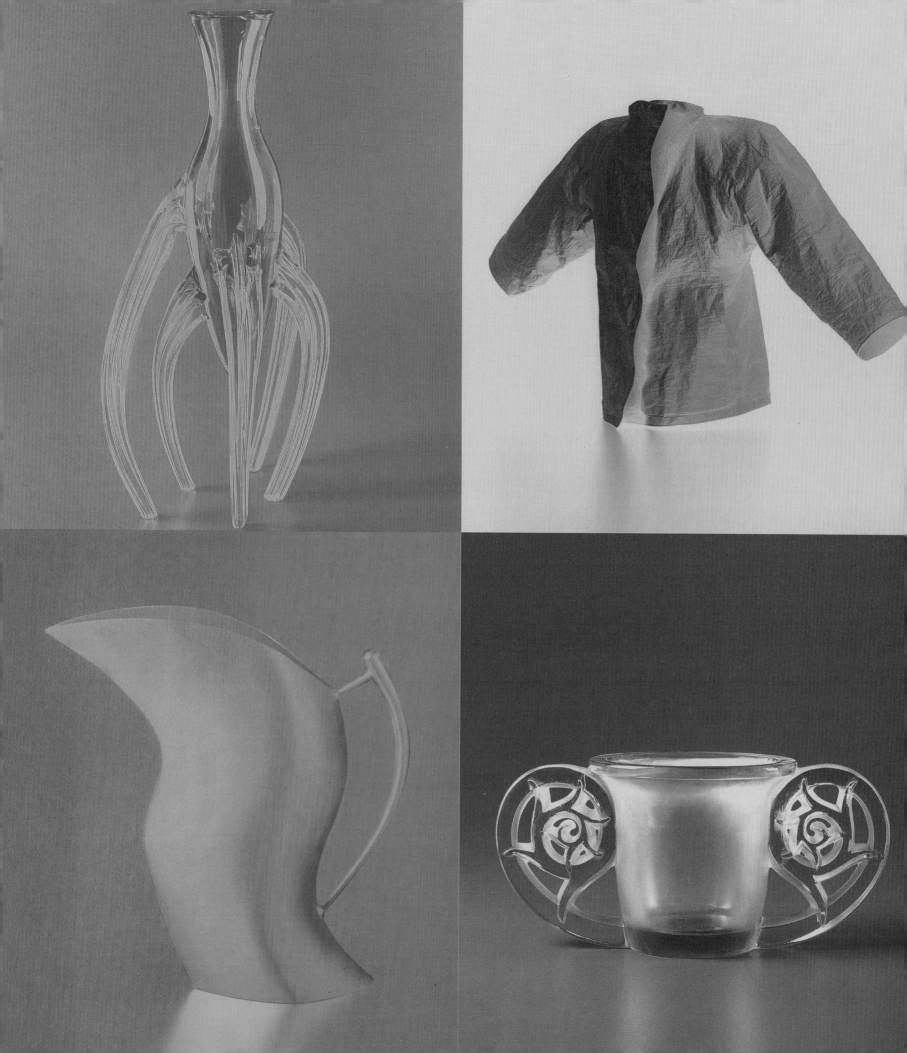

# Inversion and Transformation

# Inversion and Transformation

*by Lenore Newman and Jan L. Spak*

"Take an object. Do something to it. Do something else to it."[1] This famous proposition by Jasper Johns summarizes one of the intrinsic strategies of the modern artist. Although that tactic may be seen as a component of traditional art as well—such as reworking a Classical or biblical episode in a contemporary mode—the Modernist sensibility elevates incongruity and surprise to a degree of importance that earlier Western art conventions did not readily admit.

In the decorative arts, the idea of transforming an object into something other than what it was meant to be, thereby subverting its purpose, was a Modernist taboo. The very words "inversion" and "transformation" are antithetical to such Modernist dictums as "form follows function." These oft-quoted principles of design had their roots, of course, in nineteenth-century reform theory which stressed morality and fitness for purpose. As Augustus W. N. Pugin wrote, "How many objects of ordinary use are rendered monstrous and ridiculous simply because the artist, instead of seeking the most convenient form … has embodied some extravagance to conceal the real purpose for which the article has been made."[2] By the 1920s, the premise of strict functionalism reigned supreme among trendsetters, and by mid century, the functionalist credo had exerted a significant influence on industrial design. Even so, proselytizers like Edgar Kaufmann, jr., still found it necessary to remind the public that "Modern design should express the purpose of an object, never making it seem to be what it is not."[3]

Yet throughout the century, and even within the parameters of Modernist rhetoric, designers have ventured beyond function to create objects that subvert expected notions of form and challenge our traditional assumptions about the behavior of materials. The ways in which twentieth-century designers have transformed common objects into creative new visions are seemingly infinite yet they conform to certain basic formulas. Often, functional elements such as bases, handles, and openings are inverted in meaning or exaggerated in scale. Elsewhere, designers play upon what we normally expect from metal, glass, and other standard materials: making hard materials seem soft, making soft materials seem hard, transferring techniques appropriate for one material to another. Although certain of these tendencies are often ascribed to a specific period, in fact, designers of the later twentieth century used the same devices as those of earlier decades, thus revealing the unity of this century's design and the pervasive desire to provoke surprise and joy.

Earlier generations had established rules governing the structure of buildings and objects. For example, not only did the preponderant weight have to be at the bottom, but also the base had to be suitably wide, and there needed to be visual assurance of structural firmness. Given these traditional and logical strictures, it was inevitable that the base would be a prime target for whimsical expression. Viennese design offers a prime example. Kirk Varnedoe has pointed out that in the Wiener Werkstätte's designs, a recurring element was "a spherical form, a ball that quickly became a stylistic accent separate from, or even opposed to, structural logic."[4] The Austrian designers of that era used them structurally as well. A glass bowl by the Loetz Witwe firm (cat. no. 50) and a ceramic bowl from the Wiener und Gmündner pottery (cat. no. 49), both from the early years of the century, rest on round balls typical of this amusing Viennese predilection.

Fig. 47. Josef Albers, fruit bowl, 1923.
Glass, metal, wood.
7.5 x 36.5 x 36.5 cm (2¹⁵⁄₁₆ x 14⅜ x 14⅜ in.).
Berlin, Bauhaus-Archiv.

Fig. 48. Chris Lebeau, three bowls on stands,
1924–25. Glass.
Leerdam, Stichting Nationaal Glasmuseum Leerdam.

By virtue of their perfect shape, these spheres also fitted within the minimalist parameters of Bauhaus guidelines, as in a fruit bowl designed by Josef Albers (fig. 47); lacquered wood balls might seem an improbable form of base from a rational standpoint, but they certainly add a distinctive note to Albers's ascetic decoration. Similarly, at the end of the century, spherical forms were chosen to support Masanori Umeda's triangular vase (cat. no. 51), but here they refer directly to male sexuality in a manner uncannily reminiscent of Man Ray's *Priapus Paperweight* (fig. 9).

By over- or underscaling, designers can also play with expected notions of proportion and order, and challenge the norm of stability. Wilhelm Kåge's *Terra Spirea* vase (cat. no. 52), thrown as a single piece, and Chris Lebeau's vase and stand (cat. no. 53), two distinct entities, evidence the designers' strategy of making disproportionately small bases. In Kåge's vase, the body tapers miraculously to a slender point and seems to balance precariously on its dainty base, resembling a spinning top abruptly halted in motion. The stepped base for the Lebeau vase rests on its narrowest diameter rather than its widest. The same base could also be used the opposite way, with the widest diameter at the bottom to support other glass shapes in a more traditional way (fig. 48, right side). Lebeau created an inventive series of many interchangeable components. However functionalist in concept, his treatment of the base becomes an element of both style and ornament, and the dark purple color adds a sense of drama and weight. Likewise, an Art Deco form designed by Jacques-Émile Ruhlmann for the Sèvres manufactory (cat. no. 146) similarly trifles with the sense of stability by miniaturizing the base.

At the opposite extreme are bases that are overscaled or excessive in relation to any supposed function of support. This counters the Modernist notion that structure be simplified and minimalized. The paradigm of the Modernist desire for simplicity is an illustration prepared for the magazine *Bauhaus, Zeitschrift für Gestaltung* showing a sequence of chairs designed by Marcel Breuer (fig. 50). The pseudofilmstrip goes from a carved wooden chair with African-inspired decoration to simpler wooden and then tubular steel chairs. It progresses from elaborate decoration to unadorned structure, and from traditional materials to modern industrial materials. Most important of all, the last photo shows a woman seated on seemingly nothing — a resilient column of compressed air. These images register the Bauhaus's actual and theoretical "progress" — a word weighted with positivist significance. While this minimalist form of air seating was a humorous exaggeration, still, the theory of progressive design went in just this reductivist direction. Breuer's famed *B55* chair, with its cantilevered frame of tubular steel (fig. 49), reduced the number of vertical supports from four to two and, several decades later, Eero Saarinen's pedestal chair of plastic, fiberglass, and aluminum reduced the support still further to a single slender element.

Whereas Saarinen was troubled by the "clutter of legs" of traditional furniture, many modern designers have veered in the opposite direction, incorporating superfluous elements. The multiple, insect-like legs of Gaetano Pesce's *Greene Street* chair (cat. no. 54) and David Palterer's *Little Dipper* vase (cat. no. 55), both designed in recent years, make a virtue of superfluity and amusingly lend a sense of animation; one can envision them spiritedly crawling away. Ironically, Pesce's humor is not so mirthful in intent; with these extra legs, he wants us to consider instability in seating as a metaphor for our uncertain times. Max Schmidt's *Elephant Trunk Table* (cat. no. 56), designed some eighty years earlier, also has what appears to be an excessive display of legs, and for no seeming purpose other than to delight the eye. Traditionally attributed to Modernist pioneer Adolf Loos, who used it in several interiors, the *Elephant Trunk Table* has the starkness of

Fig. 49. Marcel Breuer, armchair, *B55*, 1928–29.
Chrome-plated tubular steel, steel-thread fabric, wood.
87.8 x 51.8 x 63 cm (34⅝ x 20⅜ x 24¹³⁄₁₆ in.).
Berlin, Design Collection Ludewig.

**1921**

**1921¹/₂**

**1924**

**1925**

**19??**

Fig. 50. Marcel Breuer, "Bauhaus film, five years long.
Every day we are getting better. In the end we
will sit on resilient air columns," 1926. Photomontage.
New York, The Museum of Modern Art.

Fig. 51. English Chippendale table, c. 1750,
in the office of Friedrich Otto Schmidt, Vienna.

surface that characterized reform Viennese design at the turn of the century, but its eight legs seem unnecessarily redundant until one compares it with its eighteenth-century English Chippendale prototype (fig. 51); complexity and simplicity emerge as highly subjective terms.

Superfluidity in addition to superfluity invest Shigeru Uchida's *Nirvana* chair (cat. no. 57) and Dale Chihuly's goblet (cat. no. 58) with sinuous vitality. Both designs feature unexpectedly undulant bases, and Uchida not only persuades metal to appear in a manner quite opposed to its expected form, but also irreverently plays on the iconic, rigid forms of Modernist tubular steel furniture such as Breuer's *B55* chair (fig. 49). So, too, does Shiro Kuramata's stool (cat. no. 59), which was inspired by the tension spring, an image deriving directly from machine Modernism. When Kuramata proposed this design for the luncheon counter of Tokyo's Seibu department store, he fancifully imagined the patrons bouncing on the stools while sipping soda pop, an entertaining concept that runs counter to our usual notion of equilibrium while eating.

Handles are another functional element that designers have used in provocative ways to attract attention, to amuse us, and to relieve the monotony of the expected. Humans have been applying gripping mechanisms to objects from the earliest times. These handles, especially in the last two centuries, have been a fundamental target of functionalist dogma, with multifarious attempts at dictating size, shape, and position. And this has continued to be of concern to design theoreticians and educators throughout the century. Nonetheless, there have proved to be endless amusing variations devised for this ostensibly functional element.

At the turn of the century, for example, the Rozenburg pottery created wonderful forms for vases and a large portion of their charm was due to the exaggeration of the handle. In the vase presented here, for example (cat. no. 62), the dramatic arcing of the handle changes our perception of the form of the entire vase; the lavishness of this example is made only more apparent by looking at a group of such vases set side by side, or, as it were, handle by handle (fig. 52). In Vienna of the 1920s, the same extravagant liberties were taken. In Josef Hoffmann's justly celebrated centerpiece (cat. no. 63), the ribbon-like handles sum up how perfectly useless these lifting devices can become; they are startling not only because we do not expect metal to loop, especially not when used for handles, but also because of the overly generous proportions — factors that certainly exceed the modest demands of function. Similarly, what is René Lalique's *Pierrefonds* vase (cat. no. 64) but two magnificently large and decorated handles with a vessel attached? These examples argue for the existence of vessels as mere excuses for their glamorous appendages.

Equally arresting is the application of more handles than necessary. Such superabundance was not uncommon in Vienna in the 1920s; it can be seen in a Wiener und Gmündner vase (cat. no. 66) and in so many of the numerous vases by Vally Wieselthier and Gudrun Baudisch of the Wiener Werkstätte (fig. 53). Likewise, such overendowment is not an uncommon motif among the Memphis group and the Postmodernists in general. A ceramic vase designed by Alessandro Mendini (cat. no. 67) and a glass vase with polychromatic handles by Ettore Sotsass (cat. no. 65) are but two of many possible examples. These several works, spaced across the twentieth century, speak of similar concerns and whimsical creativity; the more things change, the more they stay the same!

Quite the opposite of excess but no less potent is the single, piercing handle on Philippe Starck's water kettle (cat. no. 68); *Hot Bertaa* is virtually impaled by this element. Looking back and without prejudice, we find that even Bauhaus designers gleefully experimented with handles — provided they conformed to geometric

Fig. 52. Group of Rozenburg vases, c. 1900.
Glazed porcelain. Height of tallest: 27.5 cm ($10^{13}/_{16}$ in.).
Rotterdam, Museum Boymans van Beuningen.

Fig. 53. Wiener Werkstätte vases, c. 1920–25:
Vally Wieselthier (left). Glazed earthenware. Height:
39.4 cm (15½ in.); Gudrun Baudisch (right).
Glazed earthenware. Height: 25.4 cm (10 in.).
New York, private collection.

Fig. 54. Marianne Brandt, teapot, *MT49*, 1924.
Brass, silverplated brass, ebony.
Height: 7.5 cm (2¹⁵⁄₁₆ in.).
Berlin, Bauhaus-Archiv.

shapes (fig. 54). Less extreme, finally, are the infinite variety of handles that confer distinction on coffee and tea services. In a group of services ranging in date from prewar to Postmodern, Jean Puiforcat (cat. no. 69) and Hans Hollein (cat. no. 70) create unconventional handles by overscaling them, and Rudolf Lunghard (cat. no. 71) imparts novelty not only through scale but also through an improbable oval shape. Masanori Umeda introduces an unorthodox handle inspired by the bulging eyes of a fish (cat. no. 72).

Another functional element that has received a fair share of experimentation is the opening of a vessel. Through an exaggeration of proportion or through redundancy, these elements have been used to surprise or delight us but, as in the previous examples, the designs have little to do with functionalism. Toshiko Takaezu's two-spouted ceramic bottle (cat. no. 73) is a fine expression of an extravagance particular to the postwar years when multiple spouts became a hallmark of studio ceramics. In fact, many of her other vessels toy with openings by incorporating minuscule apertures that contrast with the volumetric, globular bodies. A parallel development, whereby the opening becomes the focus of a piece through its play on proportion, is seen in Alfredo Barbini's vase (cat. no. 76). He provides a robust contrast to the clear but dense form through the intense, darkly outlined void, in essence exposing the teardrop-shaped cavity as though seen by x-ray. Maurice Marinot's incomparable bubble-glass flacons, with their broad shoulders and miniature stoppered openings (cat. no. 74), are a fascinating commentary on notions of containment and proportion. In their mass and volume they are not unlike other Art Deco objects (such as the dense stoneware vessels of Henri Simmen that are set with small ivory stoppers by his wife, Eugénie O'Kin), since the volume of the vessel is emphasized by the smallness of the finial. Likewise, the generously proportioned furniture of Ruhlmann often rests on small feet, even small balls of precious ivory. A generation after Marinot, Fulvio Bianconi obtained a similarly exaggerated but opposite effect in his narrow-necked bottle with wide, oversized stopper (cat. no. 75) that became one of Venini's most illustrious designs of the 1950s. Ironically, Marinot and Bianconi designed objects that have become icons of twentieth-century design, yet icons that are not useful and were not intended to be useful; Takaezu's vase is not much different. Obviously, there is a certain esprit in design that responds to very different imperatives than functionalism.

Postmodern design has been especially suffused with antirational theory. In Italy, where much of this theory was first promulgated, designers have sought to tease the principle of verticality. The canting of forms plays with our sense of stability in the same way as tampering with the base. Andrea Branzi's tea set (cat. no. 79), Alessandro Mendini's *Perilloide* vase (cat. no. 78), and Matteo Thun's *Volga* vase (cat. no. 77) are alike in their off-center balance of vertical form, perilously poised to tip over. Branzi even comments on his intentional reversal of perspective as a challenge to established rules. Gaetano Pesce cants the legs of his *Samson* table (cat. no. 80) to the brink of collapse as a metaphor for the designer's challenge to the prevailing design establishment and rejection of Modernism's rigidity. The table is part of Pesce's effort to individualize mass-produced objects: each worker is responsible for pouring the different colored resins into the molds, thus having a hand in determining the final, variegated results. As Pesce explained, with the *Samson* table he tried to create "... an industrial series in which each one is different.... Until today I used to consume goods that everybody owned or everybody liked to own. But now people, I think, will consume and like to have objects that they own in a personal way, personalized ..."⁵

Designers have also been drawn to exaggerated bowed forms as another means of defying the rigid rectilinearity and rational uniformity of mainstream Modernism.

The bookcase, potent symbol of rationalized information, makes an especially appealing target, and Ron Arad's *One Way or Another* (cat. no. 81) displays exhilarating disregard for the uprightness of the traditional library shelf. Its inherent instability is an ironic commentary on the fate of printed matter in the information age. Shiro Kuramata's *Side 1, Side 2* chests of drawers (cat. no. 82) similarly pit the modularity of stacking against the potentially precarious nature of undulating form, accentuated by the eighteen drawer divisions. One swerving sideways, the other front to back, these pieces pose dizzying challenges to our senses of balance and perspective, much like Branzi's tea set.

Undulating form can complement the intent of a design. In a mid-century vase from the Rosenthal factory (cat. no. 83), as well as in Massimo Iosa Ghini's *Simulated* pitcher of several decades later (cat. no. 84), the fluidity of liquid finds an appropriate reflection in the undulations of the vessels' forms. Even Lino Sabattini, known for his utilitarian approach to design, could not resist injecting a touch of whimsy into the handles of his *Sculptura* cutlery (cat. no. 87), although the design has been explained in rational, functional terms — as a diagram of the act of eating and the attendant up and down movement of the hand.[6] Serpents are alluded to in Livio Castiglioni and Gianfranco Frattini's ingenious *Boalum* lamp (cat. no. 85), its flexible, tubelike form capable of snaking up the wall or humorously curling across the floor and which, when combined in multiples, forms a continuous "boa" of indefinite length. Similarly, Elizabeth Browning Jackson has broken away from the rigid perimeters of traditional floor coverings, thereby injecting whimsy into an often ignored area of the Modernist interior. The ground-hugging convolutions of her *Endless Point* rug (cat. no. 86) refer to the universal symbol of the spiral, used in ancient cultures as well as in such recent environmental sculptures as Robert Smithson's *Spiral Jetty* (fig. 55).

The blurring of directional indicators in design permits a function that can take place in either position; it is akin to the lack of orientation in much abstract painting and to the idea of reversibility in clothing. Two postwar vessels that play with this idea of inversion are Flavio Barbini's sectional vase (cat. no. 88),[7] and Enzo Mari's *Pago-Pago* (cat. no. 89). A vase with a small opening can be converted to a wide-mouthed vase by inverting the object with a flick of the wrist; thus not only is a different function served but also a very different form is perceived. The idea, which could almost be hailed as superfunctionalism, is still timely today, as evidenced by Alessandro Mendini's look-alike *Godezia* jewel case and *Stellaria* vase (cat. nos. 90, 91), both comprising virtually identical components.

Traditional conceptions of overall form can be assaulted in many ways. Cubism and its concomitant plays of spatial illusion were made manifest in Kasimir Malevich's experimental tea service of c. 1922, which was as much art as it was industrial design. A slightly later example is Wilhelm Kåge's series of *Surrea* vases (cat. no. 92), in which solid and void are tantalizingly simulated in actual three-dimensional form and painted decoration. The *Surrea* series first appeared in Kåge's 1940 exhibition, which was amusingly entitled "Idyll and Panic in the Furnace." Ironically, only in recent years have Malevich's designs been produced in quantity in porcelain and silver, and some of Kåge's *Surrea* designs have been reissued as well — revealing both the overcoming of the shock of the new and the cyclic nature of taste. Less complex yet equally ingenious in its attempt at deception is the *Pouch* vase (cat. no. 93) by Stig Lindberg, who succeeded Kåge in 1949 as artistic director at the Gustavsberg factory. From one side, *Pouch* appears to be a traditional, tear-shaped vase suggestive of Chinese forms; one would never suspect the playful void that awaits on the opposite side. In this respect, both Kåge's and Lindberg's objects toy with the idea of inside versus outside.

Fig. 55. Robert Smithson, *Spiral Jetty*, Great Salt Lake, Utah, 1970. 457.2 x 4.6 m (1,500 x 15 ft.).

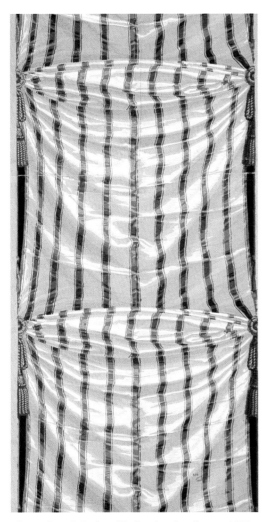

Fig. 56. Joseph Dufour, block-printed wallpaper, 1808.
Paris, Bibliothèque Forney.

Playful textile patterns are another way in which designers use confusing illusions of depth to amuse and delight the eye. Swedish designer Astrid Sampe's *Versailles* textile (cat. no. 95) is disorientingly illusionistic as it simulates a striped pattern with deep folds; although the image is computer-generated, it is strongly reminiscent of historic *trompe l'oeil* designs such as an early nineteenth-century French wallpaper simulating draped fabric (fig. 56). Junichi Arai's *Woven Pattern* textile (cat. no. 96) is also the result of advances in technology—created by photocopying a twisted bundle of fabrics and electronically scanning that image; it simulates depth through the semblance of layering.

Mainstream Modernism's reverential regard for the appropriate use of materials—the belief that specific substances demand certain formal treatments—has its origin in the mid-nineteenth century. For example, Ruskin condemned as the second of three Architectural Deceits "… painting of surfaces to represent some other material." He believed that "architecture will be noble exactly in the degree in which all these false expedients are avoided."[8] Some fifty years later, pioneering Modernist Frank Lloyd Wright expressed a similar sentiment in his 1901 lecture "The Art and Craft of the Machine." Not opposed to the machine like Ruskin, but equally adamant in his regard for the true nature of materials, Wright believed that each material had its own inherent properties and should be treated in a manner consistent with its own unique vocabulary. This idea, espoused by subsequent generations, became the ruling premise of modern design, nowhere better expressed than in Kaufmann's declaration: "Modern design should express the qualities and beauties of the materials used, never making the materials seem to be what they are not."[9]

Modernism's devotion to the doctrine of truth-to-materials created a number of design commandments waiting to be broken. Twentieth-century ceramists and glassblowers have delighted in making their forms appear soft. Fulvio Bianconi's iconic *Handkerchief* vase (cat. no. 97) implies the limpid drapery of a handkerchief frozen in time, as do the more baroque forms of Dale Chihuly's *Cadmium Yellow Seaform Set with Red Lip Wraps* (cat. no. 98). For sheer playful incongruity, Arnold Zimmerman's wildly coiled teapot (cat. no. 99) challenges a traditional ceramic technique. In this piece, "the potter's venerable coil-building tradition is thrown for a loop … the wildly spinning coils of clay meander, sag, droop, like a ball of twine after a kitten has played with it."[10]

Despite the constant emphasis on rationalism, play has proven to be an important element in twentieth-century design. The Bauhaus artist and pedagogue László Moholy-Nagy advocated creative play and spontaneity, and the interplay of materials and tools. We might recall that among the customary exercises at the school were the creation of freestanding paper sculptures and flexible springs cut from wood. The concept of creative play with materials remained an important undercurrent that found eloquent expression in future generations. For example, architect Frank Gehry delights in employing the most banal of materials and using them in novel, mischievous ways. In his *Bubbles* chaise longue (cat. no. 100), one of an important series of chairs, he used corrugated cardboard, soft and pliable by nature, and restructured it to support the weight of the human body. Inspired by commercial fruit baskets made from strips of wood, Gehry used improbably thin strips of plywood to weave durable chairs (cat. no. 101). Ordinary paper, a comparably humble material, was put to clever use in a paper dress produced as a promotion for *Time* magazine (cat. no. 102). The dress represents the surge in popularity of paper garments that occurred in the late 1960s, evidence of mainstream society's admiration for inexpensive, disposable products. Issey Miyake, an unceasingly creative fashion designer, elevated paper to haute-couture status by sculpting a jacket out of this mundane material (cat. no. 103). Challenging traditional ideas about the preciousness of jewelry in a similar fashion, Janna Syvänoja sliced and recycled printed matter to make her *Books* necklace (cat. no. 104). The offhand elegance demonstrated by these designs emerges from a creative way of thinking that dismisses stereotypical associations between material, technique, and function.

Metal, the material most often associated with the high Modernist seating of Marcel Breuer and Mies van der Rohe, is handled with much more sensuousness and lightness in Ron Arad's cascading *London Papardelle* chair (cat. no. 105), which is made of conveyor belt material (and has an odd resemblance to a rubbery stick of chewing gum). Preferring raw materials and recycled objects, Arad rejects a Bauhaus functionalist approach, drawing inspiration instead from Dada artists such as Marcel Duchamp, Surrealists such as Yves Tanguy, as well as personal experience, in this case the pasta he recently consumed. Expanded metal mesh plays with our notions of upholstered seating in Shiro Kuramata's gossamer *How High the Moon* armchair (cat. no. 106), dematerializing the mass usually associated with this form. Kuramata frequently commented on this aspect of his work: "I feel attracted by transparent materials because transparency doesn't belong to any one place in particular, and yet it exists."[11] Another example of metal handled in an unexpected way is Arline Fisch's knitted copper neckpiece (cat. no. 108). Evocative of an Elizabethan collar, the imposing jewelry reflects the artist's interest in history and demonstrates the technique she pioneered of knitting with copper, silver, or gold. Fisch manipulates metal and forces it to take a form to which it is not accustomed.

Fabrics composed of metal are yet another unexpected use of this favorite material of Modernism. Paco Rabanne's *Chainmail* (cat. no. 107), intended for apparel, was one of several versions of metallic components with which this space-age couturier rocked the foundations of the fashion world during the 1960s. Two decades later, Japanese designers were instrumental in rethinking the very nature of a textile, as well as its mode of fabrication. In Reiko Sudo's *Stainless Embossed* (cat. no. 109) and Junichi Arai's *Melted Off Contour* (cat. no. 111), the designers created techniques for depositing metal on a filmy cloth so that it is both metallic and supple.

The examples presented in this section are but a selection of objects that depart from traditionally sanctioned Modernist principles. They have been conspicuous throughout the century, as designers employed an endless variety of plays on functional elements and questioned the nature of materials. These incongruities were not mere aberrations from the norm or idiosyncratic examples. Such alternative, even antirational, expressions fell within the realm of mainstream Modernist production. As demonstrated by the major international designers and manufacturers represented in this exhibition, form often soared beyond function.

**49. Unknown designer**
Bowl
Designed c. 1920. Glazed earthenware
12 x 41.9 x 41.9 cm (4¾ x 16½ x 16½ in.)
Produced by Vereinigte Wiener und Gmündner Keramik
(Vienna, Austria), c. 1920
Unmarked
D92.186.1, The Liliane and David M. Stewart Collection

*"This bowl suggests the way in which a motif, used first in one context, can be transformed and subverted in another context. At the turn of the century, Josef Hoffmann and his Viennese colleagues utilized the square and the circle as elements of purified structure and ornament. But, once established, the motifs took on lives of their own — as in the case of this otherwise simple bowl, whose eight spherical feet almost overwhelm it. The sense of control and rationality that originally informed this simple motif has been replaced by a playful overabundance."*
Martin Eidelberg, 1993[12]

**50. Attributed to Michael Powolny**
(born 1871, Judenburg, Austria; died 1954, Vienna)
Bowl
Designed c. 1910-25. Glass
11.2 x 21.1 x 21.1 cm (4⁷⁄₁₆ x 8⁵⁄₁₆ x 8⁵⁄₁₆ in.)
Produced by Johann Loetz Witwe (Klostermühle,
Czechoslovakia), c. 1910-25
Unmarked
D94.185.1, The Liliane and David M. Stewart Collection

*"In the first years of this century, the Loetz firm produced a number of vases designed by the leading members of the Wiener Werkstätte, all of which were characterized by a reliance on sharply defined, geometric forms. Several of Kolo Moser's vases featured spherical balls at the bottom, and this concept, evidently popular and commercially viable, was then produced in countless variants by the glass company over the next two decades."*
Martin Eidelberg, 1994[13]

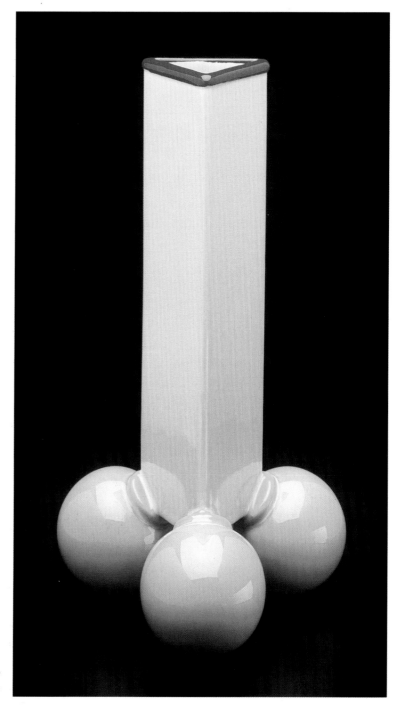

**51. Masanori Umeda**
(born 1941, Kanagawa, Japan)
Vase, *Orinoco*
Designed 1983. Glazed earthenware
27.9 x 15.7 x 11.5 cm (11 x 6³⁄₁₆ x 4½ in.)
Produced for Memphis s.r.l. (Pregnana Milanese, Italy),
1983 to the present
Unmarked
D95.156.1, The Liliane and David M. Stewart Collection

*"Tantrism is one of the cultic religious systems in India, whose*
*most important symbol is 'sex.' ... The Tantric sexual icons are*
*△ (male) and ▽ (female). This flower vase ... Orinoco, means*
*'lingam' — the symbol of the Tantric god Siva. Here you will find*
*the triangular sexual icon in three dimensions on three balls*
*installed for better balance.... Flowers put in Orinoco,*
*therefore, are ... to be the very symbol of life."*
Masanori Umeda, 1995[14]

**"Building up the base gives an entirely different feeling to this series of stoneware bowls, pots and vases designed by Wilhelm Kåge for Gustavsberg of Sweden. [The] pedestal subtly changes the scale so even the most traditional shape acquires freshness."**
*House Beautiful*, 1959[15]

**52. Wilhelm Kåge**
(born 1889, Stockholm, Sweden; died 1960, Stockholm)
Vase, *Terra Spirea*
Designed c. 1955. Glazed stoneware
15.6 x 7.6 cm x 7.6 cm (6⅛ x 3 x 3 in.)
Produced by AB Gustavsberg (Gustavsberg), c. 1955-60
Impressed on underside: FARSTA/STUDIO [within device of a hand]/GUSTAVSBERG; incised on underside:
Ä/KÅGE; painted in white on underside: 7318
D85.168.1, gift of AB Gustavsberg

*"Lebeau's work strikes us, first and foremost, as completely unusual. It almost seems as if he deliberately tried to create something that would be totally different from the work of his immediate predecessors, sometimes at the expense of being extravagant. In this way he created a series of objects that, at first, make one think of a physics laboratory."*
Karel Wasch, 1927[16]

**53. Joris Johannes Christiaan (Chris) Lebeau**
(born 1878, Amsterdam, The Netherlands; died 1945,
Dachau, Germany)
Vase and stand
Designed 1924-25. Glass
Vase: 34.2 x 14.9 x 14.9 cm (13½ x 5⅞ x 5⅞ in.)
Stand: 8 x 14.9 x 14.9 cm (3⅛ x 5⅞ x 5⅞ in.)
Produced by NV Glasfabriek Leerdam
(Leerdam, The Netherlands), 1925-30
Acid-stamped on underside of vase and on
top of stand: CLB
D94.193.1, The Liliane and David M. Stewart Collection

**54. Gaetano Pesce**
(born 1939, La Spezia, Italy)
Chair, *Greene Street*
Designed 1984. Polyurethane, stainless steel
94.3 x 54.3 x 57.6 cm (37⅛ x 21⅜ x 22¹¹⁄₁₆ in.)
Produced by Vitra GmbH (Weil am Rhein, Germany),
1984, 1986-87
Unmarked
D90.112.1, The Liliane and David M. Stewart Collection

*"The **Greene Street** chair involves two issues. One is the insecurity of this historical moment. We are living in an age when values are changing. The result is insecurity — insecurity about politics, religion, and culture, insecurity about the future of some minorities or ourselves, or about territories, or about the economic situation. I tried to represent the instability of our times with the **Greene Street** chair, which gives when you sit on it. We incorrectly assume stability for a chair, but I want people to think about instability. The **Greene Street** chair has structure but also movement. It is not as rigid as a traditional chair that gives you a feeling of security — you sit on it, you stay on it. The **Greene Street** chair is a more flexible structure. It has eight very thin legs that allow a kind of movement."*
Gaetano Pesce, 1993[17]

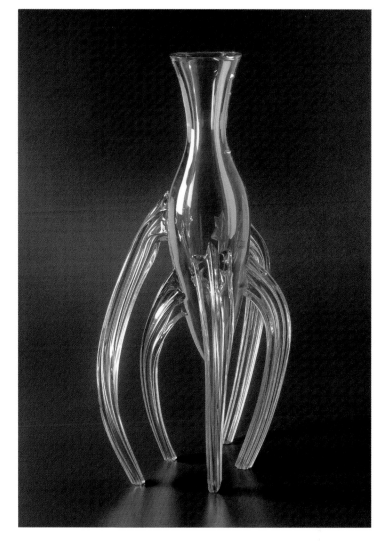

**55. David Palterer**
(born 1949, Haifa, Israel)
Vase, *Little Dipper (Orsa Minore)*
Designed 1991. Glass
71.7 x 26.4 x 34.3 cm (28¼ x 10⅜ x 13½ in.)
Executed by Pino Signoretto (Murano, Italy) for the
Galleria Paola e Rossella Colombari (Milan), 1991
Etched on rim: *002 2/9 David Palterer 1991/Pino
Signoretto*
D91.429.1, The Liliane and David M. Stewart Collection

*"... **Orsa Minore**. It's the small constellation of stars. This is the vase, classical amphora, again in memory of the very, very archetype of vases, but it can stand. It stands. It creates the possibility of standing things that you don't believe will [stand]...."*
David Palterer, 1994[18]

**56. Max Schmidt**
(born 1861, Vienna, Austria; died 1935, Budapest, Hungary)
Table, *Elephant Trunk Table (Elefantrüsseltisch)*
Designed c. 1899. Mahogany, glazed earthenware, brass
69.5 x 85.4 x 85.4 cm (27³/₈ x 33⁵/₈ x 33⁵/₈ in.)
Produced by Friedrich Otto Schmidt (Vienna), c. 1900;
tiles produced by Alexandre Bigot (Paris, France)
Unmarked
D92.190.1, gift of Paul Leblanc

*"We ourselves are of the opinion that the idea of the ... Elephant Trunk Table was taken from an antique Chippendale table, which we still keep in our office. This table ... has eight legs and one shelf below the top, but with more decorative carving. As this Chippendale table was definitely on display in our company at the turn of the century, we believe that Max Schmidt and Adolf Loos ... simplified that table."*
Claus Lorenz, 1994[19]

*"The title of this chair, Nirvana, signifies the state of mind where one is enlightened by the extinction of his or her desire and the absolute peaceful condition. In the Orient, meditating while seated means to enter Nirvana, and its seat represents the sacred space. The shape of the bottom of this chair is taken from the Renge-za (lotus flower seat) as a motif. Renge-za is a seat and a symbol of Buddha and Bodhisattva statues. The lotus flower is the beautiful entity which reflects brightly against the muddy water, that is, the chaos of today's society. The beautiful lotus flower blooms even in this chaotic situation. It is a metaphor unique to the Orient, expressing the relationship between society, human beings, and nature."*
Shigeru Uchida, 1995[20]

**57. Shigeru Uchida**
(born 1943, Yokohama, Japan)
Armchair, *Nirvana*
Designed 1981. Melamine-coated steel, chrome-plated
steel, acrylic/wool
67 x 82.6 x 69.6 cm (26³⁄₈ x 32½ x 27³⁄₈ in.)
Produced by Chairs (Tokyo), 1981 to the present
Unmarked
D93.138.1, gift of Paul Leblanc

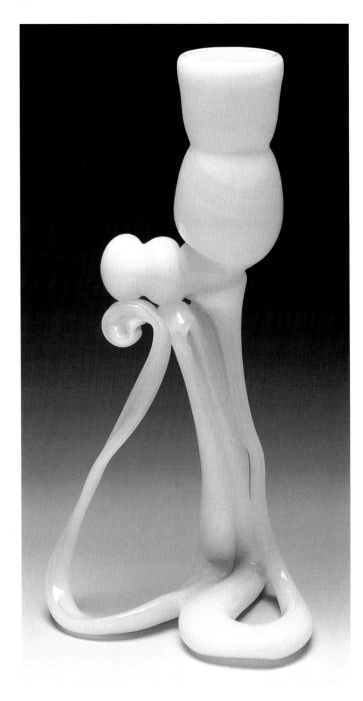

**58. Dale Chihuly**
(born 1941, Tacoma, WA, USA)
Goblet
Executed 1971. Glass
31.2 x 13.7 x 11.7 cm (12 5/16 x 5 3/8 x 4 5/8 in.)
Written in blue ink on paper label affixed to underside:
CHIHULY/GOBLET FORM #4
D91.390.1, gift of Lilliana and David Simpson

*"I've always believed that glass should do
what it wants to do. I don't like to use tools
except for the heat of the furnace, gravity,
and centrifugal force. This goblet's base
shows what glass likes to do. My work has a
lot to do with the good time had in doing it."*
Dale Chihuly, 1994[21]

**59. Shiro Kuramata**
(born 1934, Tokyo, Japan; died 1991, Tokyo)
Stool, *Spring Chair*
Designed 1968. Steel, cotton/rayon
42.6 x 38.1 x 38.1 cm (16 3/4 x 15 x 15 in.)
Produced by Ishimaru Co., Ltd. (Tokyo), 1968; fabric
produced by Yoshiko Ebihara (Tokyo)
Unmarked
D93.127.1, gift of Paul Leblanc

*"'My intuition comes from my subcon-
scious memory that throws a ball out to
my consciousness,' the designer explains.
'When the ball is caught, images within
me are born.' Such poetry, of course, is
only the beginning. Once sparked,
concepts are put through the inevitable
process of refinement: 'Ideas boil up, but
I have to think very hard to get to the
simplest form,' he says.... As early as
1968 Kuramata started subverting the
contextual meaning of his materials ...
stools were made of oversized, Pop Art-
like metal springs, ready, it seemed, to
bounce around the room...."*
Chee Pearlman, 1988[22]

**60. Ettore Sottsass**
(born 1917, Innsbruck, Austria)
Fruit dish, *Murmansk*
Designed 1982. Silver-plated brass
30.4 x 35.5 x 35.5 cm (11¹⁵⁄₁₆ x 14 x 14 in.)
Produced by Rossi e Arcandi (Vicenza, Italy) for
Memphis s.r.l. (Pregnana Milanese), 1982 to the present
Impressed on dish and base: MEMPHIS/MILANO
[within a rectangle]
D91.423.1, anonymous gift


*"If you see the sketch for this ... it's a*
*sheet of paper with many different sketches*
*around the same idea, many variations:*
*there are long proportions, short propor-*
*tions, round, square, etc. They are, again,*
*exercises, just notes."*
Ettore Sottsass, 1994[23]

**61. Philippe Starck**
(born 1949, Paris, France)
Stool, *W.W. [Wim Wenders]*
Designed 1990. Aluminum
97 x 56 x 53 cm (38¼ x 22 x 20⅞ in.)
Produced by Vitra GmbH (Weil am Rhein, Germany),
1991 to the present
Embossed in black on underside: STARCK
D93.204.1, gift of Vitra International AG


*"Wim Wenders said to me something like:*
*'... either I sleep or I work standing up,*
*maybe with a kind of stool ...' I answered:*
*'You are right, I think, good-bye' and I*
*hung up."*
Philippe Starck, 1995[24]

*"The handles played a special role in the design of pots and [vases]. They were not only solid and strong, but were also unified with the form, growing naturally from the body. The handle was indispensible to the overall shape of the vessel. When Kok drew the design for such a piece, he began, as a rule, with the handle ... the special decorative significance of these features [is that] together with the bodies [they] formed circles, ovoids, and heart shapes."*

Edvard Lehmann, 1976[25]

**62. Form: J. Jurriaan Kok**
(born 1861, Rotterdam, The Netherlands; died 1919, The Hague)
**Decoration: Samuel Jacobus de Smit**
(born 1874, Sluis; date of death unknown)
Vase
Designed 1901. Glazed porcelain
21.5 x 16.2 x 11.5 cm (8⁷⁄₁₆ x 6³⁄₈ x 4½ in.)
Produced by Koninklijke Porselein-en Aardewerk Fabriek Rozenburg (The Hague), 1901-02
Printed in black on underside: [device of crown]/Rozenburg/[device of stork with worm]/den Haag; painted in black to left: [device of ant]; to right: [square device] .490/o11
D94.121.1, The Liliane and David M. Stewart Collection

**63. Josef Hoffmann**
(born 1870, Pirnitz, Austria; died 1956, Vienna)
Centerpiece
Designed 1924-25. Brass
19 x 28.8 x 18.5 cm (7½ x 11⁵⁄₁₆ x 7⁵⁄₁₆ in.)
Produced by the Wiener Werkstätte (Vienna),
c. 1925-31
Impressed on side: MADE IN/AUSTRIA [within a square]
[monogram of conjoined JH] WIENER/WERK/STATTE
D93.307.1, gift of Paul Leblanc

*"It is Hoffmann who is responsible for this beguiling surfeit of distinction, of playfulness, of freedom from immediate goals, for which the Austrians anyway have such tripping talent...."*
Hans Tietze, 1920[26]

**64. René Lalique**
(born 1860, Aÿ, France; died 1945, Paris)
Vase, *Pierrefonds*
Designed 1926. Glass
15.7 x 33 x 17.6 cm (6³⁄₁₆ x 13 x 6¹⁵⁄₁₆ in.)
Produced by René Lalique et Cie
(Wingen-sur-Moder), 1928-57
Engraved on underside: R. LALIQUE/FRANCE NO. 990
D94.182.1, The Liliane and David M. Stewart Collection

*"An artist of classical training, René Lalique created a few glassware forms of marvelous extravagance. Either he attached voluptuous female bodies to them, whose forms harmonize perfectly with the sides, or he adorned them with knobs or extremely pronounced handles, without any reason or practical use, decoration being their only justification. Functionalism and rationalism, principles so precious to some of his contemporaries, were not his aim. The Pierrefonds vase, whose beautiful lateral, scrolling arabesques in openwork bring to mind frosted branches that seem to spring naturally from the receptacle and that contrast with the perfect geometry of its refined and classical volume, is without a doubt one of his most spectacular successes."*
Félix Marcilhac, 1996[27]

**65. Ettore Sottsass**
(born 1917, Innsbruck, Austria)
Vase, *Mizar*
Designed 1982. Glass
34 x 32.8 x 30 cm (13⅜ x 12⅞ x 11¹³⁄₁₆ in.)
Produced by Compagnia Vetraria Muranese (Murano,
Italy) for Memphis s.r.l. (Pregnana Milanese), 1982
Etched on base: MEMPHIS MILANO by COMPAGNIA VETRARIA
MURANESE
D96.103.1, The Liliane and David M. Stewart Collection

*"This was an attempt to imagine an object not based on a rotational axis ... I tried to avoid, more or less, the idea of a fixed symmetry."*
Ettore Sottsass, 1994[28]

"In the 1920s, extravagant handles became an object of
fascination for the ceramists of the Wiener Werkstätte; they
were multiplied and varied in a playful, arbitrary way, as they
became elements of decorative form rather than function.
This vase by the Wiener und Gmündner factory – a firm which
produced works designed by Michael Powolny, Berthold Löffler,
and other leading members of the Viennese school – extends
this tradition of whimsical, asymmetrical handles that serve
no purpose other than to delight the eye."
Martin Eidelberg, 1994[29]

**66. Unknown designer**
Vase
Designed c. 1920-25. Glazed earthenware
22.2 x 15.5 x 9.5 cm (8¾ x 6⅛ x 3¾ in.)
Produced by the Vereinigte Wiener und Gmündner
Keramik (Vienna, Austria), c. 1920-25
Printed in blue on underside: [device of flowerpot
flanked by G and K within a square]/AUSTRIA; incised on
underside: B/1312
D94.306.1, The Liliane and David M. Stewart Collection

*"Alchimia views objects as being both 'normal' and 'abnormal.'*
*Their ordinary side makes them part of everyday life, of real-*
*ity, and of the need for anonymity, while their extraordinary*
*side removes them from the habitual and drives them toward*
*the need for the unexpected, the accidental, difference, and*
*transgression."*
Alessandro Mendini, 1987[30]

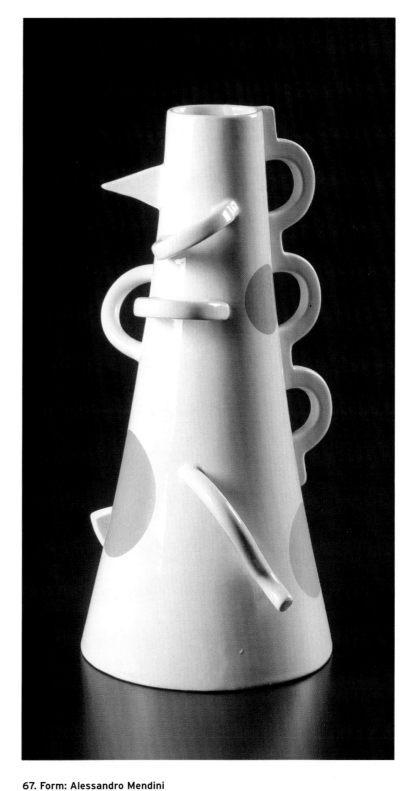

**67. Form: Alessandro Mendini**
(born 1931, Milan, Italy)
**Decoration: Giorgio Gregori**
(born 1957, Rome)
Vase, *Handles (Manici)*
Designed 1984. Glazed earthenware
29.5 x 14 x 14 cm (11⅝ x 5½ x 5½ in.)
Produced by Zabro, a division of Zanotta
(Nova Milanese), for Alchimia (Milan), 1984-85
Painted in silver on underside: ALCHIMIA/1985/2/6;
painted in blue on underside: Mendini [partially legible];
impressed on underside of vase: ZABRO
D93.223.1, The Liliane and David M. Stewart Collection

**68. Philippe Starck**
(born 1949, Paris, France)
Water kettle, *Hot Bertaa*
Designed 1987. Aluminum, polyamide
25 x 31 x 15 cm (9¾ x 12¼ x 6 in.)
Produced by Alessi S.p.A. (Crusinallo, Italy),
1990 to the present
Impressed on underside: ALESSI/Italy
D92.100.1, The Liliane and David M. Stewart Collection

*"Hot Bertaa is a kettle*
*Hot Bertaa is aerodynamic*
*Useless*
*Yes, that's its charm."*
Philippe Starck, 1995[31]

**69. Jean Puiforcat**
(born 1897, Paris, France; died 1945, Paris)
Tea and coffee service
Designed c. 1933. Silver, gilt silver, cotton thread
Coffee pot: 14.3 x 19.9 x 8.3 cm (5⅝ x 7¹³⁄₁₆ x 3¼ in.)
Produced by Puiforcat Orfèvre (Paris), c. 1933–34
Impressed on underside of each: [diamond-shaped device with knife between E and P] [octagonal-shaped .950 silver hallmark of head of Minerva facing right]/JEAN E. PUIFORCAT; device and hallmark repeated under lids of each; hallmark repeated under handles; engraved on underside of each: K
D94.285.1–4, anonymous gift

**70. Hans Hollein**
(born 1934, Vienna, Austria)
Coffeepot prototype, *Aircraft Carrier*
Designed 1980-81. Brass, plastic
17.2 x 25.4 x 13.4 cm (6¾ x 10 x 5¼ in.)
Produced by Alessi S.p.A. (Crusinallo, Italy), 1982
Impressed on underside: [device of an eagle
surmounting OFFICINA/ALESSI]/*Hans Hollein*/1982/1/1
D88.211.1, gift of Vivian and David Campbell

*"... the Alessi teaset quotes on the one hand ... the languages*
*which belong to the origins of the Viennese modern design*
*of the beginning of the century; on the other hand it also quotes*
*the already historically defined aircraft-carrier of Hollein's*
*theoretical statements. The tray represents the take-off and*
*landing strip of an aircraft-carrier ... and the teapot and the*
*other interlocking elements quote the control towers."*
Gianni Pettena, 1988[33]

**71. Rudolf Lunghard**
(born 1902, Höxter, Germany; died 1983,
Selb, West Germany)
Mocha service, *Oval*
Designed c. 1950. Glazed porcelain
Mocha pot: 23 x 18.4 x 8.5 cm (9¹⁄₁₆ x 7¼ x 3⁵⁄₁₆ in.)
Produced by Rosenthal Porzellanfabrik
(Selb-Plössberg), 1951-61
Transfer printed in green on underside of each except
sugar bowl: *Rosen* [device of crossed swords
surmounted by a crown] *thal*/SELB-PLÖSSBERG/GERMANY;
mocha pot, cup and saucer also printed: BAVARIA; mocha
pot and creamer also printed in red: M; sugar bowl
printed in green: *Rosenthal*/GERMANY/[device of two
crossed roses surmounted by a crown]
D93.218.1-4, 10, gift of Eric McLean, by exchange

*"The shapes of both the hollow and flat pieces ... are extremely dainty. The handles and knobs are not massive as elsewhere, marking the delicacy of this form. These striking features require ... careful ... almost ceremonial treatment."*
Rosenthal Verkaufsdienst, 1955[34]

**72. Masanori Umeda**
(born 1941, Kanagawa, Japan)
Coffee service, *Mudskipper (Mutsugoro)*
Designed 1984. Glazed porcelain
Coffeepot: 18.1 x 15.2 x 9.5 cm (7⅛ x 6 x 3¾ in.)
Produced by Yamaka Shouten Co., Ltd.
(Tokyo), 1984–88
Printed in black on underside of each: CERANOVA/design
M. UMEDA/YAMAKA/INTERNATIONAL/JAPAN
D89.108.1, 3, gift of Masanori Umeda; D93.100.1–3,
gift of Masanori Umeda

*"One day I saw the fish [a mudskipper, or bug-eyed mutsugoro]
in a documentary film and I was so attracted by their charming
movement that I visited the Ariake Sea in Kyushu to see them.
I must confess I ate them and found them very tasty, though
I felt guilty."*
Masanori Umeda, 1994[35]

**73. Toshiko Takaezu**
(born 1922, Pepeekeo, HI, USA)
Bottle
Executed c. 1953-54. Glazed stoneware
35 x 22.2 x 21.7 cm (13¾ x 8¾ x 8⁹⁄₁₆ in.)
Unmarked
D87.101.1, The Liliane and David M. Stewart Collection

*"The 'two-spouted bottle' originally developed from teapots and
wine bottles which were created with the images of birds in mind —
the spout being the head of the bird and the handle being its tail.
Gradually the original idea faded and the pieces evolved into more
abstract forms."*
Toshiko Takaezu, 1995[36]

*"[Marinot's] detailed use of techniques, which he pursues exhaustively, affords him the greatest diversity in his creativity; while his sense of proportion restricts him to a small number of types which seem to serve as his basis.... One type is the apple-shaped bottle with its belly rounded like a beautiful, fully ripe fruit and its straight elongated neck often topped by a globular stopper."*

René Chavance, 1923[37]

**74. Maurice Marinot**
(born 1882, Troyes, France; died 1960, Troyes)
Bottle with stopper
Executed 1929. Glass
14.6 x 11.4 x 8.3 cm (5¾ x 4½ x 3¼ in.)
Engraved on underside: *marinot*
D94.179.1, The Liliane and David M. Stewart Collection

*"The first idea for the bottle with stopper came out of Mr. Bianconi in 1950. At the Biennale that year, in Venini's display, he showed a kind of vase with a very closed neck (or a bottle without stopper).... The bottles are made just to give you the idea of a bottle, the concept. The unusually large and out-of-scale stoppers, along with the joy of color, add to the sense of festive celebration."*
Franco Deboni, 1995[38]

**75. Fulvio Bianconi**
(born 1915, Padua, Italy; died 1996, Milan)
Bottle with stopper
Designed c. 1950. Glass
40.7 x 8.2 x 8.2 cm (16 x 3¼ x 3¼ in.)
Produced by Venini S.p.A. (Murano, Italy), c. 1951–59
Acid-stamped on underside, partially legible:
*venini/murano*/ITALIA
D95.106.1, The Liliane and David M. Stewart Collection

**76. Alfredo Barbini**
(born 1912, Murano, Italy)
Vase
Designed c. 1962. Glass
15.8 x 21.9 x 9.5 cm (6¼ x 8⅝ x 3¾ in.)
Produced by Alfredo Barbini s.r.l. (Murano), c. 1962-70
Engraved on underside: *A Barbini*
D81.156.1, The Liliane and David M. Stewart Collection

*"I wanted to give this clear form a gray teardrop, just as if it*
*were a real drop of water hitting the ground. It could be a*
*decorative piece or a vase for one flower."*
Alfredo Barbini, 1994[39]

*"[I designed the vase] ... while I was drunk and
discussing [things] with Ettore Sottsass in early '81."*
Matteo Thun, 1994[40]

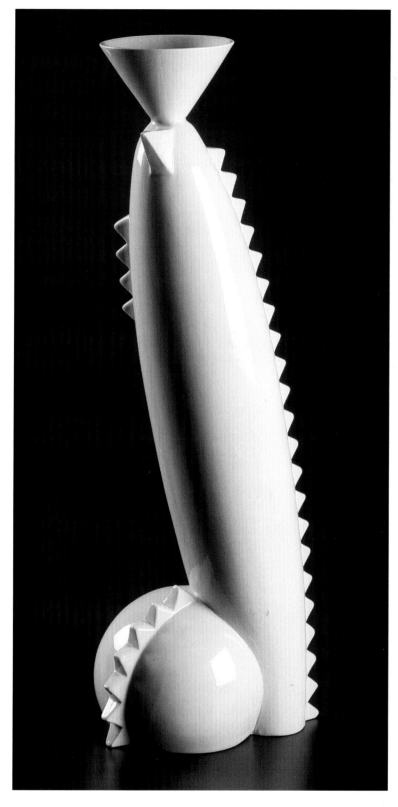

**77. Matteo Thun**
(born 1952, Bolzano, Italy)
Vase, *Volga*
Designed 1981. Glazed porcelain
55.6 x 24.7 x 17.9 cm (21⅞ x 9¾ x 7¹⁄₁₆ in.)
Produced by Porcellane d'Arte San Marco s.r.l.
(Nove) for Memphis s.r.l. (Pregnana Milanese),
1983 to the present
Printed in black on rectangular transparent label
affixed to underside: M. THUN/per/MEMPHIS
D91.425.1, anonymous gift

*"Perilloide is a vase designed together with many sketches for other vases. The idea was to develop a continuous series of shapes, each adapted for manufacture in different materials: ceramic, blown glass, porcelain, metal, turned wood, plastic.*

*As it appears to lay outside its own center of mass, the vase gives expression to a playful sense of suspense and disequilibrium, as if it were something that does not lean — rather like a rattlesnake."*

Alessandro Mendini, 1995[41]

**78. Alessandro Mendini**
(born 1931, Milan, Italy)
Vase, *Perilloide*
Designed 1985. Glazed earthenware
25.1 x 50.5 x 15 cm (9⅞ x 19⅞ x 6 in.)
Produced by Zabro, a division of Zanotta
(Nova Milanese), for Nuova Alchimia (Milan), 1985
Impressed on underside: Zabro
D91.109.1, The Liliane and David M. Stewart Collection

**79. Andrea Branzi**
(born 1938, Florence, Italy)
Tea set prototype
Designed 1974. Enameled acrylic plastic,
enameled wood
Teapot: 24.5 x 37.7 x 12.6 cm (9⅝ x 14¹³⁄₁₆ x 4¹⁵⁄₁₆ in.)
Unmarked
D91.387.1–5, gift of Andrea Branzi

**80. Gaetano Pesce**
(born 1939, La Spezia, Italy)
Table, *Samson (Sansone)*
Designed 1980. Polyester resin
77.5 x 190.8 x 117.5 cm (30½ x 75⅛ x 46¼ in.)
Produced by Cassina S.p.A. (Meda Milano), 1980
Unmarked
D91.416.1, The Liliane and David M. Stewart Collection


*"When we want something new to appear,
we have to destroy the 'temple.' Samson
did that. He reacted in a certain way to
religion, to power, to politics.
He destroyed their symbol – the temple.
The columns of that temple are the legs
of this table. They are collapsing, tired of
the old order, trying to reach for a new
one, the new order we are entering at the
end of the twentieth century."*
Gaetano Pesce, 1993[43]

**81. Ron Arad**
(born 1951, Tel Aviv, Israel)
Bookcase, *One Way or Another*
Designed 1993. Steel
255 x 180 x 30 cm (100⅜ x 70⅞ x 11¹³⁄₁₆ in.)
Produced by One Off Ltd (London, England), 1993;
produced by Marzorati Ronchetti s.r.l. (Cantu, Italy),
1994 to the present
Unmarked
D93.311.1, gift of Mr. and Mrs. Roger Labbé


*"The* Bookworm *came first ... But
because it was fixed to the wall, locking
all this tension in the sprung strip, you
immediately think of a way of locking the
spring that will still allow movement.
Then I came up with* This Mortal Coil
*[predecessor of* One Way or Another*],
where nothing is fixed solidly, so although
it is locked, it still moves and is still
allowed to spring. Gravity helps shape it
as well; when you remove a book from the
library, the whole coil is still breathing for
a while."*
Ron Arad, 1994[44]

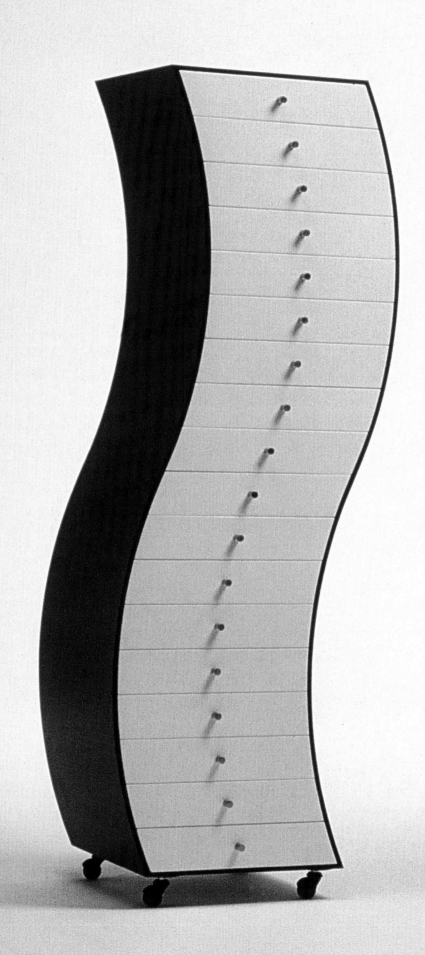

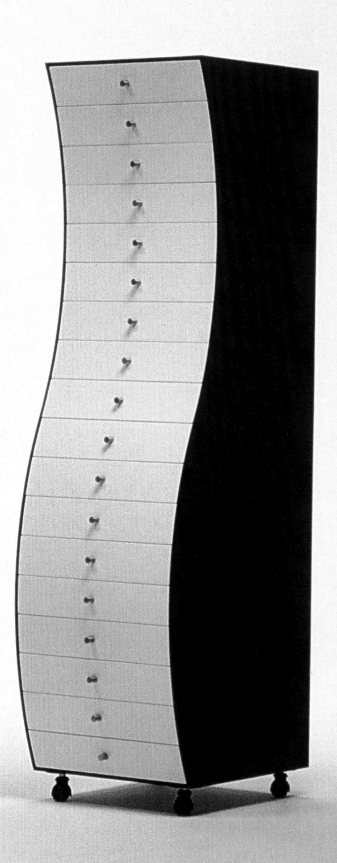

**82. Shiro Kuramata**
(born 1934, Tokyo, Japan; died 1991, Tokyo)
Chests of drawers, *Side 1, Side 2*
Designed 1970. Ebonized and lacquered ash, brushed steel
*Side 1*: 170 x 44.7 x 60.5 cm (67⅛ x 17⅝ x 23¾ in.)
*Side 2*: 170 x 63 x 49.7 cm (67⅛ x 24¾ x 19⅝ in.)
Produced by Fujiko (Tokyo), c. 1970–75; produced by
Cappellini International Interiors (Arosio, Italy),
1986 to the present
Unmarked
D91.414.1-2, The Liliane and David M. Stewart Collection,
by exchange

*"His objects are driven by an inner energy, a spasmodic
deformation of signs and surfaces; a dramatic and composed
deformation that twists forms without disintegrating objects.
If anything, it dematerializes them and transforms them into
religious icons, as quiet as gods of a sleep that brings rest but
also opens the doors to nightmares ... or comforting dreams."*
Andrea Branzi, 1989[45]

"Heidenreich ... has come through with a new creation – an asymmetrical vase. For the first time, a vase is modeled rather than turned. It is an astonishingly modern form, an entirely naturalistic porcelain creation."
*Die Kunst und das schöne Heim*, 1951[46]

**83. Fritz Heidenreich**
(born 1895, Mähring bei Augsburg, Germany; died 1966, Selb, West Germany)
Vase
Designed c. 1952. Glazed porcelain
44.6 x 13.5 x 18.4 cm (17⅝ x 5⅜ x 7¼ in.)
Produced by Rosenthal AG (Selb), c. 1952
Printed in green on underside: *Rosen* [device of crossed swords surmounted by a crown] *thal*/GERMANY/KUNSTABTEILUNG/SELB
D94.186.1, gift of Luc d'Iberville-Moreau, by exchange

**84. Massimo Iosa Ghini**
(born 1959, Bologna, Italy)
Pitcher, *Simulated (Simulata)*
Designed 1989. Silver-plated alpacca
25.1 x 24.8 x 7.5 cm (9⅞ x 9¾ x 2¹⁵⁄₁₆ in.)
Produced by Design Gallery Milano (Milan), 1989
Impressed on underside: ARGENTERIA/MERANO [within
rectangle]
D93.296.1, gift of Paul Leblanc

*"The object is part of [a large] collection – from upholstery to*
*silver pieces to wooden pieces.... And, of course, the main aim*
*was of communicating – through the shapes of the collection,*
*the shapes of the objects.... At that time, these were more*
*expressions of an extreme virtuosity with which I wanted to*
*show that ... you can give every kind of shape to material."*
Massimo Iosa Ghini, 1994[47]

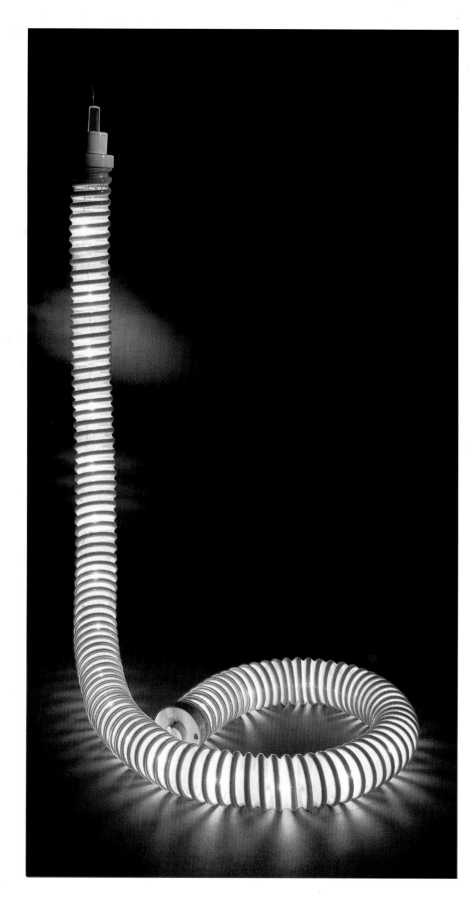

"In 1968, Livio Castiglioni and I found ourselves in Capri working on the enlargement of a hotel. Among other things, the owner wanted to illuminate the swimming pool area and we were in the process of formulating an appropriate solution. The idea came to us while we were observing the gardener, who was cleaning the lawn with a large vacuum cleaner fitted with a long flexible tube. It was the very flexibility of the tube that suggested its use to us.... The first prototype [of the lamp] had a visible electric cord and a long line of bulbs connected in series. This solution wasn't satisfactory from an aesthetic point of view — the cord being too much in evidence — and so I thought about making the electricity in the metallic armature of the tube portable, too. Together with the technical staff at Artemide, we studied a double spiral formed by one metallic structural cord and one of conductive copper covered and inserted in the transparent tube. The result was therefore a 2-meter-long module containing twenty bulbs, which was flexible and could be built up into a maximum of seven units; potentially, one could create a luminous snake 14 meters long."
Gianfranco Frattini, 1995[48]

**85. Livio Castiglioni**
(born 1911, Milan, Italy; died 1979, Milan)
**Gianfranco Frattini**
(born 1926, Padua)
Lamps, *Boalum*
Designed 1969. PVC plastic, metal
D90.130.1: 187 x 6.7 x 6.7 cm (73⅝ x 2⅝ x 2⅝ in.)
D93.283.1: 199 x 6.7 x 6.7 cm (78 5/16 x 2⅝ x 2⅝ in.)
Produced by Artemide S.p.A.
(Pregnana Milanese), 1970–84
Embossed on one end of each: Artemide/Made In Italy/Design:/Livio Castiglioni/Gianfranco Frattini
D90.130.1, The Liliane and David M. Stewart Collection;
D93.283.1, gift of Luc d'Iberville-Moreau, by exchange

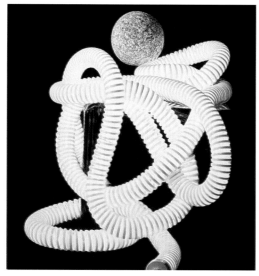

**86. Elizabeth Browning Jackson**
(born 1948, Providence, RI, USA)
Rug, *Endless Point*
Designed 1984. Wool
141 x 191.8 x 1.6 cm (55½ x 75½ x ⅝ in.)
Produced 1984 to the present
Printed in black on cloth label on underside: [device of
square monogram of stylized EJB] ELIZABETH BROWNING
JACKSON/P.O. BOX 3001 WESTPORT, MA. 02790/
508-636-6673 FAX 508-636-2966
D93.195.1, gift of Paul Leblanc

"Endless Point *was inspired by the universal symbol of the spiral, whose origins were derived from natural forms such as the snake and shell. This shape has been used throughout the world from ancient cultures to modern design.*

*Having studied environmental sculpture, I became interested in making my art more approachable. My sculptures became functional objects that pushed the limits. I started making rugs in cut-out shapes, leaving the perimeter behind. By taking the rugs out of the rectangle and adding a 3-D effect, I allowed them to float on the floor and become sculptures that people actually have fun walking on."*
Elizabeth Browning Jackson, 1994[49]

**87. Lino Sabattini**
(born 1925, Correggio, Italy)
Cutlery, *Sculptura*
Designed 1988. Stainless steel
Knife: 24.8 x 2.2 cm (9¾ x ⅞ in.)
Produced by Rosenthal Besteckfabrik (Neusorg,
Germany), 1988 to the present
Knife impressed on blade: *Rosen* [device of crossed
swords surmounted by a crown] *thal*; on reverse: 18/1
Fork and spoon, impressed on reverse of handles:
*Rosen* [device of crossed swords surmounted by a
crown] *thal*/18/10 GERMANY
D91.104.1-4, gift of Lino Sabattini

*"... Sculptura was the name that was given by the Rosenthal*
*company in Germany. In reality, Mr. Sabattini had in mind*
*the name Capricciose (the translation in English would be*
*"whimsical").... The wave form used for the handle was the*
*natural result of the search for a formal transition that would*
*allow us to make the joining of the two main components*
*in cutlery more evident."*
Guido Niest (assistant to Lino Sabattini), 1994[50]

**88. Flavio Barbini**
(born 1948, Murano, Italy)
Vase
Designed c. 1970. Glass
25.4 x 10.8 x 8.6 cm (10 x 4¼ x 3⅜ in.) each
Produced by Alfredo Barbini s.r.l. (Murano),
1970–c. 1978
Each engraved on underside: *Alfredo*
*Barbini/Murano/1970*
D84.160.1, gift of Susan Chalom


*"This one is part of a series.... They are all geometric forms —*
*superimposed, fixed, or mobile.... These involve movement. They*
*have many positions; they are not static. This one is composed*
*of two pieces, two pieces that lock together and share a single*
*axis. The position of these two pieces in the rotation allows*
*for different positions, constantly changing the look. It is like the*
*tail of a peacock — it can be open or closed ... like a zipper, or*
*a door, or a hinge."*
Flavio Barbini, 1994[51]

*"The project can be nothing but a negation of things that one considers intolerable.... I have preferred, according to the principle of negation implicit in the project (one designs new things because whatever exists is intolerable), to redefine each time a new grammar based upon whatever I see that I have to negate."*
Enzo Mari, 1993[52]

**89. Enzo Mari**
(born 1932, Novara, Italy)
Vases, *Pago-Pago*
Designed 1968. ABS plastic
30.2 x 20 x 15.5 cm (11⅞ x 7⅞ x 6⅛ in.) each
Produced by Bruno Danese s.n.c. (Milan),
1969 to the present
Embossed near base of interior: ©ENZO MARI 1969 DANESE
[device of rectangular monogram BD]
MILANO MADE IN ITALY
D87.216.1, gift of Geoffrey N. Bradfield; D88.125.1, gift of
Wistar Morris, by exchange

*"The form of the Godezia box and the Stellaria vase derive from the design of a pier in a project for a bridge in the Milan region. Reduced in scale and made from new materials, the two basic shapes of the pier (a cylinder and a fluted cone) were turned into basic elements for two elegant objects. The cylinder is aluminum painted in a black and blue checkered pattern, while the polished aluminum cone was manufactured with the aid of a laser.... The whole project is based on a principle of combined variations around a core of about ten fundamental shapes."*

Alessandro Mendini, 1996[53]

**90. Alessandro Mendini**
(born 1931, Milan, Italy)
Jewel box, *Godezia*
Designed 1993. Aluminum and enameled aluminum
45.7 x 19 x 19 cm (18 x 7½ x 7½ in.)
Produced by Design Gallery Milano (Milan), 1993
Printed in black on circular gray sticker affixed to underside: 4/24/199/*Mendini*; around perimeter of sticker: DESIGN GALLERY MILANO
D93.293.1, gift of Paul Leblanc

**91. Alessandro Mendini**
Vase, *Stellaria*
Designed 1993. Aluminum and enameled aluminum
41.5 x 19 x 19 cm (16⅜ x 7½ x 7½ in.)
Produced by Design Gallery Milano (Milan), 1993
Printed in black on circular gray sticker affixed to underside: 4/24/199/*Mendini*; around perimeter of sticker: DESIGN GALLERY MILANO
D93.294.1, gift of Paul Leblanc

**92. Wilhelm Kåge**
(born 1889, Stockholm, Sweden; died 1960, Stockholm)
Vase, *Surrea*
Designed 1940. Glazed stoneware
48 x 33 x 26 cm (18⅞ x 13 x 10¼ in.)
Produced by AB Gustavsberg (Gustavsberg), 1940, 1953
Printed in brown on underside of one section:
GUSTAVSBERG [around device of an anchor]/KÅGE [within
rectangular outline]; impressed on underside of
another section: S
D93.274.1, The Liliane and David M. Stewart Collection

*"Nowadays I am passing from a
flourishing surrealism, prompted by a
youthful inclination, to a more severe,
pure shape.... I think, however, that I can
never forget that for me beauty without
pleasure is sterile in the same way that
intelligence without humor often means a
genuine stupidity."*
Stig Lindberg, 1952[55]

**93. Frederick Sigurd (Stig) Lindberg**
(born 1916, Umeå, Sweden; died 1982, San Felice, Italy)
Vase, *Pouch (Pungo)*
Designed c. 1953. Glazed stoneware
24.2 x 14 x 12.1 cm (9½ x 5½ x 4¾ in.)
Produced by AB Gustavsberg (Gustavsberg, Sweden),
1953-64
Impressed on underside: GUSTAVSBERG/SWEDEN/283;
printed on paper label affixed to underside: STUDIO/STIG
L./PUNGO/CARRARA/283
D91.436.1, anonymous gift

*"The vases are like pure vibrations. 'Amnesie' means a (temporary) memory collapse. It doesn't mean ignorance, but free break."*
Andrea Branzi, 1993[56]

**94. Andrea Branzi**
(born 1938, Florence, Italy)
Vases, *Amnesia (Amnesie)* series:
*A 28, A 38, A 46, A 51, A 56*
Designed 1991. Aluminum
*A 28:* 22 x 13.7 x 13.7 cm (8¹¹⁄₁₆ x 5³⁄₈ x 5³⁄₈ in.)
*A 38:* 28.2 x 13.6 x 13.6 cm (11⅛ x 5³⁄₈ x 5³⁄₈ in.)
*A 46:* 34 x 14 x 14 cm (13³⁄₈ x 5½ x 5½ in.)
*A 51:* 40.3 x 13.6 x 13.6 cm (15 7/8 x 5³⁄₈ x 5³⁄₈ in.)
*A 56:* 44.2 x 11.4 x 11.4 cm (17³⁄₈ x 4½ x 4½ in.)
Produced by Design Gallery Milano (Milan), 1991
Printed around perimeter of circular aluminum disk affixed to underside of each: ANDREA BRANZI/Design Gallery Milano; printed within circle of each, respectively: 11/50/1991; 11/50/1991; 18/50/1991; 14/50/1991; 22/50/1991
D93.297.1–5, gift of Paul Leblanc

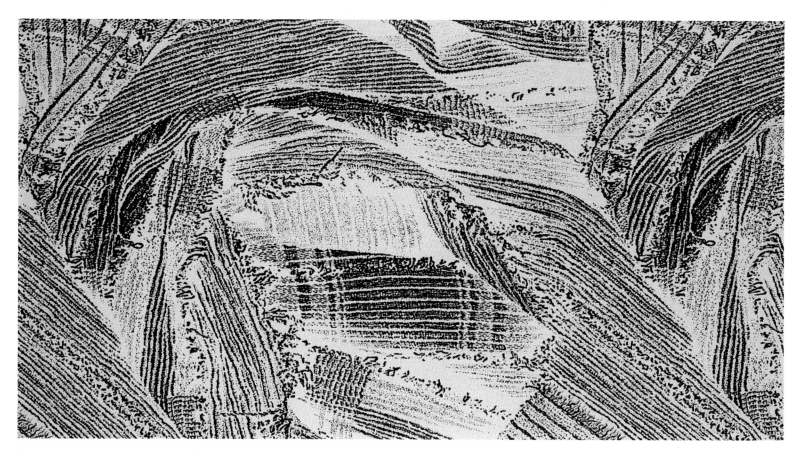

**95. Astrid Sampe**
(born 1909, Stockholm, Sweden)
Textile, *Versailles*
Designed 1972. Polyester/viscose
545.5 x 130 cm (216½ x 51³⁄₁₆ in.)
Produced by Almedahls AB (Kinna), 1972 to the present
Unmarked
D95.175.1, gift of Astrid Sampe and Almedahls AB

*"My intention for the use of* Versailles *is both for window
curtains and room dividers. I have looked many times at the
pleat[ed] curtains in the famous castle of Versailles outside
Paris [and] how they can be run up and down in horizontal
line.... Versailles is a 'romantic escape.'"*
Astrid Sampe, 1994[57]

**96. Junichi Arai**
(born 1932, Kiryu City, Japan)
Textile, *Woven Pattern (Nuno me Gara)*
Designed 1983. Cotton
284.5 x 99.1 cm (112 x 39 in.)
Produced by Nuno Corporation (Tokyo),
1983 to the present
Unmarked
D92.145.1, The Liliane and David M. Stewart Collection

*"It is called* Woven Pattern *because it uses narrow strips of cloth
in order to create the design pattern. In the style of narrow
fabrics ... used by the people living near the western coast of
Africa such as the Republic of Mali or Togo, I made some scarves
also using cotton threads of tight weave. They were bound
together into a bundle and twisted, and then synthesized with
an electronic copying machine to create a design. This design
was scanned with a scanner, and the fabric was woven with
a Jacquard loom. In other words, the design was created using
already woven fabrics as a motif, and that is why it is called*
Nuno me Gara, *a woven pattern."*
Junichi Arai, 1995[58]

**97. Fulvio Bianconi**
(born 1915, Padua, Italy; died 1996, Milan)
Vase, *Handkerchief (Fazzoletto)*
Designed c. 1949. Glass
27 x 28.8 x 25.5 cm (10⅝ x 11⁵⁄₁₆ x 10¹⁄₁₆ in.)
Produced by Venini S.p.A. (Murano), 1949 to the present
Acid-stamped on underside: *venini*/*murano*/ITALIA
D94.122.1, gift of Anthea Liontos*

*"Venetian glass from the 1950s combines a spontaneous and heartfelt affirmation of tradition with a faultless sense of style. One little Venini handkerchief vase is typical. The Muranese glassmaker's skillful manipulation of glass is instantly evident in the graceful undulations of the rim.... The rim is extraordinary because each curve seems 'aware' of the existence of all the others. An edge that folds in is echoed on the opposite side by an edge that folds out, as if the two were dancing together."*
William Warmus, 1984[59]

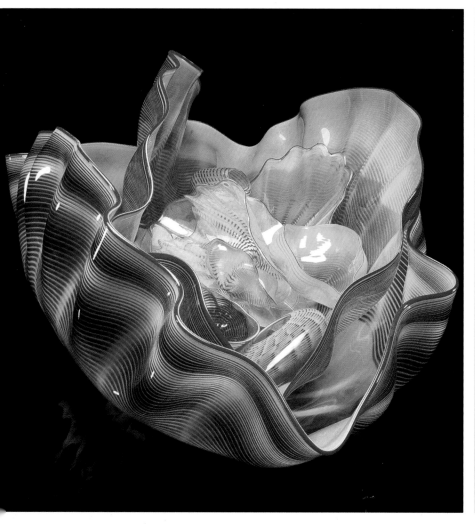

**98. Dale Chihuly**
(born 1941, Tacoma, WA, USA)
*Cadmium Yellow Seaform Set with Red Lip Wraps*
Executed 1990. Glass
43.2 x 61 x 91.5 cm (17 x 24 x 36 in.)
Engraved under base of small closed form: *Chihuly 90*
D90.219.1, gift of Jay Spectre

"The piece is always moving while it's in progress, and
one has to make decisions very quickly.... I like the
work to reflect those quick decisions, the end result
being a frozen fluid thought – as direct as at drawing.
My work ... relies on spontaneous combinations of
fire, molten glass, air, and gravity."
Dale Chihuly, 1993[60]

**99. Arnold Zimmerman**
(born 1954, Poughkeepsie, NY, USA)
Teapot
Executed 1984. Glazed stoneware
35.3 x 15.3 x 31.8 cm (13⅞ x 6 x 12½ in.)
Incised on underside: *Zimmerman/84*
D85.118.1, The Liliane and David M. Stewart Collection

"In 1984, at the time this series of teapots was made,
I was also working on nine 10-foot-high carved vessels
weighing two tons each. I moved between ponderous
glacial manipulation of tons of clay and the seemingly
effortless, split-second improvisations of throwing
a four-pound ball of clay. In this smaller scale, teapots,
jars and plates provided a sense of 'comic relief,'
farcical diversions from the ever-waiting, demanding
monuments looming over me in my studio."
Arnold Zimmerman, 1994[61]

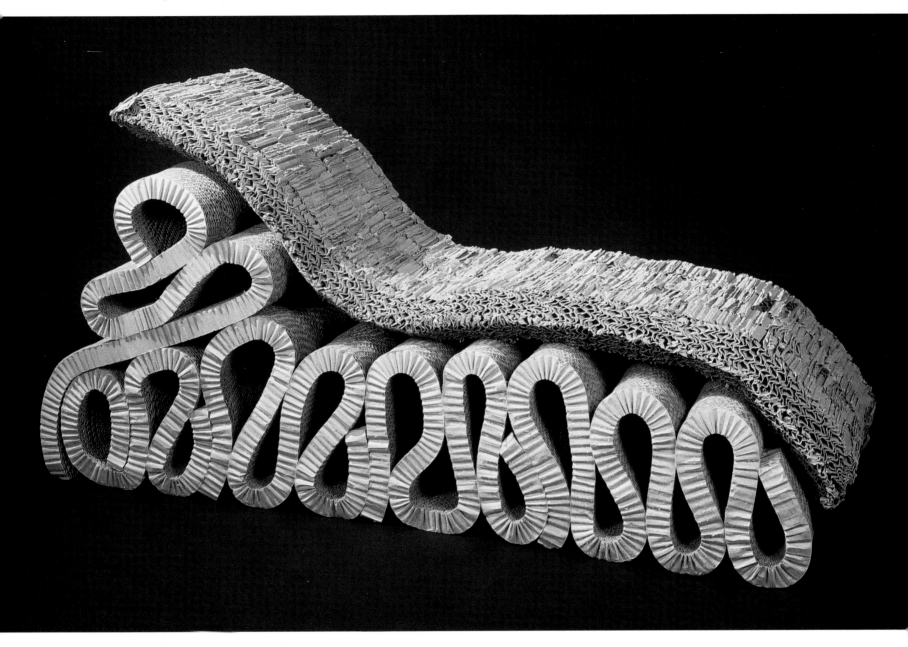

**100. Frank Gehry**
(born 1929, Toronto, Ontario, Canada)
Chaise longue, *Bubbles*
Designed 1979. Cardboard, wood
91.5 x 70.6 x 198 cm (36 x 27¹³/₁₆ x 77¹⁵/₁₆ in.)
Produced by New City Editions
(Venice, CA, USA), 1979-86
Written in black ink on paper label affixed to
underside: BUB 22/50/*Gehry* [indecipherable]
D93.271.1, gift of Caroline Moreau

*"I got interested in paper furniture when I was designing for
department stores and had to invent display furniture that
nobody really had to sit on, and then could be easily disposed of.
It led to the* Easy Edges *furniture, which evolved in a shop in my
studio. I would draw and my assistants and I would then make
them. I never expected to sell these things until someone from
Bloomingdales saw them and suggested I develop them."*
Frank Gehry, 1991[62]

**101. Frank Gehry**
Side chair prototype, *Steam-Bent Pillow Chair*
Designed 1989. Maple, basswood, birch plywood
96.5 x 69.8 x 99.1 cm (38 x 27½ x 39 in.)
Produced by the Gehry studio (Los Angeles, CA, USA)
Unmarked
D92.110.1, gift of Frank Gehry and The Knoll Group

*"The objects I started fantasizing about were baskets. When I was a kid, my father used to bring home a lot of wicker furniture, and maybe that stuck in my memory. I used to play with wooden bushel baskets, too, but I don't think the design came from that. . . . What makes this all work and gives it extraordinary strength is the interwoven, basketlike character of the design. Now structure and material have freed bentwood furniture from its former heaviness and rigidity. It really is possible to make bentwood furniture pliable, springy, and light."*
Frank Gehry, 1991[63]

**102. Walter Lefmann**
(date of birth unknown)
**Ron DeVito**
(date of birth unknown)
Dress
Designed 1967. Printed paper
86.6 x 64.6 cm (34⅛ x 25⁷⁄₁₆ in.)
Produced for Time, Inc. (New York, NY, USA), 1967
Unmarked
D94.176.1, gift of Toni and Wesley Greenbaum*

*"The dress is good for four or five wearings, depending on the clemency of the weather and the intensity of the wearer's frug. Gone are laundry and cleaners' bills: all that is needed is a good eraser. Gone, too, are needle and thread and painstaking alterations. A quick snip of the scissors and the hem is shortened, the neckline lowered, while cutouts sprout all over. As for rips, Scotch Tape is all that's needed for instant repairs."*
Time, 1966[64]

**103. Issey Miyake**
(born 1939, Tokyo, Japan)
Jacket
Designed 1988. Paper
73 x 148.6 cm (28¾ x 58½ in.)
Produced by Issey Miyake Inc. (Tokyo), 1988
Woven in white on black label sewn inside collar: ISSEY
MIYAKE/PⵑRMANⵑNTⵑ
D94.207.1, gift of Yvonne Brunhammer

*"We have clothes made of iron, paper, cane, bamboo, stones.
There are any number of possibilities once you let your
imagination roam. And in that way, the area of my work is
expanded. That's enough to achieve, I feel."*
Issey Miyake, 1985[65]

**104. Janna Syvänoja**
(born 1960, Helsinki, Finland)
Necklace, *Books*
Executed 1990. Paper, wire
29.7 x 36.9 x 1 cm (11¹¹⁄₁₆ x 14½ x ⅜ in.)
Impressed in gold on edge: VAHAN
D92.155.1, The Liliane and David M. Stewart Collection

*"When you open a book and start to interpret it, you find an adventure, a trip to jump into. I wanted to open this usual object in an unusual way, as we cut a fruit and find the seeds.... I made it with respect. I didn't want to respect only written knowledge, but also the knowledge of how to make paper from wood, to bind a book. It was also respect for curiosity to see existing things in a new way."*
Janna Syvänoja, 1995[66]

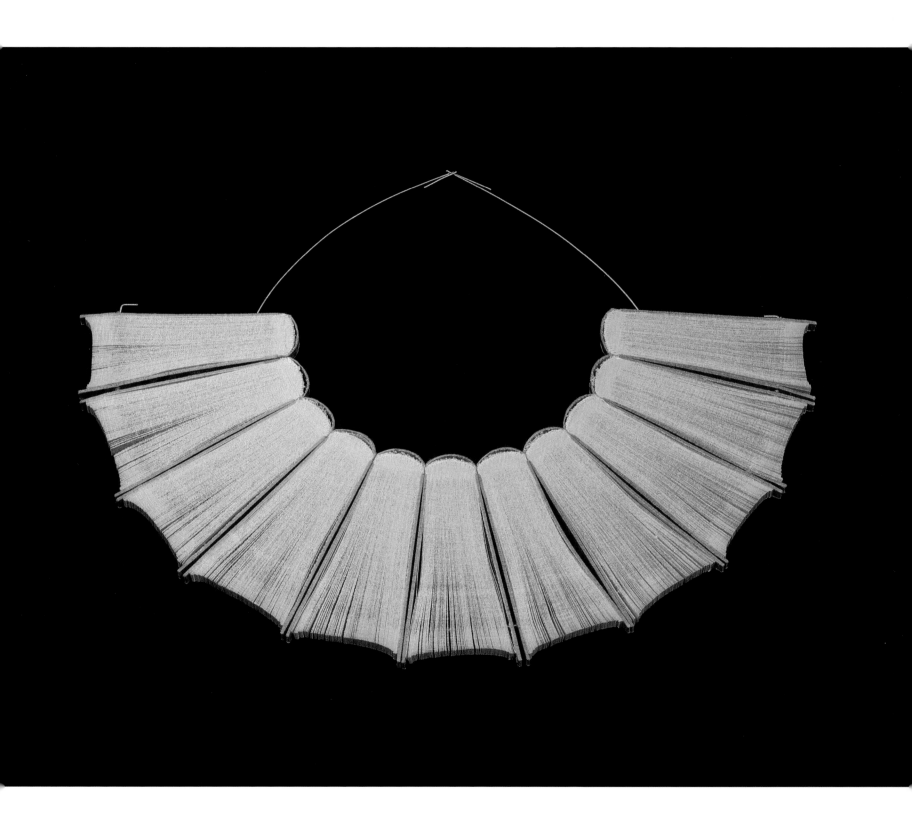

*"That was the title in which the word 'London' was added because there was an Italian restaurant near us [where] they serve a kind of pasta that's like a long black tape and it reminded us of the pappardelle.... After working for a long time in metal ... you make metal soft.... The material itself is, you know, most of the delight.... It's very minimal."*
Ron Arad, 1994[67]

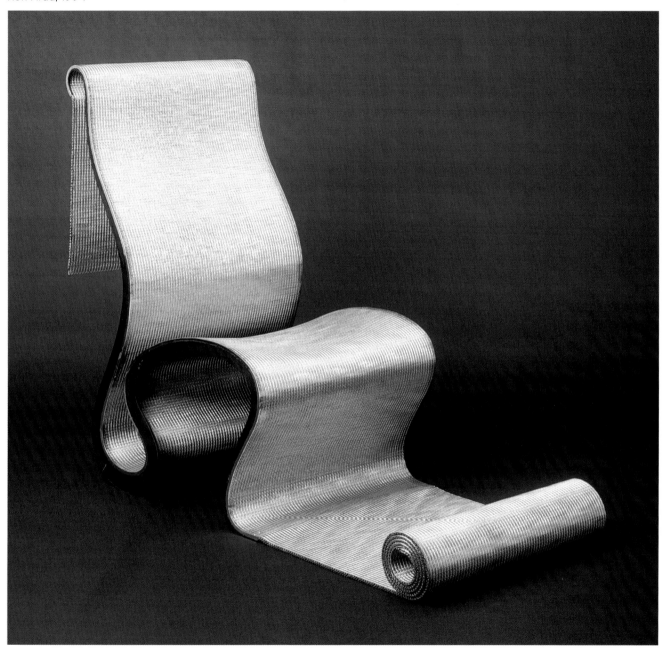

**105. Ron Arad**
(born 1951, Tel Aviv, Israel)
Chair, *London Papardelle*
Designed 1992. Steel, stainless steel
105 x 59.6 x 90 cm (41⁵⁄₁₆ x 23⁷⁄₁₆ x 35⁷⁄₁₆ in.); extended:
273 cm (107½ in.)
Produced by One Off Ltd (London, England), 1992-93;
produced by Marzorati Ronchetti s.r.l. (Cantu, Italy),
1994 to the present
Unmarked
D93.310.1, anonymous gift

*"How High the Moon ... marks the beginning of Kuramata's use of expanded metal. It is an armchair — a shimmering phantom of a chair, really. It's as though there was once a chair inside ... 'I like expanded metal for its transparency,' says Kuramata ... 'It doesn't shut out the space or the world. It looks very light, and therefore, it looks as if it floats.'"*

Adele Freedman, 1988[68]

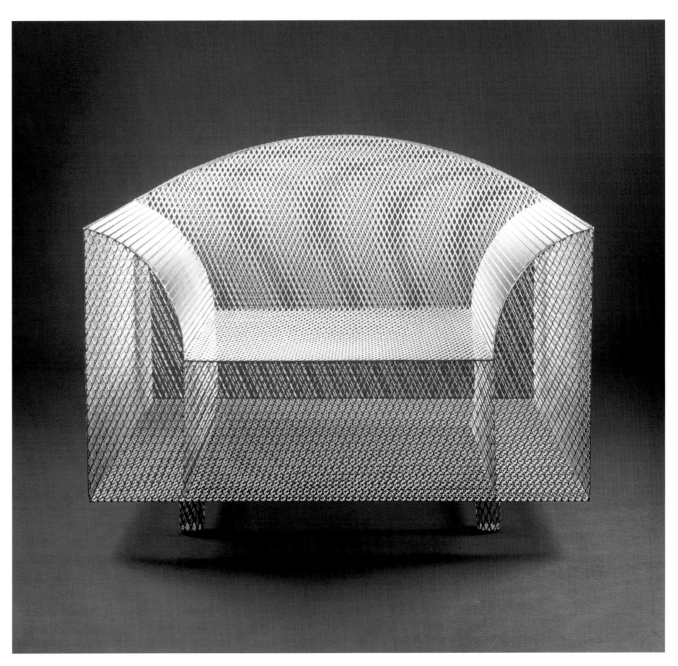

**106. Shiro Kuramata**
(born 1934, Tokyo, Japan; died 1991, Tokyo)
Armchair, *How High the Moon*
Designed 1986. Nickel-plated steel
72.4 x 95 x 81.8 cm (28½ x 37⅜ x 32¼ in.)
Produced by Idée Co. Ltd. (Tokyo), 1987–95;
Vitra GmbH (Weil am Rhein, Germany),
1987 to the present
Unmarked
D90.114.1, The Liliane and David M. Stewart Collection

**107. Paco Rabanne**
(born Francisco Rabaneva-Cuervo, 1934, San Sebastian,
Spain)
Textile, *Chainmail*
Designed c. 1967. Plastic
101.6 x 101.6 cm (40 x 40 in.)
Produced by Paco Rabanne (Paris, France), c. 1967
Unmarked
D91.441.1, gift of Louise and George Beylerian*

*"The 1960s were in their turn the arena for an
astonishing revolution in the arts. New forms of
expression evolved, such as Op Art and Kinetic Art,
every single direction was explored, though one
thing remained constant: traditional materials were
always abandoned ...*

*Fascinated and fired by these amazing develop-
ments, I resolved to apply to fashion – a minor art –
all the things the designers I most admired were
doing. I, too, would take the plunge and abandon cloth,
which had been invented fifteen thousand years ago
by the Egyptians, replacing it with the most up-to-
date materials. That's how I became interested in
plastic, in Rhodoid and in aluminum, which had never
before been used in fashion design. I laid my needle
and scissors aside and took up pliers and blowtorch."*
Paco Rabanne, 1991[69]

**108. Arline M. Fisch**
(born 1931, New York, NY, USA)
Collar, *Collar MKC43*
Executed 1985, Copper, silver, carnelian
50 x 31 x 24.5 cm (19¹¹/₁₆ x 12³/₁₆ x 9⁵/₈ in.)
Impressed on reverse of clasp: STERLING/A [within device
of a stylized fish] 85
D95.180.1, The Liliane and David M. Stewart Collection

*"Metal is hard, fabric is soft, yet the two can develop
an interrelationship that allows new concepts to
develop. I am intrigued by the idea that metal can be
soft to the touch at the same time that it maintains
a structured form, a visual contradiction that poses
many questions. When is a collar a piece of clothing?
When is it a costume? When does it become a piece
of jewelry? What is this collar of knitted metal? ...
It refers to Elizabethan grandeur in its appearance,
but it is machine knitted in coated copper wire manufactured for industrial use, automatically placing
it in the twentieth century and presenting another
contradiction, another question."*
Arline M. Fisch, 1995[70]

**109. Reiko Sudo**
(born 1953, Niihari, Japan)
Textile, *Stainless Embossed*
Designed 1990. Polyester, nickel, iron, chrome
285.7 x 115 cm (112½ x 45¼ in.)
Produced by Nuno Corporation (Tokyo),
1990 to the present
Unmarked
D92.187.1, The Liliane and David M. Stewart Collection

*"I had wanted to express the cold and clear shine of stainless steel in fabric. My encounter with the technique of 'sputtering' (ordinarily used for automobile production) allowed me to create an entirely new fabric that is soft and permeable and has the appearance of stainless steel, by spraying a mixture of steel, chrome, and nickel onto a cloth.... The surprised faces of the technicians at the automotive factory were unforgettable as they looked at the thin cloth I brought there."*
Reiko Sudo, 1994[71]

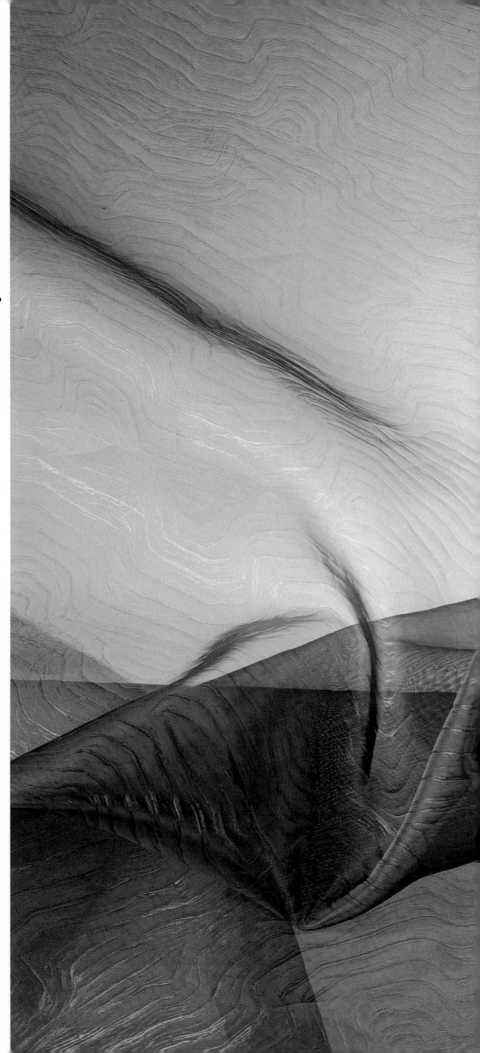

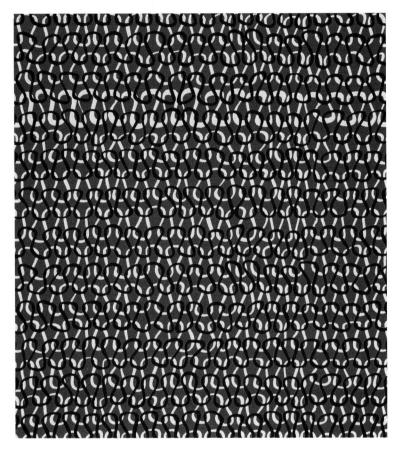

**110. Oliver Lundquist**
(born 1916, Westbury, NY, USA)
**Abel Sorensen**
(born 1915, Charlottedal, Denmark; died 1982, New York)
Textile, *Tricot*
Designed 1947. Printed cotton
129.5 x 120.5 cm (51 x 47⁷⁄₁₆ in.)
Produced by Schiffer Prints, Division of Mil-Art Co., Inc.
(New York), 1947-c. 1950
Printed in black along one selvage: TRICOT-ABEL SORENSEN
& OLIVER LUNDQUIST; along other selvage: © SCHIFFER PRINTS
VAT DYE HANDPRINT
D83.129.1, gift of Geoffrey N. Bradfield

"Tricot *was so-named because of its derivation from
the knit pattern and was intended to be 'natural'
rather than slick modern.... I believe the fabric was
intended for both draperies and upholstery — certainly
for slip covers.*"
Oliver Lundquist, 1994[72]

**111. Junichi Arai**
(born 1932, Kiryu City, Japan)
Textile, *Melted Off Contour*
Designed 1958. Nylon, aluminum-plated polyester
290.5 x 93.6 cm (114³⁄₈ x 36¹³⁄₁₆ in.)
Produced by Nuno Corporation (Tokyo),
1988 to the present
Unmarked
D92.149.1, The Liliane and David M. Stewart Collection

"*I obtained about twenty patents for the process
of vacuum-plating polyester film with aluminum, and
dissolving it in a weak alkali solution ... I used this
design as an experiment to see how thin lines could
be deposited.... The design was born from an experimental need, but the realization had to wait for thirty
years because of other related conditions such as the
structural problem of the fabric and the availability of
chemical adhesives.... The* Contour *design ... was also
derived from the fact that I had the good fortune to
be pursuing patterns that were created accidentally
and selecting from them.*"
Junichi Arai, 1995[73]

# Is Ornament a Crime?

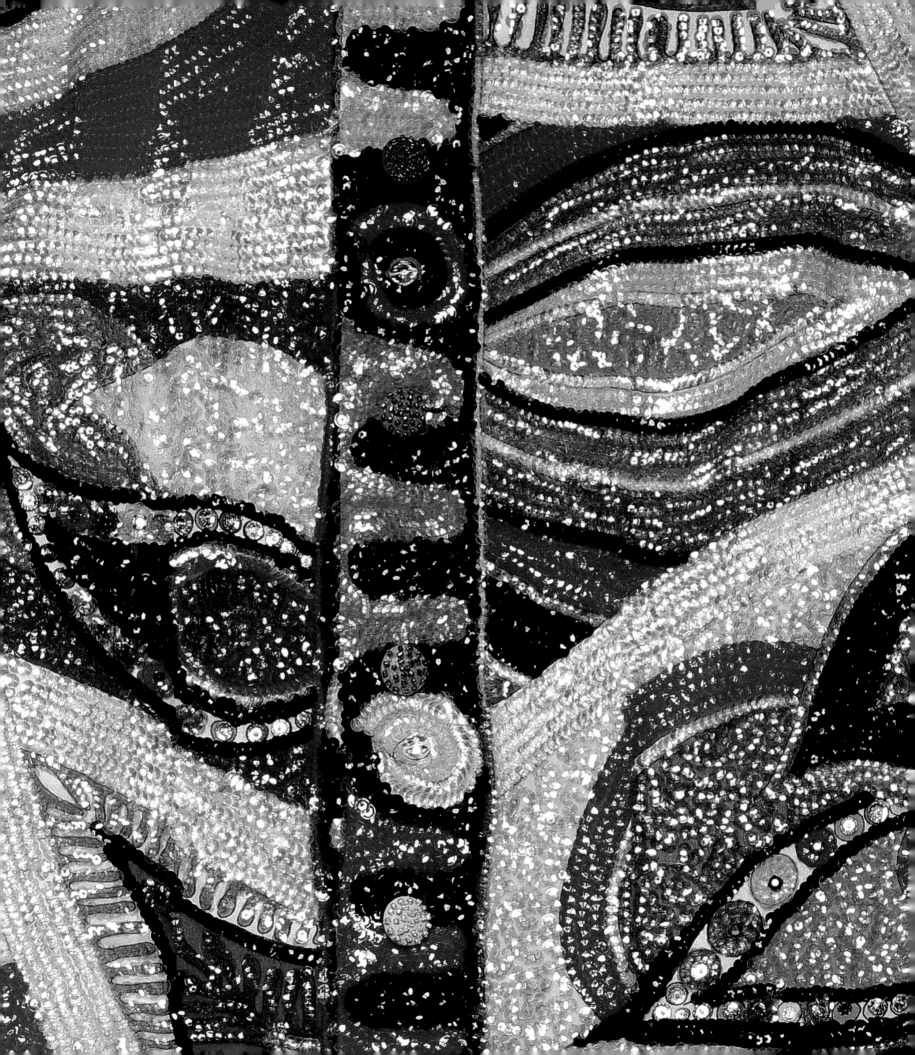

# Is Ornament a Crime?

*by Lenore Newman and Jan L. Spak*

Fig. 57. Christopher Dresser, jugs, c. 1884.
Glazed and transferprinted earthenware.
Height of tallest: 19 cm (7½ in.).
Produced by Old Hall Earthenware Co.
New York, Marc O. Rabun Gallery.

Fig. 58. Charles F. A. Voysey, detail of rug, c. 1905.
Wool. 5.49 x 2.85 m (18 ft. x 9 ft. 4 in.).
New York, The Metropolitan Museum of Art,
Gift of Cyril Farny, in memory of his wife,
Phyllis Holt Farny, 1976.

"I have evolved the following maxim, and pronounce it to the world: the evolution of culture marches with the elimination of ornament from useful objects."[1] So decreed Adolf Loos, the preeminent Austrian Modernist, in a didactic essay entitled "Ornament and Crime" published in 1908. Loos's proclamation, which essentially equated decorating an object with committing a felony, would become the battlecry of Modernist theorists and practitioners throughout the succeeding decades of our century. To these purists, form took precedence over all other considerations; ornament was banished to the closet to languish alongside its fellow criminals—historicism and individualized expression.

In the mature phase of the Bauhaus, an emphasis on machine production mandated simple, geometric shapes and primary colors, the same principles that guided the influential Dutch de Stijl group. In Germany, the notion that all surface decoration should be excluded was proclaimed in bold, defiant terms by the important exhibition *Form Without Ornament* staged by the Deutsche Werkbund in 1924.[2] This had a profound influence on the development of design theories in other industrialized nations as well. In the catalogue to the *Machine Art* exhibition mounted in 1934 at the Museum of Modern Art in New York City, the museum's director, Alfred Barr, Jr., reiterated this machine-driven philosophy: "Machine art, devoid as it should be of surface ornament, must depend upon the sensuous beauty of porcelain, enamel, celluloid, glass of all colors, copper, aluminum, brass and steel."[3] As the repository and promoter of good modern design, the museum continued to promulgate these ideas through important didactic exhibitions and publications. In 1950, Edgar Kaufmann, jr., codified Modernist principles in *What is Modern Design?*, a text in which he formulated twelve precepts, one of which counseled that "Modern design should be simple, its structure, evident in its appearance, avoiding extraneous enrichment."[4] While the use of the word "extraneous" tempered the original prohibition against *any* ornament, objects with pure, undecorated surfaces still represented, in his view, a paradigm of Modernism.

Nonetheless, ornament has remained an important element in much of modern design throughout the century. Indeed, the impulse to enrich form with pattern, both floral and geometric, has never died at any point. For example, the boldly rendered, brilliantly colored textiles of Paul Poiret and the École Martine of Paris (fig. 63) are justly renowned. But there are other equally brilliant designs from the Art Nouveau and Art Deco periods, as well as from the postwar and Postmodern periods. What era cannot claim practitioners of decoration? Moreover, ornament is a universal phenomenon: in the simplest of cultures and in the most highly developed industrial civilizations. Still, the principles of ornament and ornamentation have been part of a strident discourse in the twentieth century. In hindsight, the issue of whether or not to decorate has not been the major issue. If anything, the issue has been what style of ornament to use.

The debate about ornament has been a long and lively one. Decades before Loos's proclamation, British design reformers such as Henry Cole, Dr. Christopher Dresser, and Owen Jones, appalled by the decorative excesses of Victorian manufactured objects, set out to codify new principles of modern ornament that could guide designers of the burgeoning industrial revolution. Their conviction that decoration should be appropriate to an overall design—that "no decoration is tolerable which militates against the general beauty of the shape"[5]—was a principle that remained fundamental to Modernism even in periods when it seemed as though all ornament or surface enrichment had been expunged.

Underlying nineteenth-century reform theories was the fervent belief that the only appropriate source of decoration lay in nature, the truest form of beauty. This point of view derives directly from the ideas of John Ruskin and William Morris, who saw Nature as the best designer: "...all noble ornamentation is the expression of man's delight in God's work."[6] While the reformers recoiled from fully modeled, naturalistic representations of motifs taken from nature, they recognized that such virtuous qualities as symmetry, balance, and other geometric principles could be divined through close observation of her creations. Thus, highly conventionalized motifs derived from the real world were not merely legitimate but even desirable models for decoration, as seen in two jugs whose form and decoration were created by Dresser (fig. 57). In England, the trend toward stylized floral and foliate motifs continued, finding eloquent expression at the turn of the century in the work of Charles F. A. Voysey (fig. 58), an architect who advocated abstraction in his belief that "natural forms have to be reduced to mere symbols."[7]

On the Continent, too, nature had assumed a dominant role as the primary source of inspiration for creators of pattern. A wealth of design manuals sought to convey the principles of design to an increasingly sophisticated industrial world. The graphic artist and teacher Eugène Grasset, whose 1899 treatise *The Plant and its Ornamental Applications (La Plante et ses applications ornementales)* was one of the most important on the subject, was instrumental in reinforcing nature's preeminence in France. While maintaining a basis of botanical specificity, Grasset demonstrated how plants could be conventionalized in varying degrees of abstraction (fig. 59).

Indeed, nature remained predominant in European design at the turn of the century. In France and most of Europe, much Art Nouveau design consisted of an amalgam of a floral motif with the "wavy line" of 1900. For example, the porcelain objects designed by Edouard Colonna and Georges de Feure for S. Bing's L'Art Nouveau store show how skillfully floral and linear elements could be conjoined in rhythmic union (fig. 60). Likewise, the vase by Algot Eriksson (cat. no. 112) for the Swedish firm Rörstrand shows a graceful compromise between a naturalistic rendering of the floral motif and a repetitive decorative scheme. Whereas most modern twentieth-century designers adhered to schools of thought that required conventionalization of some sort, there were those who did not retreat from naturalistic renderings. Instead, they reveled in portraying the wonders of the natural world in all its minute and varied details. Among the most significant practitioners of this genre were Émile Gallé (fig. 61) and Louis C. Tiffany (cat. no. 199), whose works, both in form and ornament, brought naturalism to its apex.

The dichotomy between naturalistic and conventionalized renderings of floral patterns proved to be a central issue in twentieth-century design. Among those who embraced the latter approach in the early twentieth century were the Wiener Werkstätte designers in Vienna, who were very adept at applying stylized floral motifs to two- and three-dimensional surfaces. Of particular appeal to this group, especially during the 1910s, was a silhouetted bell-shaped flower; it is featured prominently in Carl Otto Czeschka's engaging *Pouter Pigeon* textile (cat. no. 113), Josef Hoffmann's cased glass vase (cat. no. 114), and an enameled pendant (cat. no. 115) that shows the impact of this Viennese approach to design. These works illustrate how the contours of a flat, schematized floral motif provided suitable

Fig. 59. Eugène Grasset, *Columbine* (from *La Plante et ses applications ornementales*, 1899).

Fig. 60. Georges de Feure, ice bucket, c. 1902. Glazed porcelain. 20 x 13 cm (7⅞ x 5⅛ in.). Paris, Musée des Arts Décoratifs.

Fig. 61. Émile Gallé, vase, *Autumn Crocus*,
c. 1897–1904. Glass with wheel-carved marquetry.
Height: 44.8 cm (17⅝ in.).
New York, The Metropolitan Museum of Art,
gift of Lloyd and Barbara Macklowe, 1984.

Fig. 62. Louis Süe and André Mare, detail of armchair,
c. 1912. Painted wood, leather.
125 x 50 cm (49¼ x 19¹¹⁄₁₆ in.).
Paris, Musée des Arts Décoratifs.

Fig. 63. École Martine, textile, c. 1919. Silk.
179.5 x 129 cm (70¾ x 50¾ in.).
New York, The Metropolitan Museum of Art,
Purchase, Edward C. Moore, Jr., Gift, 1923.

Fig. 64. Mimbres, bowl, c. A.D. 1000. Earthenware.
10 x 22.5 cm (3¹⁵⁄₁₆ x 8⅞ in.).
Syracuse, Collection of the Everson Museum of Art,
gift of Mr. and Mrs. Kenneth Siebel, Jr.

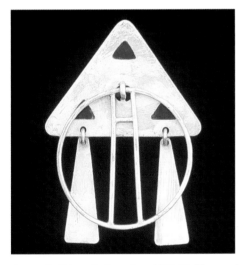

Fig. 65. Emil Bäuerle, brooch, c. 1900-05. Silver and
enamel. Pforzheim, Schmuckmuseum.

embellishment to a wide range of materials. And, though cast in the form of a bold paisley design with the brashness appropriate to the tastes of a half century later, such bellflowers appear in Emilio Pucci's sequined bodice (cat. no. 125). Throughout the teens, these geometric and even spiky floral treatments remained a constant of Austrian and German design. They can be seen, for example, in Emanuel Margold's graphic work at Darmstadt, as represented by the biscuit boxes he designed for the bakery firm of Bahlsen (cat. nos. 117, 118).

Floral patterns remained equally popular in other countries. In France in the teens, for example, flowers were symmetrically bunched and given sharper forms (though not as flat or hard-edged as the Austrian or German ones). Arranged with a lush profusion, they appear on the crest of a chair (fig. 62) designed by Louis Süe and André Mare for their influential Compagnie des Arts Français as the symbol of the new French style that they were promoting.[8] Similarly stylized flowers are to be found in the boldly conceived patterns of Paul Poiret and the École Martine (fig. 63), as well as on such sumptuously decorated deluxe objects as the Léon Jallot clock (cat. no. 120). Another bold example is the energetically-patterned linen textile dating to the 1920s by the Fauve painter Raoul Dufy (cat. no. 121); its flat pattern and strong contrasts are as vibrant as his works on canvas. Such stylized bouquets are also discernible in the patterns for dinnerware conceived by Suzanne Lalique (cat. no. 122), daughter of the jeweler and glass designer René Lalique.

Nor were such floral patterns restricted to the first half of the century. A flamboyant example of the Art Nouveau revival that began in the 1960s is Peter Max's textile (cat. no. 124), which explodes with the "flower power" of a decidedly psychedelic generation. Also extensively popularized by Max's graphics, the flower became emblematic of the peaceful qualities of life and hope for the future during this idealistic period. Turning from "flower children" to the other end of the social scale, the clothing of Italian fashion designer Emilio Pucci, which appeared on the backs of the world's best-dressed women, shows a similarly dynamic approach to floral pattern. His sequin- and rhinestone-encrusted evening top (cat. no. 125) radiates opulence while updating the large, foliate forms of the paisley motif amidst a field of geometric designs.

The architect Robert Venturi, perhaps the most influential theorist of the Postmodern period, together with his partner Denise Scott Brown, have also been influential in the revolt against the minimalism of early Modernism. Their spirited *Queen Anne* dining chair (cat. no. 126), which Venturi described as "Queen Anne in front and Mary Anne behind, but ... Alvar Aalto from the side,"[9] pays homage to an eighteenth-century chair form as well as to modern technology; at the same time, Venturi appropriated and updated an old and purposely banal type of floral pattern. As he put it, "It was difficult achieving an ordinary, sentimental, pretty floral pattern."[10] Tellingly, he called it *Grandmother*, although such patterning was not truly the prerogative of that older, sentimental generation.

As styles wax and wane in favor, cycles of taste often lead back to similar starting points. Lush patterns may give way to more stringent ones, and hot colors may give way to cooler palettes, but inevitably the pendulum returns full swing. Two examples bear eloquent witness to the way tropical climes stimulated exotic patterns. The Longwy factory, known for its ceramic wares imitating cloisonné enamel, created a spherical vase for the 1931 Colonial Exposition in Paris (cat. no. 128) that captures that age's fascination with tropical luxuriance and exoticism; the exuberant colors and profuse layering of leafy jungle foliage are rendered in a polychromatic tour de force. Pucci's design for a porcelain vase of a half century later is somewhat more modest but no less intense (cat. no. 129). Bursting with tropical lushness, its pattern was created, in effect, by wrapping one of the designer's signature scarves around the cylindrical form.

Throughout the evolution of style, floral ornament has experienced an everlasting bloom of popularity, often offering relief from the mundane. By providing a burst of color, and through its associative values—its sweet perfume, the evocation of spring and summer, and the eternal beauty of natural forms—the flower has transcended the fickle nature of taste.

The major alternative to floral decoration was a system of ornament based upon geometric configurations. Enriching objects for pure pleasure with regular geometric shapes—squares, rectangles, and triangles—has been sanctioned since earliest times. Archaic Greek art, African tribal art, and Native American cultures, for example, are particularly renowned for pottery of this type (fig. 64), and many of man's most coveted creations during the present century carry this basic form of ornament. Already in the mid-nineteenth century, Owen Jones and his fellow reformers believed that, even when derived from natural forms, "All ornament should be based upon a geometrical construction."[11] Given the emphasis in modern design theory on geometric form, it was natural that those designers who were interested in ornamenting objects would employ such shapes for decoration as well.

At the turn of the century, reformers in Vienna, Glasgow, and Chicago demonstrated how a shockingly new style of modern ornament could be derived wholly from straight lines and circles, sometimes to the amusement of critics. In a review of "The Set Table," a 1906 exhibition of tablesettings by Hoffmann, Kolo Moser, and others of the Wiener Werkstätte, one skeptical critic facetiously remarked: "The geometric factor guides both of our artistic table-setters in their creations, and the new mealtime grace may well have to be: 'Make me draw the right lines' …dumplings have to be reshaped by a master turner and the only stylistically correct black-and-white starch dish consists of poppyseed noodles perfected by Kolo Moser…here madness and geometry conjoin."[12]

In Germany, designers such as Peter Behrens created wonderfully complex patterns of geometric configurations in which angles and straight lines were combined in dense patterns for textiles, ceramics, and metalware. This can be seen in a brooch of strikingly simple, yet sophisticated, geometric arrangements (fig. 65) conceived by Emil Bäuerle, one of the teachers at the decorative arts school at Pforzheim, a center for jewelrymaking. Unwittingly, one might think it had been created two decades later. Throughout the twentieth century, geometric shapes were promoted as fitting motifs for modern objects in simple and complex schemes, ranging from Jutta Sika's spare design from turn-of-the-century Vienna (cat. no. 141) to Ralph Bacerra's recent charger (cat. no. 154) on which the densely overlapping stripes, squares, triangles, diamonds, and circles use geometry to complicate rather than define planar realities.

Even just straight lines can produce exceptionally striking patterns. Stripes, the simplest of graphic devices, have found wide application throughout the last hundred years. Around 1900, Vienna was known for witty designs conceived with only black and white stripes—such as Josef Hoffmann's glassware for the Wiener Werkstätte (fig. 66). In the 1920s, brightly colored stripes could exaggerate the overall geometric effect of an object, as in Lili Schultz's tea caddy (fig. 67), and patterns of similarly bright stripes were often employed on lamp shades. In the 1930s, striped bandings became the hallmark of streamlining—as in the ultramodernistic table lamp probably made by Pattyn Products of Detroit (fig. 68). Stripes remained a favored solution in the postwar years. They were used with bright

Fig. 66. Josef Hoffmann, decanter and glasses, 1912–13. Enameled glass. Height of decanter: 21.5 cm (8½ in.). Produced by J. & L. Lobmeyr.

Fig. 67. Lili Schultz, tea caddy, c. 1928. Enameled tombac. Height: 10.4 cm (4⅛ in.). Utsunomiya, Utsunomiya Municipal Museum.

Fig. 68. Pattyn Products Co., table lamp, c. 1935.
Chrome-plated and enameled steel, brass, and glass.
Height: 50.5 cm (20 in.).
New York, The Brooklyn Museum,
H. Randolph Lever Fund.

Fig. 69. Ettore Sottsass, vases, 1957–59.
Glazed and unglazed earthenware.
Height of tallest: 46.8 cm (18⅜ in.).
Montreal, Montreal Museum of Decorative Arts.

intensity on Venini's *a fasce* series of glass bottles (cat. no. 75), and with less vibrancy but no less impact on glassware designed by Floris Meydam for Leerdam (cat. no. 131) and by Vicke Lindstrand for Kosta (cat. no. 132). Like so much postwar design, the bands on these objects are less mechanistic than their prewar forebears but they still remain stripes. Hard-edged stripes reappeared in the 1960s: they were used as a bold accent or the focal point of a design, much as Gunnar Cyrén did in his *Pop* goblets (cat. nos. 134, 135), the name of which succinctly suggests its historical and artistic references. And in the Postmodern world, hard-edged stripes were featured with a vengeance, as in a group of vases by Ettore Sottsass (fig. 69). Likewise, Roseline Delisle's ceramics (cat. nos. 137, 138) are characterized by striped patterns which define the contrasting proportions of body and finial, and which the artist also sees as echoing the technique of throwing on the wheel. For Dorothy Hafner, who popularized brightly patterned dinnerware in the 1980s, the bold black and white racing stripes of her typically vivid coffee service *Blue Loop with Headdress* (cat. no. 139) were intended to suggest parallels with a wide range of visual sources, from primitive art to highway barricades. Each person has his or her own explanation for what seems to be a universal, recurring form of ornament.

Other members of Modernism's elite have been fascinated by the endless possibilities derived from the square and the rectangle. The Bauhaus weavings of Anni Albers from the 1920s (fig. 70), with their regular repetition of similar geometric shapes, are splendid examples of the acceptance of this type of ornament. They remind us of one of the exercises in the Bauhaus foundation course — deriving complex forms and patterns from just the rectangle.

The repetition of a single, geometric element is also characteristic of primitive art, which had an especially profound influence on some examples from the second half of the twentieth century. It was Hopi patterning, for example, that specifically inspired the design of Jack Lenor Larsen's bravura textile, *Magnum* (cat. no. 142). Originally designed as a theater curtain, the fabric employs repeating squares highlighted with reflective silver vinyl in order "to entertain the audience with thrusts of reflected light while waiting for the curtain to rise."[13] Primitivism also exerted its influence on the work of jeweler Earl Pardon, whose necklace (cat. no. 143) is a tapestry of repeating and overlapping squares and rectangles. Sven Palmqvist took advantage of the visual merit of geometric repetition as well, but he looked instead to Byzantine antecedents. The internally colored bowl (cat. no. 144) from his *Ravenna* series, in which graduated rectangular units within the glass shimmer with light, were inspired by the sumptuous mosaics of that Italian city.

Many designers juxtaposed different geometric forms in complex combinations. Developments in the fine arts during the first several decades of the century and, above all, Cubism in its various manifestations contributed to the dynamic new modes of geometric patterning. Sonia Delaunay, for example, translated the overlapping, transparent Cubist planes and bright colors of her Orphist paintings to the world of fashion, producing patterned textiles and accessories of stunning effect (fig. 71). Likewise, Czech and Italian Cubists and Futurists transposed the vivid forms of this art-oriented imagery into the world of decorative functional objects (fig. 72).

Although Cubism may have been born in France, its impact on French decorative arts was essentially delayed until after World War I. But when it finally took hold, especially after the great success of the Paris Exposition of 1925, it became a universal standard of Modernist chic. As can be seen in one of the enameled vases by Camille Fauré and his daughter Andrée Fauré-Malabre (cat. no. 145), and in the

Fig. 70. Anni Albers, wall hanging, 1927. Silk.
182.9 x 122 cm (72 x 48 in.).
Cambridge, Massachusetts, Harvard University,
Busch-Reisinger Museum.

Fig. 71. Models in street ensembles
by Sonia Delaunay, 1928.
Paris, Bibliothèque Nationale de France.

Fig. 72. Giacomo Balla, screen, 1916–17.
Oil on wood. 124 x 115.5 cm (48¹³⁄₁₆ x 45½ in.).
Rome, private collection.

Fig. 73. Alexander Girard, textile, *Feathers*, 1957.
Cotton/linen. 73.1 x 66.7 cm (28¾ x 26¼ in.).
Produced by Herman Miller, Inc.
Montreal, Montreal Museum of Decorative Arts.

Fig. 74. American, detail of evening coat,
c. 1928. Silk.
New York, The Metropolitan Museum of Art,
gift of the Fashion Group, Inc., 1975.

ornament conceived by Adrien-Auguste Leduc for the Manufacture Nationale de Sèvres (cat. no. 146), Cubism could be turned into a piquant interplay of geometric motifs and chromatic richness that gave a sense of fashionable luxury. The following decade, in the United States, the geometric basis of modern ornament was frequently proclaimed. It was both preached and practiced by one of its leading advocates, Walter Dorwin Teague, as is witnessed in the rectilinear, Cubist-oriented patterns that he created for a deluxe version of the Kodak camera (cat. no. 147). As Teague wrote: "We are learning to value an exactly straight line, a perfect circle, a precise arc, a definite curve."[14] Likewise, Ruth Reeves's printed textiles (cat. no. 149) reveal her tremendous debt to School of Paris painting. Several decades later, the Canadian-born painter Rolph Scarlett, who designed jewelry throughout his career, acknowledged the ancient antecedents of geometric composition, translating into three dimensions his non-objective approach to canvas (cat. no. 150).

In the years preceding and following World War II, the nature of much geometric design evolved into rounder forms and softer curves under the impact of abstract Surrealism and Biomorphism. As can be seen in Ruth Adler Schnee's textile *Bugs in Booby Trap* (cat. no. 151), the impact of Arp, Miró, and Calder was quite potent. Likewise, Ross Littell's pattern for Hallcraft dinnerware (cat. no. 152) evidences a similar approach; the design shows both an engineer's concern for mathematic organization and the "freeform" parabolic curves so popular in the postwar years.

On the other hand, many postwar designers retained the hard-edged geometry of prewar Modernism, but with postwar restraint. Sven Markelius's *Pythagoras* textile (cat. no. 153), named after the Greek mathematician who developed the theorem involving the right triangle, reflects geometry's place in this architect's thoughts. The furnishing fabrics of Alexander Girard (fig. 73) show a similar approach. The sharply fragmented geometry of Cubism remained a cogent force in later decades, especially from the 1970s onward when designers started to look back to the heroic origins of twentieth-century Modernism. In its overlapping geometric planes, for example, Fujiwo Ishimoto's fabric *Rocky Landscape* (cat. no. 155) recalls the paintings of Paul Cézanne, while Alessandro Mendini's *Museum Market* textile (cat. no. 156) shows the designer's appreciation of Czech Cubism. Nathalie Du Pasquier's agitatedly fractured pattern, *Gabon* (cat. no. 157), is characteristic of Memphis design in its cacophony of color and form; its name also reminds us of the enduring allure of the geometric forms of African art and its close relation to modern design.

The highly chromatic surface decorations of Memphis designs epitomize the Postmodern revolt against the principles of Modernist austerity; if anything, the Memphis group has evolved riotous schemes of pattern and color. Late twentieth-century designers have had the benefit of this century's richness of changing styles to choose various points of reference. This approach is evident in Mendini's *Calamobio* cabinet (cat. no. 158), whose pattern brings to mind graphics plucked from both the computer age and from Kandinsky's work of the 1920s. Peter Chang's bracelet (cat. no. 159) exhibits parallel tendencies. His typically brilliant colors and compartmentalized geometric patterning impart a vivid sense of joy to jewelry that is fashioned through the use of a thoroughly modern material, PVC, but which makes reverential allusions to the intensity of Art Deco patterns, such as those seen on Fauré's vase (cat. no. 145). Chang's bracelet is but one reminder of the revival of interest in Art Deco design that occurred after 1970. Another such reminder is seen in Eddie Squires's *Archway* textile (cat. no. 160), whose stepped motif and witty, syncopated vitality recalls textiles of the 1920s (fig. 74). These later works testify to the cycles of taste that have given continuity to the century.

As should be evident, Modernist rhetoric was not sufficiently convincing to completely banish ornament from the repertoire of twentieth-century designers, even those with whom we most associate the principles advanced in its cause. Frank Lloyd Wright, for example, the American master whose seventy-year career began during the Arts and Crafts Movement and ended during the zenith of the International Style, never lost his conviction that surface enrichment is fully compatible with the modern aesthetic, as long as it "… was an integral feature of the whole."[15] As it turns out, floral and geometric patterning were often used to enhance the objects of our daily lives. It was not until the end of this century, however, that we were able to truly grasp the significance of Siegfried Giedion's poignant words of 1948: "The wish for adornment is innate in man and proves ineradicable, like hunger or love."[16]

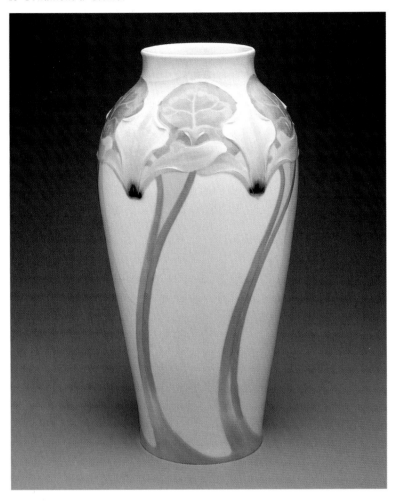

**112. Per Algot Eriksson**
(born 1868, Stockholm, Sweden; died 1937, Stockholm)
Vase
Designed c. 1900. Glazed porcelain
49.5 x 26.3 x 26.3 cm (19½ x 10⁵/₁₆ x 10⁵/₁₆ in.)
Produced by Rörstrand Porslinsfabrik AB (Lidköping), c. 1900-10
Painted in green on underside: [device of two crowns]/*Rörstrand*/[device of crown]/AE; impressed: 10113
The Montreal Museum of Fine Arts Collection, purchase, Horsley and Annie Townsend Bequest

*"As there has been no tradition since the end of the last century that we could continue and that could be our support, it is much better immediately to turn back to the rational origins of Art, taking as our compositional basis the constructive necessities, and adopting an ornament borrowed from nature. But natural forms can only be used if they are modified in such a way as to be adapted closely to the medium in which they are made."*
Eugène Grasset, 1899[17]

**113. Carl Otto Czeschka**
(born 1878, Vienna, Austria; died 1960, Hamburg, West Germany)
Textile, *Pouter Pigeon* (*Kropftaube*)
Designed c. 1910. Printed linen
104.7 x 73.7 cm (41¼ x 29 in.)
Printed by Gustav Ziegler (Vienna) for the Wiener Werkstätte (Vienna), c. 1910-11
Unmarked
D93.262.1, gift of Esperanza and Mark Schwartz, by exchange

*"Czeschka ... reaches out beyond the bounds of graphic art and reveals an exceptional wealth of imagination. He is bursting with decorative sense. His feeling for space, his assortment of colors, his linear perception, reveal a tense, forceful temperament which is alien to every kind of sentimentality and reveals a yearning for the strong accents of ancient German woodcarving and the vivid color display of incunabula miniatures."*
Berta Zuckerkandl, 1905[18]

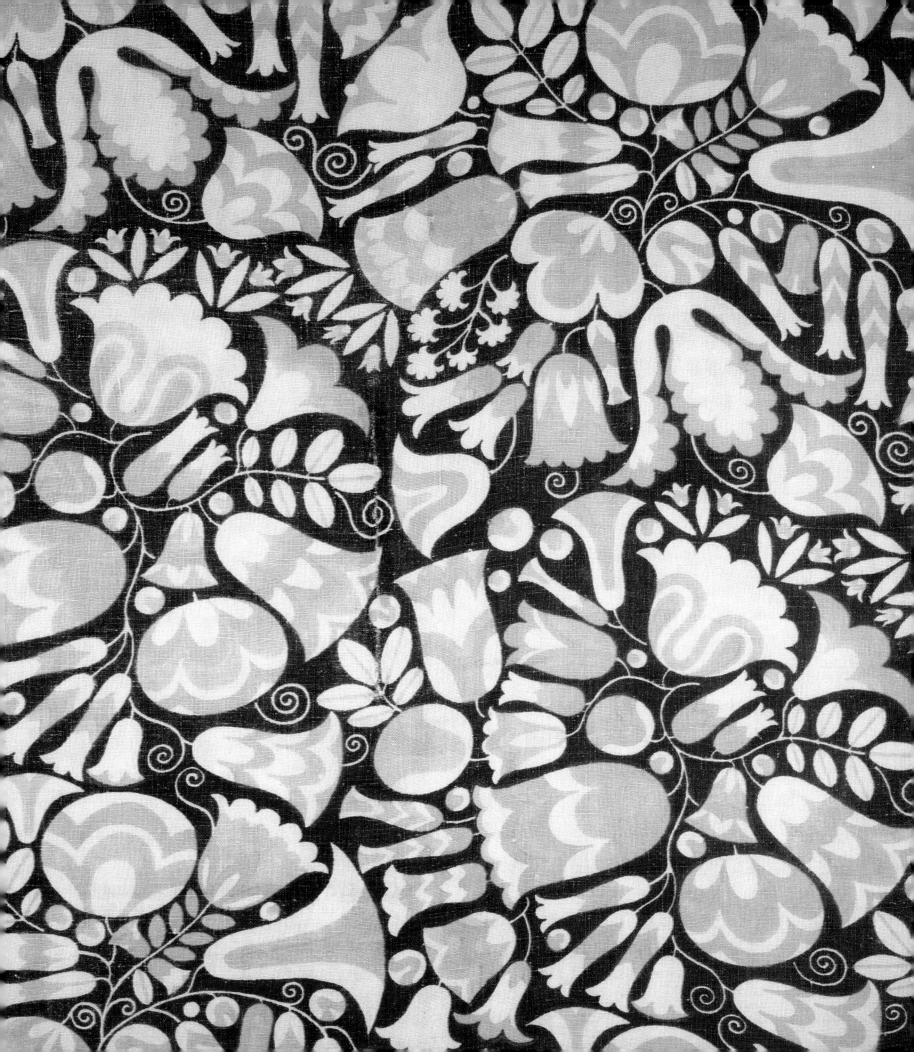

**114. Josef Hoffmann**
(born 1870, Pirnitz, Austria; died 1956, Vienna)
Vase
Designed 1912. Glass
26 x 11.2 x 11.2 cm (10¼ x 4⁷⁄₁₆ x 4⁷⁄₁₆ in.)
Produced by Johannes Loetz Witwe (Klostermühle), c. 1912–15
Unmarked
D94.171.1, gift of Mr. and Mrs. Roger Labbé

*"Using a few decorative variations, he [Hoffmann] organized the surface of the vessel geometrically, into individual fields in which ornamental plant forms alternated with geometric shapes. This transitional motif, between vegetable ornament and pure geometry ... was very successful and frequently paraphrased, particularly by Hans Bolek, in the following years."*
Helmut Ricke, 1989[19]

**115. Unknown designer (Austria?)**
Necklace
Executed c. 1910–20, Silver, enamels
Pendant: 7 x 3.5 cm (2¾ x 1⅜ in.);
extended: 47.5 cm (18¹¹⁄₁₆ in.)
Unmarked
D93.226.1, anonymous gift

*"Only a fairly good design, founded on some flower or leaf
which can be satisfactorily reproduced in, and is, so to speak,
en* rapport *with, the jewels to be used, can succeed in pleasing
through beauty of form alone, independently of any association.... Working in enamel is of course an independent art in
itself ... beautiful are the colour effects produced by the Viennese
craftsmen ... very good results can ... be obtained by what
the French call* émail à jour, *or émail translucide, as well as in
the old-fashioned opaque enamel."*
W. Fred, 1901[20]

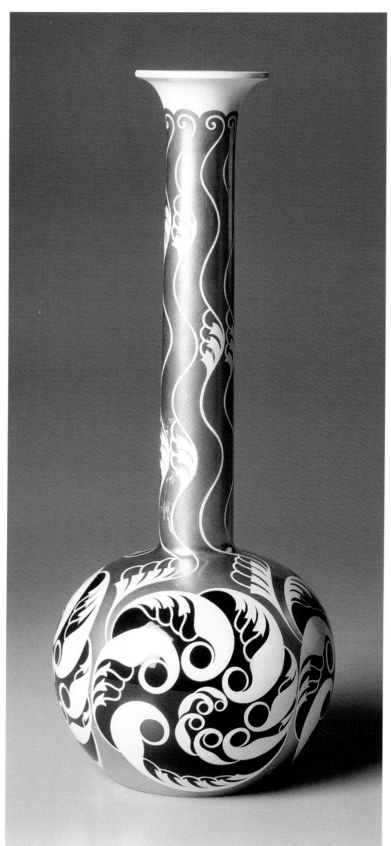

"*Tones of such strong luminosity, clarity, and depth are applied under the glaze next to a velvety black, that the graceful imagination of the decorative artist is given free rein.... Besides this, however, gold and platinum are used under the final glaze to emphasize the sheen and to distinguish the layers and contours of the ornament. This strengthens the clarity and decisive nature of the decorative rhythm.... Clearly, [this type of] faience suggests new artistic opportunities.... It stands between the elegant and noble luster-faience of the Orient and the naive but effective peasant majolica of the countryside as an appropriately strong accessory in a modern interior.*"
Hartwig Fischel, 1912[21]

**116. Albin Müller**
(born 1871, Dittersbach, Germany; died 1941, Darmstadt)
Vase
Designed 1910. Glazed and partially gilt porcelain
38.8 x 16.2 x 16.2 cm (15¼ x 6⅜ x 6⅜ in.)
Produced by Ernst Wahliss Porzellanfabrik
(Vienna, Austria), c. 1910
Painted in gold on underside:
53/F.10166./S.3002./Nach Entwurf/VON/
PROF. A. MÜLLER/ARCHITEKT/Darmstadt.;
printed in blue-green: SERAPIS/WAHLISS; impressed: 10166
D94.172.1, gift of Mr. and Mrs. Roger Labbé

"*[Margold] does not begin with natural form and stylize it to create surface ornament. On the contrary, he begins with the surface and develops appropriate rhythmic linear ornaments that merely recall flowers and leaves.... Some critics dispute this. They look at his panels, carpets and tapestries and say with an ironic smile, these are stylized blooms, stems and blades of grass! They may be reminiscent of natural forms, but, through the conscious process of the artist, they have been transformed into abstract ornament.*"
Arthur Roessler, 1911[22]

**117. Emanuel Josef Margold**
(born 1889, Vienna, Austria;
died 1962, Bratislava, Czechoslovakia)
Biscuit container
Designed 1914-15. Printed tin
4.2 x 21.2 x 11.9 cm (1⅝ x 8⁵⁄₁₆ x 4¹¹⁄₁₆ in.)
Produced by H. Bahlsens Keksfabrik
(Hannover, Germany), c. 1915
Embossed in fluted oval frame on underside:
H. BAHLSENS/KEKS-FABRIK HANNOVER/KONIGL. PREUSS.
STAATSMEDAILLE/WELTAUSSTELLUNGEN- /
1904-1910-GROSSER PREIS - 1911-1913/
BALTISCHE AUSSTELLUNG
MALMO 1914/DIE KONIGL. MEDAILLE
D94.174.1, gift of Mr. and Mrs. Roger Labbé

**118. Emanuel Josef Margold**
Biscuit container
Designed 1914-15. Enameled tin
11.5 x 17.5 x 17.5 cm (4½ x 6⅞ x 6⅞ in.)
Produced by H. Bahlsens Keksfabrik
(Hannover), c. 1915
Embossed in fluted oval frame on underside:
H. BAHLSENS/KEKS-FABRIK HANNOVER/KONIGL. PREUSS.
STAATSMEDAILLE/WELTAUSSTELLUNGEN- /1904-1910-
GROSSER PREIS - 1911-1913/BALTISCHE AUSSTELLUNG MALMO
1914/DIE KONIGL. MEDAILLE
D94.175.1, gift of Mr. and Mrs. Roger Labbé

**119. Dario Ravano**
(born 1876, Casale Monferrato, Italy;
date of death unknown)
Cup and saucer
Designed c. 1930. Glazed earthenware
Cup: 6.7 x 11.5 x 10 cm (2⅝ x 4½ x 3¹⁵⁄₁₆ in.)
Saucer: 2 x 16 x 16 cm (¾ x 6¼ x 6¼ in.)
Painted in black on underside of each: R./
[device of stylized flower]/D.
D95.109.1, gift of Lenore and Mark Newman

*"The major centre is Albisola (province of
Savona) where numerous factories have
turned to contemporary art for inspiration,
especially to the best Italian painters of the
past twenty years.... Today's production,
usually in majolica, consists in ornamental
and decorative pieces, lamp bases, etc., as
well as in tableware — both with traditional
patterns and with styling inspired by the
modern Cubist and abstract schools."*
*Italian Ceramics*, c. 1950[23]

**120. Léon Albert Jallot**
(born 1874, Nantes, France; died 1967, Nantes)
Clock
Designed c. 1920. Lacquered and gilt wood, bronze
27.3 x 27.8 x 11 cm (10¾ x 10¹⁵⁄₁₆ x 4⁵⁄₁₆ in.)
Incised on underside: [device of L/J in semicircle]
D95.143.1, The Liliane and David M. Stewart Collection

*"While writers describe humankind, while
painters choose images from their milieu,
the decorative artists borrow their themes
from nature, which they group into a basket
or plait into garlands of flowers and fruits;
and nothing gives a better account of an
individual's imagination. In this way, the
basket and the garland of flowers and fruits
come to constitute the trademark of a new
style, as did the torch, bow, quiver and
arrows in the eighteenth century."*
André Véra, 1912[24]

*"Though this awareness is particularly evident in furniture, it
can also be recognized in fabrics and textiles, added to a certain
tenderness toward the grace of roses and foliage with which the
printed fabrics of 1840 so charmed our forefathers. The most
recent fabrics by André Mare and Raoul Dufy seem to be the
most eminent examples of this trend. Finally, these latest variations on flower motifs exhibit an influence of children's art whose
freshness and ingenuity has never before been so extolled and
for which the Martine School, especially, has been responsible.
It is surely undeniable that such an art, in which such a lively
spontaneity of the imagination is evident, in its guileless sincerity
and awkward grace, can provide some useful signposts to any
artist who might wish to reinvigorate his work in the charm of
the primitives."*
Léon Moussinac, 1921[25]

**121. Raoul Dufy**
(born 1877, Le Havre, France; died 1953, Forcalquier)
Textile, *Leaves (Feuilles)*
Designed c. 1920. Printed linen
59.4 x 81.3 cm (23⅜ x 32 in.)
Produced by Bianchini-Ferier (Lyons), c. 1920
Unmarked
D85.124.1, gift of the Société des Décorateurs
Ensembliers du Québec

*"I am enclosing a few lines inspired by memories I have of my mother creating her decorations for plates on a big table where bouquets of wildflowers (her favorites) would be slowly wilting. Outside the window, through the branches of the chestnut trees on the Cours la Reine, we could see the Seine flow by.*

*Her designs express an extraordinary youthful delight, their rhythms expressing the life of the flowers with sharply defined lines and fresh colors. They are little visual poems, evocative of their era."*

Nicole Maritch-Haviland, 1996[26]

**122. Suzanne Lalique**
(born 1892, Paris, France; died 1989, Bédoin)
Dinnerware, *Pinks (Mignardise)*
Designed 1928. Glazed porcelain
Dinner plate: 2.9 x 24.6 x 24.6 cm (1¼ x 9¹¹⁄₁₆ x 9¹¹⁄₁₆ in.)
Produced by Theodore Haviland (Limoges, France),
c. 1928-40
Printed on underside of each, in green:
THEODORE HAVILAND/FRANCE [arranged in the shape of a
horseshoe]; in black: THEODORE/HAVILAND/FRANCE
[device of ochre-colored shield]; in blue: décor de/
*Suzanne Lalique*; impressed on underside of each:
T[device of star and bracket]H
D95.149.1-3, The Liliane and David M. Stewart Collection

**123. Birger Kaipiainen**
(born 1915, Pori, Finland; died 1988, Helsinki)
Charger
Designed c. 1964. Glazed earthenware
15.2 x 65.2 x 65.2 cm (6 x 25⅝ x 25⅝ in.)
Produced by Arabia Oy (Helsinki), c. 1964
Incised and painted in black on front: KAIPIAINEN . ARABIA
Printed twice in brown on underside: [device of crown]/
ARABIA/MADE IN/FINLAND
D93.272.1, gift of Andrea and Charles Bronfman

*"Unique among modern Finnish ceramists, Kaipiainen approaches
the medium as a painter, bringing the surfaces of simple forms to
life with radiant color and iridescent glazes. Drawing on Eastern
design traditions, Kaipiainen decorates his work with naive and
stylized representations of flora and fauna, expansively celebrat-
ing the forms, colors, and textures of nature."*
David Revere McFadden, 1982[27]

**124. Peter Max**
(born 1937, Berlin, Germany)
Textile
Designed c. 1968. Printed cotton
149.9 x 102.9 cm (59 x 40½ in.)
Produced by Cameo Curtains (New York, NY, USA), 1968-69
Printed in black lozenge in the repeat of the design: peter max ©
D88.153.1, The Liliane and David M. Stewart Collection

*"I remember once looking down into a pool and seeing images reflected from leaves onto the floor ... That [was] the beginning of ... these particular [petal] shapes which I used to call 'zooples' — these beautiful little shapes that move; that ... look animated and ... have a friendliness ... [Inner peace] was the mood in my heart, that was the mood in the street, the mood in the country, in the music, and I think that these friendly shapes I created fit very well."*
Peter Max, 1994[28]

**125. Emilio Pucci**
(born 1914, Naples, Italy; died 1992, Florence)
Bodice
Designed c. 1965. Silk, sequins, rhinestones
50.9 x 47 cm (20 x 18½ in.)
Produced by Emilio Pucci (Florence), c. 1965
Woven in white on black label: EMILIO PUCCI/FIRENZE;
written on paper label affixed to black label: 9029; woven in gold on white label: MADE IN ITALY EXCLUSIVELY FOR/ *Saks Fifth Avenue*; woven throughout lining: *Emilio*
D91.381.1, The Liliane and David M. Stewart Collection

*"Prints used to be staid, tame. I started the wild geometrical prints with wild colors."*
Emilio Pucci, 1976[29]

*"... we wanted a floral pattern that was something different and we began casting around for ways to make it interesting. It wasn't enough just to have a floral pattern; it was too simple. We looked around for something to make it more complex.... At some point during that process we discovered the final way to do the roses through the tablecloth that our associate ... brought in from his grandmother. We evolved a good pattern for the roses based on that and began to match them to different zipatones. The pattern that we eventually used we tended to call the ant pattern (the Japanese call it the chopsticks pattern). It was orderly but also random and went well in its own clashing way with the flowers. Someone has since called that pattern a mixed metaphor and that seems like a very good definition for it."*
Denise Scott Brown, 1990[30]

**126. Denise Scott Brown**
(born 1931, Nkana, Northern Rhodesia)
**Robert Venturi**
(born 1925, Philadelphia, PA, USA)
Dining chair, *Queen Anne*
Designed 1984. Plywood, plastic laminate, rubber
98 x 69 x 63.5 cm (38⁹⁄₁₆ x 27½ x 25 in.)
Produced by Knoll International (New York, NY), 1984–89
Printed in black on paper label attached to base of apron:
KNOLL INT. *DO NOT REMOVE* 1OF 1/CC=4215234-001
YOUR=DESIGN/N.Y./PATT0/CTY-6621/PATT1/CTY-/*** VENTURI
CHAIR (TM)***/DR=33001-23 REV=3 DTE=/
KNOLL INTERNATIONAL, INC./655 MADISON AVE./
ATTN STEVE SMITH/SHOWROOM DISPLAY/NEW YORK/
NY 10021/APR 1 1985/KNOLL/INSP/53
D85.117.1, gift of Knoll International

**127. Ettore Sottsass**
(born 1917, Innsbruck, Austria)
Dinner plate, *Renaissance*
Designed c. 1985. Glazed porcelain
3.4 x 30.5 x 30.5 cm (1⁵⁄₁₆ x 12 x 12 in.)
Produced by Swid Powell (New York, NY, USA), 1985-89
Printed in black on underside: © SWID POWELL/
ETTORE SOTTSASS/'Renaissance'/*Ettore Sottsass*
D93.244.1, The Liliane and David M. Stewart Collection

*"The idea to use floral ornaments comes from tradition, but the traditional way flowers are put together is mostly realistic. My idea was to keep the tradition but to break the logic with which flowers are traditionally put together. In the Renaissance, flowers were designed sort of meta-physically and not realistically. I mean they were designed mostly with a certain abstract idea about movement, lines, the structure with which flowers are arranged in the air. That's why I took Renaissance flowers, broke them into pieces, and put them in a different order, as in a collage. More or less."*
Ettore Sottsass, 1995[31]

"At the 1931 Exposition Coloniale in Paris, the host nation presented a romantic view of her overseas possessions, especially those in Indo-China and West Africa. In this vase, the artist-decorator has responded to the Exposition's theme with a fanciful interpretation of the equatorial forest rendered in a bright contrasting palette that captures the lush fertility of its undergrowth.

The festive mood engendered by this vibrant composition did not reflect the real world of 1931, however. The depression sparked by the Wall Street crash two years earlier had by then settled like a pall over Europe, forcing people sharply to rein in their optimism. The vase therefore belongs stylistically more to the 1920s — that of the Jazz Age, Folies Bergère and Josephine Baker — than to the anxiety-ridden 1930s."
J. Alastair Duncan, 1996[32]

**128. Maurice Paul Chevallier**
(born 1892, Paris, France; died 1987, Longwy)
Vase, *Colonial Sphere (Boule Coloniale)*
Designed 1931. Glazed earthenware
37 x 34.5 x 34.5 cm (14⅝ x 13⅝ x 13⅝ in.)
Produced by Faïenceries de Longwy (Longwy), 1931-48
Transfer-printed in black on underside: [in a rectangular device] F-B- 5660/C-/EMAUX DE LONGWY [on a scroll within a circular device containing the coat of arms of the d'Huart family, the firm's original owners]/FRANCE
D95.176.1, The Liliane and David M. Stewart Collection

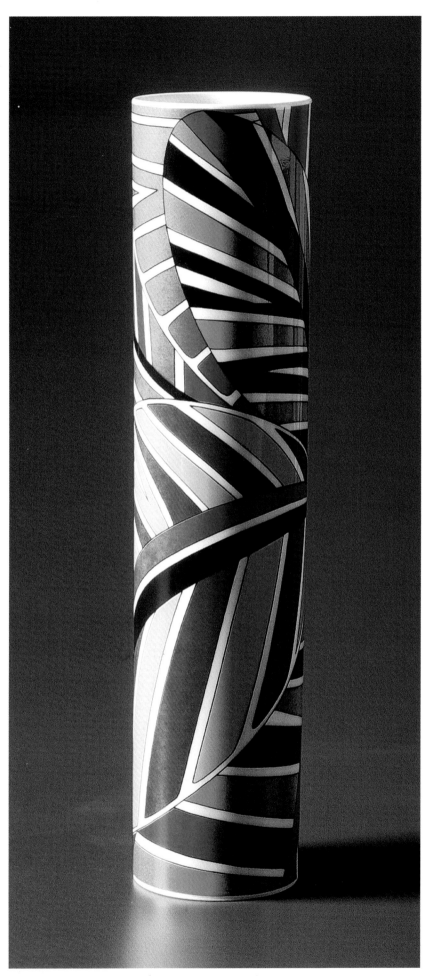

"A Pucci print was immediately recognizable and, although often based on medieval heraldic banners of the sort waved at the Siena Palio, so utterly of the moment that it could be taken as a classic symbol of the late 1950s and the early 1960s.... He was a brilliant colourist and his colour scheme became the colours of the decade (hot pink, lime, blue, purple) ... his protean talents have spread into many different areas of design, including pottery, motor cars and linens."
Colin McDowell, 1985[33]

**129. Emilio Pucci**
(born 1914, Naples, Italy; died 1992, Florence)
Vase
Designed 1968. Glazed porcelain
35.8 x 8.5 x 8.5 cm (14⅛ x 3⅜ x 3⅜ in.)
Produced by Rosenthal AG, Porzellanfabrik Selb
(Selb, West Germany), 1968-74
Printed in black along side: *Emilio*; printed in green on underside: *Rosen* [device of crossed swords] *thal*/Germany; printed in black: *Emilio Pucci*; printed in gold: studio linie [within large s]
D93.268.1, The Liliane and David M. Stewart Collection, by exchange

"Jungnickel's design concept is purely decorative. Sharp borders are used to build contours and provide ornamental structure. Strong areas of local color stand in sharp contrast to one another, creating a lively mood suggestive of Austrian folk art."
Berta Zuckerkandl, 1913[34]

**130. Ludwig Heinrich Jungnickel**
(born 1881, Wunsiedel, Germany; died 1965, Perchtoldsdorf, Austria)
Textile, *Jungle (Urwald)*
Designed c. 1910-11. Printed linen
106.7 x 90.8 cm (42 x 35¾ in.)
Printed by Gustav Ziegler (Vienna) for the Wiener Werkstätte (Vienna), c. 1910-11
Unmarked
D93.263.1, gift of Esperanza and Mark Schwartz, by exchange

**131. Floris Meydam**
(born 1919, Leerdam, The Netherlands)
Vase
Designed 1953. Glass
27.2 x 20.3 x 11.8 cm (10¹¹⁄₁₆ x 8 x 4⅝ in.)
Produced by NV Koninklijke Glasfabriek Leerdam
(Leerdam), 1953–c. 1960
Engraved on underside: leerdam 21/M
D86.149.1, gift of Lynn Brows, by exchange

*"After I started industrial design, I gradually abandoned vignette and figurative decorations. I tended more toward an enrichment of the surface which follows the shape of an object, and/or strengthens it, or which fills the whole surface as a structure.... The lines on the vase were originally intended 'to please' and were, as such, a reaction to the severe nature of industrially mass-produced designs. The two colored spirals follow and accentuate the shape as well as decorate and provide an all-over structure."*
Floris Meydam, 1995[35]

**132. Viktor (Vicke) Emanuel Lindstrand**
(born 1904, Göteborg, Sweden; died 1983, Åhus)
Vase
Designed c. 1954. Glass
24.2 x 8.5 x 8.5 cm (9½ x 3⅜ x 3⅜ in.)
Produced by Kosta Glasbruk (Kosta), 1954–c. 1959
Engraved on underside: LH1209; acid-stamped within
square: LIND/STRAND/KOSTA
D95.152.1, The Liliane and David M. Stewart Collection

*"In Sweden, Kosta's romantic, careful work seems to derive from Marinot, while the works of Orrefors exhibit a plasticity related to sculpture. These two tendencies, which are intertwined some-what, lend their originality to these varied forms, which deal with volumes of floating black stripes and fine, frosted lines, used delicately, particularly in Kosta's work."*
P.-M. Grand, 1951[36]

**133. Massimo Vignelli**
(born 1931, Milan, Italy)
Table lamp, *Mushroom (Fungo)*
Designed 1955. Glass
35.4 x 25.4 x 25.4 cm (13¹¹⁄₁₆ x 10 x 10 in.)
Produced by Venini S.p.A. (Murano),
c. 1955 to the present
Unmarked
D86.237.1, gift of Massimo Vignelli

*"Traditionally lamps were made of a base and a separate lamp shade. The basic concept behind this design was to make it into one object, by combining the two elements into a unified form, top to bottom, with lines flowing from one element to the other. The lamp is made of a type of ornamental glass, vetro a canna, developed at the Venini glassworks, with numerous narrow vertical stripes of white opaque glass over colored glass, which is then blown into a mold. The lines in the glass become wider or narrower following the shape of the lamp. This pattern is an integral part of the material used in making the object."*
Massimo Vignelli, 1995[37]

*"In 1965, after visiting several big aquariums with all their fantastic exotic fishes, I began to enjoy myself by doing these goblets with multicolored stems. We made them in a hundred different color combinations."*
Gunnar Cyrén, 1995[38]

**134. Gunnar Cyrén**
(born 1931, Gävle, Sweden)
Goblet, *Pop*
Designed 1965–66. Glass
16.2 x 10.2 x 10.2 cm (6⅜ x 4⅛ x 4⅛ in.)
Produced by AB Orrefors Glasbruk (Orrefors), 1966–c. 1976
Acid-stamped on underside: ORREFORS/[indecipherable device of two vertical lines between two horizontal lines]
D95.203.1, The Liliane and David M. Stewart Collection

**135. Gunnar Cyrén**
Goblet, *Pop*
Designed 1965–66. Glass
20.5 x 11.5 x 11.5 cm (8¹/₁₆ x 4½ x 4½ in.)
Produced by AB Orrefors Glasbruk (Orrefors), 1966–c. 1976
Acid-stamped on underside: ORREFORS EXPO B.548-67
*Gunnar Cyren*
D84.156.1, gift of Susan A. Chalom

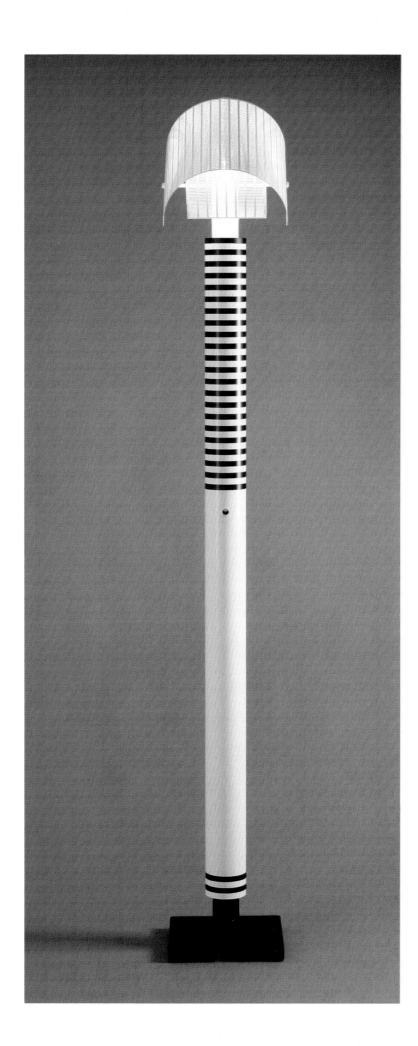

*"Geometry is balance."*
Mario Botta, 1995[39]

**136. Mario Botta**
(born 1943, Mendrisio, Switzerland)
Floor lamp, *Shogun Terra*
Designed 1985. Painted aluminum, steel, cast iron
217 x 32 x 31.5 cm (85⁷⁄₁₆ x 12⁹⁄₁₆ x 12³⁄₈ in.)
Produced by Artemide S.p.A. (Pregnana Milanese, Italy),
1985 to the present
Unmarked
D91.378.1, gift of Artemide S.p.A.

*"My work evolves from the concept of the unity of opposites ... black and white, strength and fragility, movement and stillness.... Still maintaining the minimal qualities but desiring to add color, I experimented with vitreous engobes. Wishing to obtain the same smooth surface, I applied the engobes to the vessel while on the wheel. The stripe pattern was a natural outgrowth of the application process. It seems to capture the spinning quality which refers back to its initial means of conception."*
Roseline Delisle, 1995[40]

**137. Roseline Delisle**
(born 1952, Rimouski, Quebec, Canada)
Covered jar, *Trilogy: 3.87 (Trilogie: 3,87)*
Executed 1987, Unglazed porcelain, pigmented slip
26 x 11.5 x 11.5 cm (10 x 4½ x 4½ in.)
Incised on underside: roseline delisle/Trilogie: 3,87
L96.102.1, extended loan from Anne Davis

**138. Roseline Delisle**
Covered jar, *Quadruple 7 Lightning Rod (Quadruple 7 Paratonnerre)*
Executed 1989, Unglazed porcelain, pigmented slip
52 x 22.2 x 22.2 cm (20½ x 8¾ x 8¾ in.)
Incised on underside: *Roseline Delisle*/QUADRUPLE 7 PARATONNERRE/89
D96.154.1, anonymous gift

*"In Fred Flintstone, Flash Gordon and Marie Antoinette, there are combinations of decoration that seem modern, regimented. But things like checkerboard, which we think are really modern, go back to medieval heraldry and beyond. And we associate the racing stripes with highway barricades, but they're in primitive art, on baskets and gourds. So each is both modern and primitive. It was interesting to contrast them so that the beauty and dynamic of each was enhanced. For instance, the blue loop — I love music and rhythm — comes from the path that a conductor's baton would take through the air. Or that your fingers would trace if you were to take an elaborate bow. The loop has more élan when it's backed up with these stripes. Some of the gestures are celebratory; others represent speed or frivolity. The blips come from a radar scanner; they create a scattered, firecrackery kind of pattern....*

*What is 'of my time' that can link them together? Television! I chose television because it embodied the primitive (Fred Flintstone) and the aerodynamic (Flash Gordon). As for the rococo — Marie Antoinette just seemed like the right gal because she commissioned so much really frivolous tableware."*

Dorothy Hafner, 1994[41]

**139. Dorothy Hafner**
(born 1952, Woodbridge, CT, USA)
Coffee service, *Fred Flintstone, Flash Gordon and Marie Antoinette* (form);
*Blue Loop with Headdress* (decoration)
Designed 1984. Glazed porcelain
Coffeepot: 26.9 x 30.2 x 10.1 cm (10 9/16 x 11 7/8 x 4 in.)
Produced by Dorothy Hafner (New York, NY), 1984-88
Painted in black on underside of each: *Dorothy Hafner '88*/© 1984
D94.305.1-3, The Liliane and David M. Stewart Collection

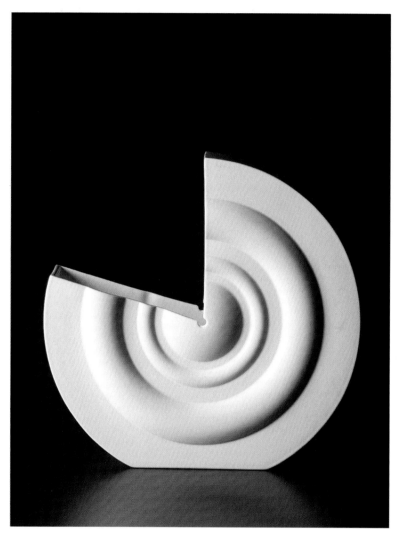

**140. Sergio Asti**
(born 1926, Milan, Italy)
Vase, *Wheel (Ruota)*
Designed 1972. Glazed earthenware
38.1 x 40.6 x 12 cm (15 x 16 x 4¾ in.)
Produced by Cedit (Lurago d'Erba) for Knoll International
(New York, NY, USA), 1972–74
Unmarked
D92.134.1, anonymous gift

**141. Jutta Sika**
(born 1877, Linz, Austria; died 1964, Vienna)
Mocha service
Designed c. 1901. Glazed porcelain
Plate: 3.3 x 24.9 x 24.9 cm (1⁵⁄₁₆ x 9¹³⁄₁₆ x 9¹³⁄₁₆ in.)
Produced by Josef Bock Wiener Porzellanmanufaktur
(Vienna) for the Wiener Werkstätte (Vienna), c. 1901–05
Painted in red on underside of each: *D501*; printed in green on
underside of plate and saucers: *.SCHULE PROF. KOLO MOSER.*
D94.173.1–3, gift of Mr. and Mrs. Roger Labbé

*"… surprise, curiosity … the reference to other shapes, the
sense of metaphor, the meaning of chakra in Hindu thought …
We share the belief that adding fantasy, ornament and emo-
tional involvement (raga=strong emotion) to what we make
(especially when they are objects close to us), beyond pure
function, beyond a rational critical analysis (on the borders
of a scientific approach proper to laboratories) carries a
conspicuous weight, today as well as it did yesterday. I would
even say one could not do without it."*
Sergio Asti, 1994[42]

*"Jutta Sika's coffee and tea service [another, closely related in
design] is original in form and decoration; without depending on
the help of a border, it is relaxed and light in form and ornament."*
Josef Folnesics, 1902[43]

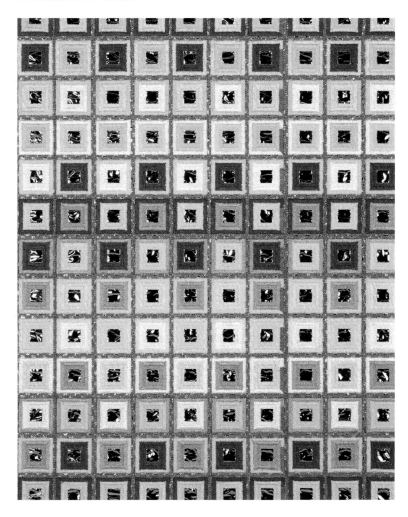

**142. Jack Lenor Larsen**
(born 1927, Seattle, WA, USA)
Textile, *Magnum*
Designed 1970. Mylar, cotton, vinyl, nylon, polyester
136.5 x 140.7 cm (53¾ x 54⅜ in.)
Produced by Jack Lenor Larsen, Incorporated
(New York, NY), 1970-80
Unmarked
D86.110.1, gift of Jack Lenor Larsen

*"Originally designed as a theater curtain
for the Phoenix, Arizona, Opera House in
colors reflecting Southwest Native
American traditions, the starting place
was the mirrored cloths of India attached
with stitches.... The square came from
Hopi patterning; the repeat and modulation of color from the restrictions and
options within Schiffli embroidery
equipment.... I feel geometric patterns
are as old as time.... Their inherent
sense of structure is the more welcome
now when most spaces are without a
sense of structure, and more adhesive
than cohesive."*
Jack Lenor Larsen, 1995[44]

**143. Earl Pardon**
(born 1926, Memphis, TN, USA; died 1991,
Saratoga Springs, NY)
Necklace
Executed c. 1965. Silver, enamels
Pendant: 12.5 x 16.4 x 1.5 cm (4¹⁵⁄₁₆ x 6⁷⁄₁₆ x ⅝ in.);
extended; 55.2 cm (21¾ in.)
Impressed on reverse of clasp: [device of encircled
dot]/STERLING/*Pardon*
D94.257.1, gift of Paul Leblanc

*"[My wall sculpture is] a multitude of focal
points which culminate in an overall
decorative sculptural arrangement ...
A feeling of ... elegance is present in its
rich ... color distribution."*
Earl Pardon, 1960[45]

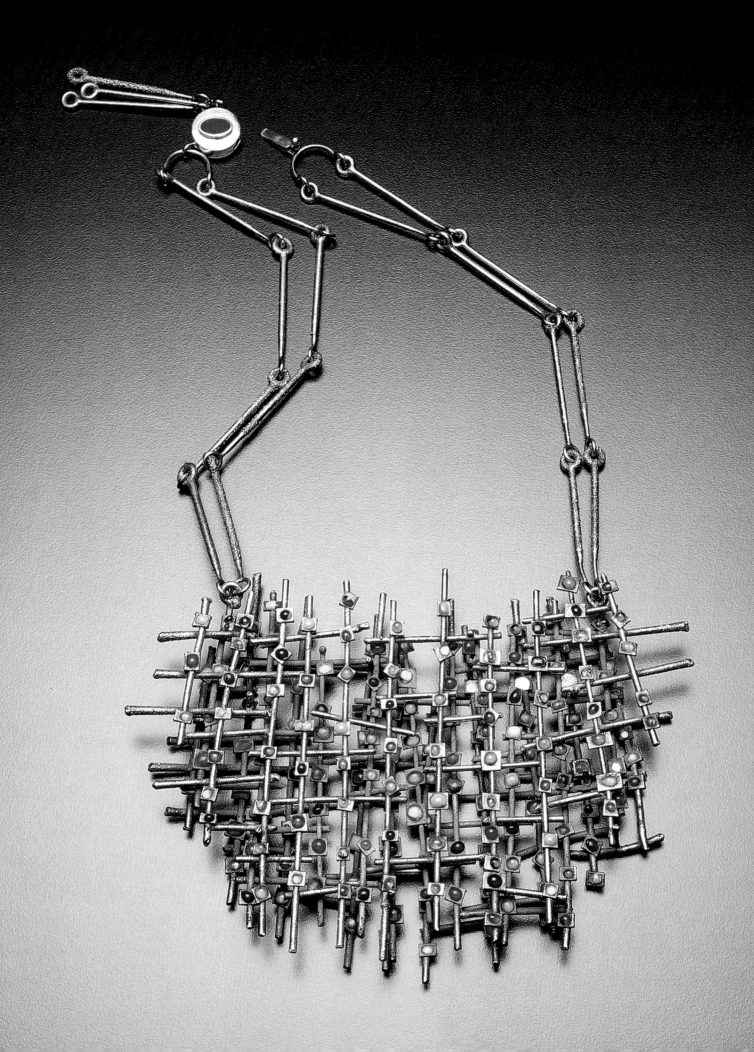

**144. Sven Palmqvist**
(born 1906, Lenhovda, Sweden; died 1984, Orrefors)
Bowl, *Ravenna*
Designed c. 1948-60. Glass
12.5 x 26.7 x 26.7 cm (4$^{15}$/$_{16}$ x 10½ x 10½ in.)
Produced by AB Orrefors Glasbruk (Orrefors), 1948-81
Engraved on underside: ORREFORS/Ravenna Nr 1682/*Sven Palmqvist*
D95.157.1, The Liliane and David M. Stewart Collection

**"Sven Palmqvist ... has captured the magnificence of ancient Roman millefiori or so-called 'mosaic' glass in his Ravenna bowls in which glowing colors are suspended like a veil between layers of crystal accentuating its brilliance."**
Jeanne Anne Vincent, 1953[46]

**145. Camille Fauré**
(born 1874, Périgueux, France; died 1956, Limoges)
**Andrée Fauré-Malabre**
(born 1904, Limoges; died 1985, Limoges)
Vase, *Sidney*
Designed c. 1925. Enamels on copper
31 x 24.5 x 22.8 cm (12¼ x 9¾ x 9 in.)
Produced by Camille Fauré (Limoges), c. 1925-30
Painted in gold near base: c. FAURÉ/Limoges
D95.145.1, The Liliane and David M. Stewart Collection

**"Since the 1925 Exposition of Decorative Arts ... surfaces
have been covered with regular or staggered, symmetrical or
asymmetrical geometric figures – juxtaposed, interlocking,
or overhanging. In a word, ornamentation has become Cubist."**
Léon Werth, 1927[47]

*"Cubist ornament was a compromise between the need for
ornament and its satisfaction by means that seemed outdated.
Whereas the arbitrary use of a rose might have appeared
intolerable, the arbitrary use of a triangle or a sphere gave the
illusion of rigor and necessity. The caprice was disguised as
geometry. The caprice of fashion itself."*
Léon Werth, 1927[48]

**146. Form: Jacques-Émile Ruhlmann**
(born 1879, Paris, France; died 1933, Paris)
**Decoration: Adrien-Auguste Leduc**
(born 1901, Vassy-Etaules; died 1967, Versailles)
Vase
Designed 1926 (form); 1930 (decoration)
Porcelain, silver-plated bronze
22.3 x 24.9 x 24.9 cm (8¾ x 9¹³⁄₁₆ x 9¹³⁄₁₆ in.)
Produced by the Manufacture Nationale de Sèvres (Sèvres),
1931-c. 1935
Impressed near base: A. Leduc; printed in black on underside:
[letter s within a rose/SEVRES/MANUFACTURE/NATIONALE/FRANCE/d;
written in black on paper label affixed inside upper edge:
*F/18-3/2.050/Ruhlmann-Leduc*
D95.137.1, The Liliane and David M. Stewart Collection

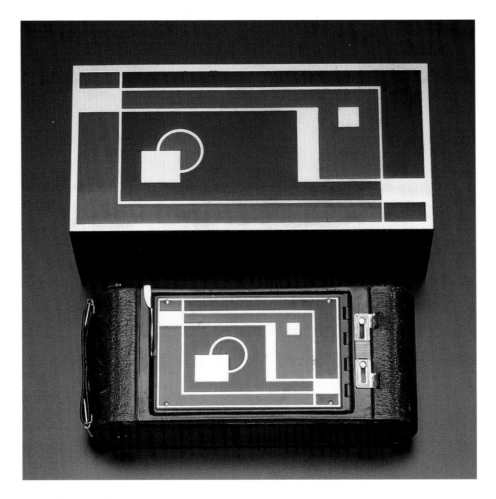

**147. Walter Dorwin Teague**
(born 1883, Decatur, IN, USA; died 1960, Flemington, NJ)
Camera and box, *No. 1A Gift Kodak*
Designed 1930
Camera: nickel-plated and enameled brass, steel,
leatherette, composite bellows
Box: cedar, nickel-plated and enameled brass
Camera: 21.2 x 9.6 x 4.4 cm (8⁵⁄₁₆ x 3¾ x 1¾ in.)
Box: 22.5 x 11.2 x 6.3 cm (8⅞ x 4⁷⁄₁₆ x 2½ in.)
Produced by Eastman Kodak Co. (Rochester, NY), 1930-31
Embossed on brown-enameled metal label affixed
to underside of camera lid: NO.1A GIFT KODAK/MADE IN U.S.A.
BY/EASTMAN KODAK CO./ROCHESTER NY; around lens: SHUTTER
MADE IN U.S.A. BY EASTMAN KODAK ROCHESTER N.Y.
D95.135.1, The Liliane and David M. Stewart Collection


*"We have rediscovered the moving power of a straight line and an exact angle;
the meeting of planes is again dynamic; a curve acquires value if it is a definite
arc or parabola; the relationship of visual forms and lines reveals the harmonic
possibilities of musical chords; and above all we require that these things should
derive their sanction from something more necessitous than a designer's
fancy.... Design is geometry made visible, and 'Euclid alone saw beauty plain.'"*
Walter Dorwin Teague, 1940[49]

**148. After Gilbert Poillerat**
(born 1902, Mer, France; died 1988, Paris)
Radiator cover
Designed c. 1935. Wrought iron
86.8 x 129.5 x 32.3 cm (34½ x 51 x 12¾ in.)
Executed by students of the École Technique
(Montreal, Quebec, Canada) under the direction
of Albert Colpron, c. 1935-40
Unmarked
D90.213.1, gift of Jean Boucher, by exchange

*"Since the war, modern life has evolved considerably; it is a period of movement, of change, of novelty. Moreover, mechanical engineering rules supreme: all these influences have necessarily had an effect on the decorative arts.... Wrought-iron craftsmen followed this rhythm. In their compositions, they seek the expression of the essential and look for a way of making it crystallize through unfussy and meticulous workmanship and the use of new materials — geometrical forms, pure, harmonious lines. This is a new and most beguiling vision."*
Edna L. Nicoll, 1931[50]

"... Miss Reeves ... is perhaps inspired by the industrial spirit to a certain extent, but she does not allow too much genuflection to it to subdue and crush the leading ideas of her designs. One of the most important requirements in fine fabric design today is that it shall have great vitality, pulsating movement, vivacity and verve. Lacking a distinct spirit of motion, rhythm, and living interest, the design becomes dead in appearance and less than useless for its purpose. Dynamic devices in design for fabrics will always triumph over static, inert types, just as lively, interesting people are inevitably more attractive than those who seem indifferent, over-nonchalant, lacking in inner excitement."
Blanche Naylor, 1933[51]

**149. Ruth Reeves**
(born 1892, Redlands, CA, USA; died 1966, New Delhi, India)
Textile
Designed c. 1940. Printed linen
89 x 65 cm (35 1/16 x 25 9/16 in.)
Unmarked
D85.108.1, gift of Kelvyn Grant Lilley

**150. Rolph Scarlett**
(born 1889, Guelph, Ontario, Canada; died 1984,
New York, NY, USA)
Pendant
Executed 1966. Silver, malachite, tiger-eye, synthetic
stones
Pendant: 16.2 x 24.5 x 4.4 cm (6³/₈ x 9⁵/₈ x 1³/₄ in.);
extended: 40.2 cm. (15¹³/₁₆ in.)
Engraved on front: ROLPH SCARLETT; on underside: ROLPH
SCARLETT/7-10-66 [partially obscured]
L96.103.1, extended loan from Mr. and Mrs. Samuel A.
Esses

*"Man knew how to make circles, how to make*
*squares, how to make a triangle. He put*
*these things together.... These are the basic*
*fundamental, aesthetic conceptions of how*
*to interpret space.... Kandinsky worked that*
*way.... After... being completely lyrical, he*
*was eventually able to get rid of the trees,*
*the houses, the barns and everything else....*
*Kandinsky was challenging all the concep-*
*tions of art that existed from the Egyptians*
*on. He was challenging the whole damn*
*thing and I was fortunate enough to see it*
*at a very early age."*
Rolph Scarlett, 1979[52]

**151. Ruth Adler Schnee**
(born 1923, Frankfurt am Main, Germany)
Textile, *Bugs in Booby Trap*
Designed c. 1947. Printed cotton
160 x 125.6 cm (63 x 49⁷/₁₆ in.)
Produced by Ruth Adler (Detroit, MI, USA), 1947
Printed in black along one selvage *'BUGS IN BOOBY*
*TRAP' HAND PRINT A RUTH ADLER DESIGN*
D84.170.1, gift of Geoffrey N. Bradfield

*"For a few years after World War II, I was*
*fascinated by rounded and pierced shapes.*
*This was, no doubt, a reaction from the*
*austere, square graphics which the Bauhaus*
*produced.... I relished this expression, and*
*the resultant shapes and lines came to look*
*like living organisms. Undulating shapes and*
*rounded holes played against each other in*
*my dreams and then were put to paper and*
*then to printing silk-screens:* **Bugs in Booby**
**Trap** *... and a score of other early designs*
*are very much a part of this dream and my*
*'then' world."*
Ruth Adler Schnee, 1994[53]

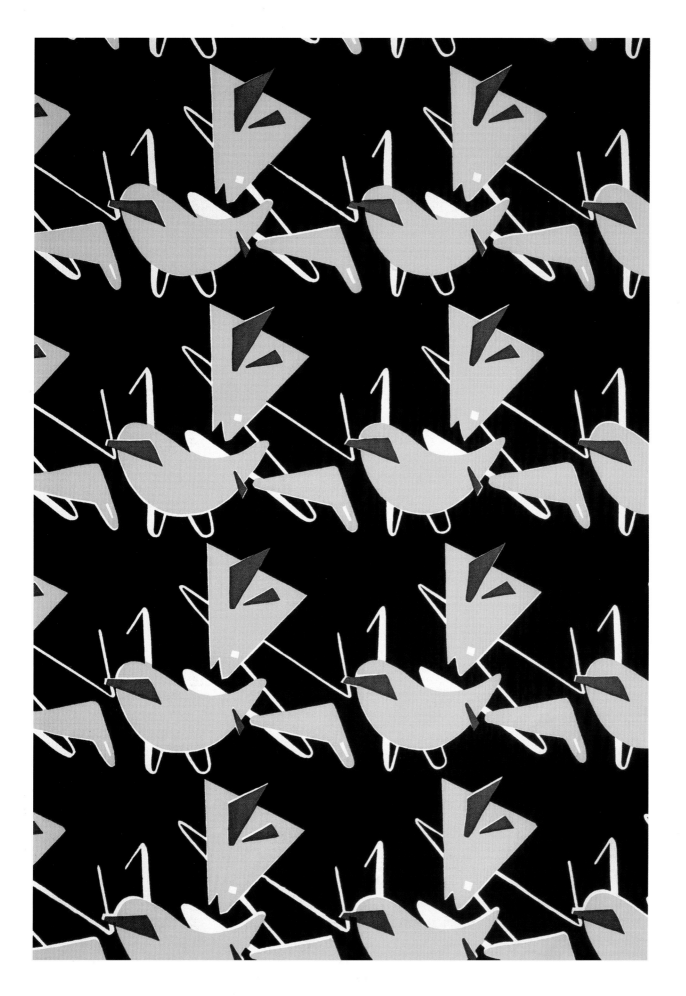

**152. Form: Eva Zeisel**
(born 1906, Budapest, Hungary)
**Decoration: Ross Littell**
(born 1924, Hollywood, CA, USA)
Dinnerware, *Fantasy*
Designed c. 1950 (form); c. 1951 , (decoration). Glazed earthenware
Teapot: 14.5 x 22.5 x 13.6 cm (5¹¹⁄₁₆ x 8⅞ x 5⅜ in.)
Produced by Hall China Company (East Liverpool, OH), 1951–c. 1960
Teapot, saucer, and platter printed in blue on underside: HALLCRAFT/SHAPE
 BY/Eva Zeisel/[device of white letters HCC in a gray rectangle with
round corners]/MADE IN U.S.A. BY HALL CHINA CO.; cups printed in gold on underside:
FANTASY/2169
D95.150.1, gift of Mr. and Mrs. Charles O'Kieffe, Jr., by exchange; D95.151.1, 3,
gift of Eldon Wong; D95.181.1-3, The Liliane and David M. Stewart Collection


**"Ideally the goal is a marriage of form and pattern. 'Fantasy' as
a name suggested flight, a letting go or release.... Based on a
grid of equally spaced points, the curved connections formed a web-
like pattern by avoiding the center point — each a variation by
circuitous route. The enhancement through variation squelches
out repetitive monotony — in essence, warming up a grid."**
Ross Littell, 1995[54]

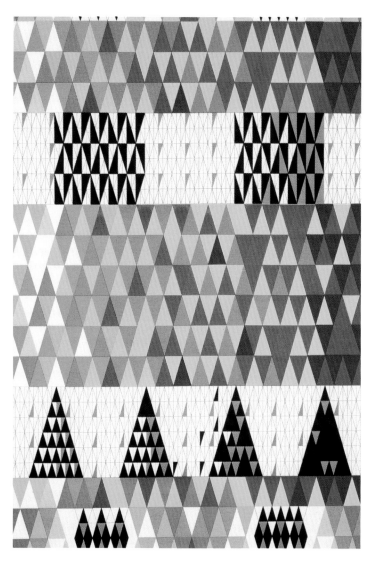

**153. Sven Gottfrid Markelius**
(né Sven G. Jonsson: born 1889, Stockholm, Sweden;
died 1972, Stockholm)
Textile, *Pythagoras*
Designed 1952. Printed cotton
299.7 x 130.7 cm (118 x 51½ in.)
Printed by Ljungbergs Textiltryck (Floda) for Nordiska
Kompaniet (Stockholm), 1952, 1965, and 1984
Printed in black along selvage: LJUNGBERGS TEXTILTRYCK
1984 "PYTHAGORAS" DESIGN SVEN MARKELIUS
D85.160.1, The Liliane and David M. Stewart Collection

*"All Markelius' patterns were based on abstract, geometrical
figures and never on naturalistic subjects. This vocabulary
tallies well with his architecture, and practically all the
patterns were in fact designed for a particular position and
function in the room. While work was in progress on ... the
Linköping Folkets Hus, the need for textiles to harmonise with
the character of the building became more and more pressing.
Markelius found nothing suitable on the market and therefore
began sketching his own patterns ... the result was Pythagoras,
[a] pattern based on triangular shapes. The triangle theme
gave [this] pattern a dynamic, mobile character which came
into its own in large formats."*
Eva Rudberg, 1989[55]

**154. Ralph Bacerra**
(born 1938, Garden Grove, CA, USA)
Charger
Executed 1986. Glazed and lustered earthenware
8.9 x 56.5 x 56.5 cm (3½ x 22¼ x 22¼ in.)
Incised on underside: *Bacerra/86*
D93.202.1, The Liliane and David M. Stewart Collection

*"By using simple geometric shapes, I transform a two-
dimensional plane into a three-dimensional surface. I let the
basic circle, square and triangle evolve into shapes and
forms to disorient the viewer. Pattern and color enhance the
new orientation. My interest in Asian ceramics, Chinese
cloisonné, and Persian painted miniatures have all enhanced
my way of dealing with clay surfaces."*
Ralph Bacerra, 1994[56]

**155. Fujiwo Ishimoto**
(born 1941, Ehime, Japan)
Textile, *Rocky Landscape (Kalliomaa)*
Designed 1988. Printed cotton
299.8 x 147.4 cm (188¹⁄₁₆ x 58¹⁄₁₆ in.)
Produced by Marimekko Oy (Helsinki, Finland), 1989-91
Printed in blue along one selvage: MARIMEKKO
® FUJIWO ISHIMOTO: "KALLIOMAA" © MARIMEKKO OY 1988
SUOMI-FINLAND 100% COTTON [devices of laundering instructions]
D92.138.1, gift of Marimekko Oy

*"Nature is a very important source of inspiration in my work, and Kalliomaa, a picture of a rocky landscape, is one example of the many designs inspired by nature.... Kalliomaa depicts an austere landscape, without any vegetation.... To some people the cubes of the pattern may look like ice floes, but the design also reflects warmth and reciprocity. When the sun is shining, rock both absorbs and radiates heat. It takes, but it also gives. The same idea or feeling also applies to the fabric's material, pure cotton."*
Fujiwo Ishimoto, 1994[57]

**156. Alessandro Mendini**
(born 1931, Milan, Italy)
Textile, *Museum Market*
Designed 1993. Printed cotton
201 x 143.5 cm (79¾ x 56⅝ in.)
Printed by Assia (Briosco) for Design Gallery Milano (Milan),
1993 to the present
Printed in red along one selvage: ASSIA PER DESIGN GALLERY
MILANO MUSEUM MARKET ALESSANDRO MENDINI 1993
D96.111.2, gift of Geoffrey N. Bradfield*

*"This fabric comprises a system of a series of various marks which I designed over a period of years. Their assemblage gives rise to a decor with Futurist overtones, composed on various supports (canvas, satin, silk) and each with variants in polychrome and monochrome (ochre and brown tones). The inspiration for this fabric came from the Futurist material that I employed in my first Kandissi sofa (1979).... Assia also produced clothing and scarves in this material."*
Alessandro Mendini, 1995[58]

**157. Nathalie Du Pasquier**
(born 1957, Bordeaux, France)
Textile, *Gabon*
Designed 1982. Printed cotton
399.4 x 153.2 cm (157¼ x 60½ in.)
Printed by Rainbow B and B S.p.A. (Milan, Italy) for Memphis s.r.l. (Pregnana
Milanese), 1982 to the present
Printed in black along selvages: NATHALIE DU PASQUIER FOR MEMPHIS - 1982 - PRODUCED
IN ITALY BY RAINBOW ®
D86.166.1, gift of Geoffrey N. Bradfield

*"[The] geometric motifs are the result of a jerky dance my
imagination was engaged in, and which I wanted to communicate
to anyone willing to plunge into this Gabon decoration.*
*I used the language I learned during my training: important
journeys in Africa, in Australia, and in India ... and the culture
of people of my age based on rock music and the graphics of
certain comic books — an 'ethnic-metropolitan' mix. In Africa,
the early, traditional textiles and the modern ones gave me
the impetus to work on decoration ..."*
Nathalie Du Pasquier, 1995[59]

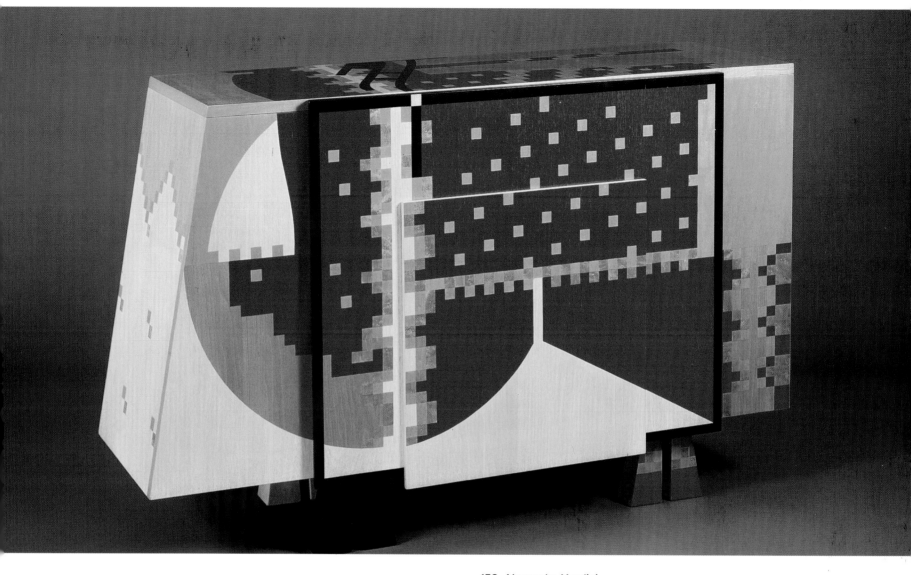

**158. Alessandro Mendini**
(born 1931, Milan, Italy)
Cabinet, *Calamobio*
Designed 1985. Inlaid and stained koto, maple, tulipwood
83.5 x 131.8 x 43.2 cm (32⅞ x 51⅞ x 17 in.)
Produced by Zabro, a division of Zanotta (Nova Milanese),
for Nuova Alchimia (Milan), 1985-87
Printed in black on metal label affixed to underside: AM ZABRO
/0170989 [device of insect] DIVISIONE NUOVA ALCHIMIA 1985
D91.107.1, The Liliane and David M. Stewart Collection

*"This piece of furniture forms part of a series designed for Zabro.*
*Although the majority of this range of furniture was conceived*
*in lacquered wood, Calamobio's surfaces are composed of fine*
*natural wood inlay or wood treated with aniline.... The decora-*
*tive pattern was developed using an instrument called the*
*'Mendinigrafo,' applied onto a squared-up layout.*

*As in other investigations into vibrations, colors, and*
*geometry undertaken in other objects, here, too, the basic idea*
*is to render the volume of the furniture evanescent and indefi-*
*nite. The hint of an atmosphere overlays and replaces the form,*
*giving the work an immaterial appearance."*
Alessandro Mendini, 1995[60]

**159. Peter Chang**
(born 1944, Liverpool, England)
Bracelet
Executed 1988, Acrylic plastic, PVC plastic
16.5 x 15.9 x 6.4 cm (6½ x 6¼ x 2½ in.)
Unmarked
D90.204.1, The Liliane and David M. Stewart Collection

*"The form of this particular bracelet is based upon a recurring triaxial image.... Within this triangulated shape, aspects of organic and man-made reticulated tessellations are used in conjunction with nature's warning colours and the subtleties of camouflage to construct both a metamorphic and contrasting object. Contradiction comes in the serpent symbolism where the 'head' is delineated by the checker-board stripe, which is, in a British context, a badge of authority.... Contrasts of different heights and shapes, some rounded, some soft, some faceted, some hard, help give textural significance to the differentiation of the three main elements."*
Peter Chang, 1995[61]

**160. Eddie Squires**
(born 1941, Anlaby, England; died 1995, London)
Textile, *Archway*
Designed 1968. Printed cotton
91.5 x 125.8 cm (36 x 49½ in.)
Printed by Stead McAlpin & Co., Ltd (Carlisle) for
Warner & Sons Ltd (London), 1968-71
Printed in purple along selvages : ARCHWAY :
A STEREOSCOPIC SCREENPRINT : Warner's Studio Range :
D90.142.1, gift of Eddie Squires

*"Several factors influenced this design—1930s cinema architecture, the painter Roy Lichtenstein, colour blind test charts. Both Sue Palmer and myself made three-dimensional models as further induction inspirations. These we painted with dots and bright hues."*
Eddie Squires, 1994[62]

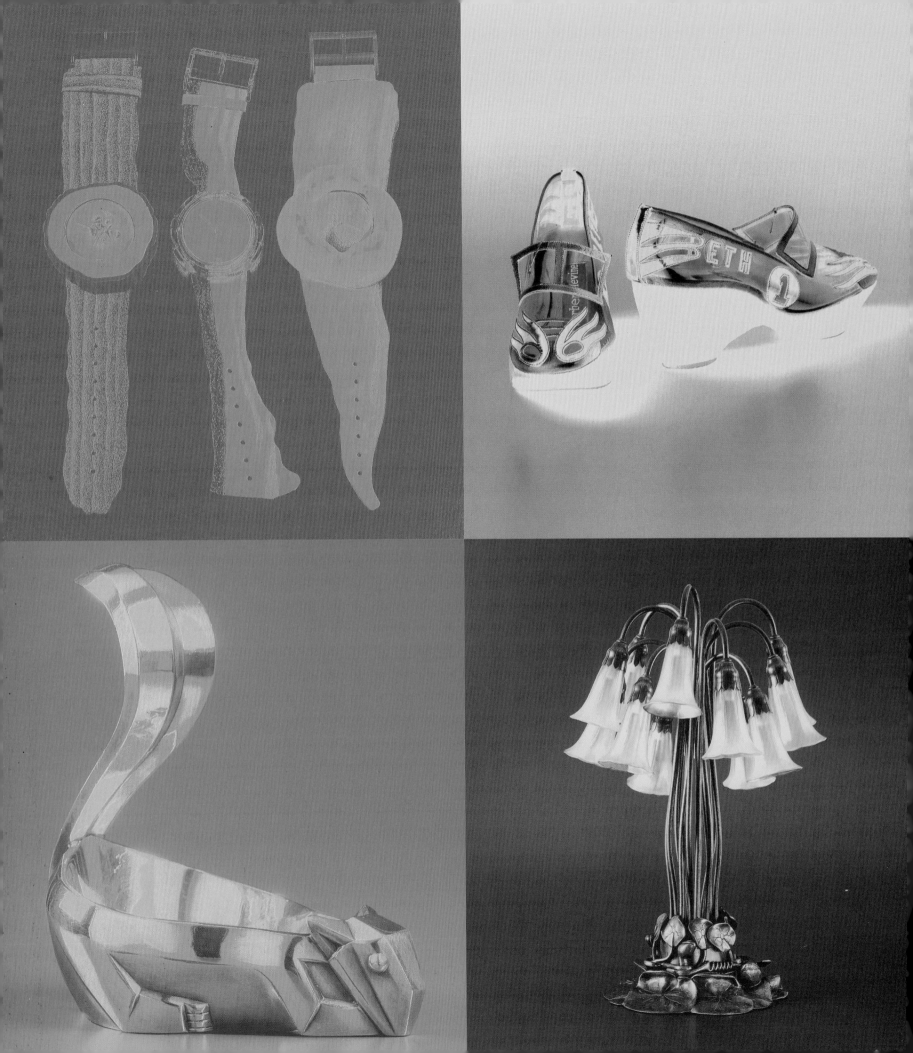

# Flights of Fantasy

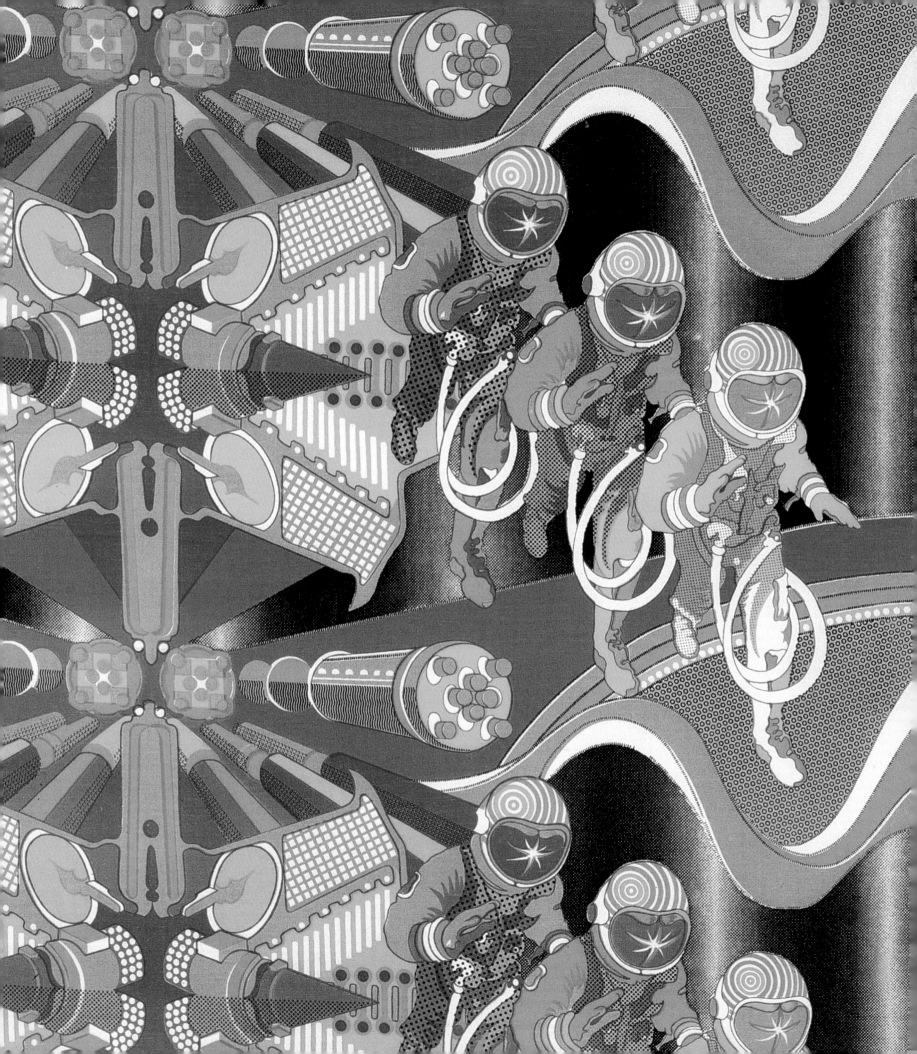

# Flights of Fantasy

*by Lenore Newman and Jan L. Spak*

If Modern design has had one overriding principle, it is that people are rational and that their objects should be rational as well. Objects were to be useful and meet the needs of function — nothing more. As mechanization took command and standardization became an attainable goal, designers spun out endless theories, trying to make sense of the enormous changes that were overtaking the production and consumption of man-made goods. Individual expression and especially fantasy were understandably excluded. The eccentric and the irrational were outlawed not only because they defied standardization, but also because they challenged the basic definition of a rational mankind. In 1925, Le Corbusier summed up a Modernist sentiment that was to permeate the century:

> Leaving behind the unquiet reign of fantasy and the incongruous, we can regain possession of a comforting set of norms ... to define human needs. These needs are few in number, identical in all men, since from time immemorial man has been made from the same stamp ... *These needs are standard*, that is, they are the same for everybody ...[1]

However, as Freud's theories have shown, it is impossible to deny the ego, an entity incapable of succumbing to standardization. Despite the Modernists' rigorous rejection of fantasy, this forbidden fruit has remained a constant element of twentieth-century culture. The wide variety of objects presented here represent subjective interpretations of the modern world, expressions of the individual in a mechanized and supposedly standardized society. These interpretations range from narrative expressions of personal experiences and dreams, to nostalgic glances at the past, to satirical designs in which objects imitate other objects. Some appeal to a specialized (one might even say elitist) audience, but many are mass-produced and thus intended for the general populace; these objects reveal much about both the designer and the purchaser.

Many objects that demonstrate flights of fantasy reflect the influence of the fine art movements that defined the last hundred years. An early manifestation can be seen in the way in which Art Nouveau design assimilated poetic Symbolist imagery, such as evocative female heads (cat. nos. 19–22) and motifs drawn from nature, such as Tiffany's *Pond Lily* lamp (cat. no. 199). Yet this imagery was used in a largely decorative context. It took the more assertive incongruities of the Dadaists and Surrealists — both groups were especially object-oriented — for designers to begin to exploit more fully the rich ore of fantasy.

Salvador Dalí, perhaps the most visible proponent of Surrealism, frequently crossed the boundary between the fine and decorative arts. In his brooch, *The Persistence of Memory* (cat. no. 161), based on a motif in a painting of several decades earlier, Dalí's melting timepiece symbolizes his belief in the fluid nature of time. The stretched and elongated timepiece reminds us of the way in which memory contorts the reality of an event, allowing individual interpretation. Indeed, the subjective nature of time, coupled with the pressures imposed by modern phenomena such as standardized time, fueled the fantasies of many twentieth-century writers, artists, and designers. The way in which personal, inner time conflicts with chronometric time inspired writers such as Franz Kafka to remark, "... The clocks don't agree. The inner one rushes along in a devilish or

Fig. 75. Giorgio de Chirico,
*The Philosopher's Conquest*, 1914.
Oil on canvas. 125.8 x 99.1 cm (49½ x 39 in.).
Chicago, The Art Institute of Chicago,
the Joseph Winterbotham Collection.

Fig. 76. Jean-Michel Frank and Christian Bérard,
room in the Institut de Beauté Guerlain, Paris, 1939.

demonic — in any case inhuman — way while the outer one goes, falteringly, its accustomed pace."[2]

The disquieting nature of modern life and nostalgia for the Classical world were poignantly expressed early in the century in Giorgio de Chirico's paintings, such as *The Philosopher's Conquest* (fig. 75), which, like Dalí's painting, symbolically features a timepiece. A similar sense of displacement and nostalgia is seen in much of Italy's Novecento movement; prime examples are the designs for ceramics created by Gio Ponti in the 1920s, such as *The Classical Conversation* (cat. no. 162), with its elusive classical references. As Ponti later explained,

> Interpreters, in the most concrete ways, of the stuff of dreams, the Italians have always made, with their arts, the most powerful invitation to the peoples of the whole world to translate fantasy, without fear, into poetic reality, waking from sleep and capturing dreams, all dreams …[3]

Italy, however, was not the sole country to be concerned with such dreamlike imagery. Surrealist fantasies became a chic taste in Europe in the 1930s. In Paris, for example, the neo-Romantic artists Eugène and Léonid Berman and Christian Bérard extended the imagery of the easel onto the stage, as did Cecil Beaton, Rex Whistler, and Oliver Messel in England. Likewise, Jean-Michel Frank and Syrie Maugham created splendid and very special interior decoration using the same language of architectural fantasy and irrational juxtaposition (fig. 76). In the postwar years, elegiac ruins and plunging perspective lines were the common stock of musical numbers in the cinema and on television, and, as Peter Todd Mitchell's wallpapers and textile designs affirm (cat. nos. 163, 164), they became the fare of more ordinary interior decoration and fashion as well.

Indeed, one of the surprising aspects of the role of fantasy in twentieth-century design is not only its ubiquitousness but also the way in which daring, outré ideas of an earlier decade were domesticated and distributed to a wider audience. The impact of Surrealism is nowhere more evident than in postwar New York, where textile firms such as Fuller Fabrics and Schiffer Prints recast the paintings of Picasso, Dalí, Miró, Chagall, and the other masters of the School of Paris into fabric designs for an art-minded bourgeoisie. Fuller Fabrics' *Women and Birds* textile (cat. no. 165), for example, features Miró's characteristic hieroglyphs within a matrix of lyrical line. Other artist-designed textiles, equally witty, were more closely allied with popular culture, such as cartoonist Saul Steinberg's *Wedding Picture* textile (cat. no. 166) which portrays a humorously capricious view of a traditionally sober rite of passage.

From Sigmund Freud's *The Interpretation of Dreams,* published in 1900, through André Breton's first *Surrealist Manifesto* of 1924, the dream has increasingly become a central focus of the arts; scenes of personal reverie materialized not only on canvas but also on ceramics, glass, and other decorative arts. Edward Hald's romantically poignant evocation of love in his relatively straightforward and perhaps even sentimental design for the Swedish firm of Orrefors (cat. no. 167) suggests an innocent first stage. Encouraged by the craft revival of the mid-twentieth century, many artists expressed their dreams and fantasies through age-old craft traditions. Rudy Autio, who has been described as the Matisse of ceramics,[4] draws upon the ancient tradition of decorating vessels with women and animals (cat. no. 168). Rather than portraying a straightforward scene of reverie, he expresses a much more highly charged narrative in which the writhing figures envelop the vessel. Joyce Scott, who in other instances uses her art to force awareness of powerful issues of feminism and racism, evokes the power of the dream in her neckpiece *Frosted* (cat. no. 169).

Not only does she offer a new interpretation of the traditional necklace of strands of beads but, as her accompanying poem suggests, the image is meant to evoke a stream-of-consciousness, a very personal sort of narrative. Another artist who demonstrates the communicative power of jewelry is Robert Ebendorf, a pioneer in the art of assemblage. He uses found objects of a disturbingly common order — an old eyeglass frame and commercial ball-link metal chain like the kind used for key chains — and combines them with vintage tintype photographs to create haunting images (cat. no. 170). These objects invite, almost demand, active interpretation on the part of the viewer/consumer, as much as they express artistic intent.

Mythology — a domain of antirational forces — was especially dear first to the Symbolists and then to the Surrealists; it was a staple in the works of Odilon Redon, Jean Cocteau, and Dalí. And its repertoire of fabled beasts has never lost its appeal in the twentieth century. Borrowing from Greek mythology, a pair of mid-century Sèvres vases (cat. no. 171) depict the winged horse Pegasus flying among the stars of heaven. Ramón Puig Cuyás returns to the siren, one of the fabled creatures he remembers from childhood, to create an idiosyncratic image for his brooch, *The Choral Mermaid* (cat. no. 172).

A uniquely twentieth-century mythology has been built around the theme of space travel and extraterrestrial life. Space, the final frontier, is a fantasy that became a reality in the 1960s. Both Sue Palmer's *Space Walk* (cat. no.174) and Eddie Squires's *Lunar Rocket* (cat. no. 175) commemorate the momentous event of landing on the moon, and though these images were based on photographic and factual data, they were also given mythic power.

Before space captured our imagination, the modern city was an omnipresent symbol of optimism, speculation, or sometimes, satirical commentary. Novels and movies attempted to glorify the city of today or envision the city of tomorrow, as in the futuristic film classic *Metropolis*. Designers were quick to adapt images of urban density and the mesmerizing abstraction of soaring verticals to the decorative arts. An American textile (cat. no. 176) tells an enraptured tale of New York in the 1930s, using a photomontage technique that parallels similar experiments by avant-garde photographers of the period. Now, at the end of the century, the initial optimism has faded and has been replaced by disillusionment. In his sofa, *Sunset in New York* (cat. no. 178), Gaetano Pesce seems to evoke positive associations of the New York City skyline, but the designer is really reflecting on what he perceives to be the decline of the city's cultural importance. Despite a change in visual language, the melancholy of Pesce's vision is strangely reminiscent of the nostalgia expressed in de Chirico's paintings and Ponti's ceramics from the early part of the century.

Pesce's disillusionment reminds us that cynicism and satire have long been staples of artistic inspiration. In the twentieth century, as the definition of art has continued to expand, the decorative arts have increasingly become an outlet for satirical expression. Some of the most witty examples have involved satires of fabled icons of Western art, such as Marcel Duchamp's *L.H.O.O.Q.*, featured in the Dada Manifesto of 1920, in which the artist defiantly drew a mustache on a reproduction of the *Mona Lisa* (fig. 77) and retitled the work with a naughty pun that suggests the enigmatically smiling lady is sexually charged. Also tweaking this Leonardo icon, Polish graphic designer Maciej Urbaniec's *Cyrk* poster (cat. no. 179) presents the *Mona Lisa* as a carnival contortionist. In his charger, *Describing the Diameter* (cat. no. 180), American ceramist Robert Arneson, known for his biting self-portraiture, follows in this rich tradition with a play on Leonardo's image of *Vitruvian Man* (fig. 32) by substituting his own less-than-perfect proportions for those of the ideal Renaissance figure.

Fig. 77. Marcel Duchamp, *L.H.O.O.Q.*, 1919. Rectified Readymade: reproduction altered with pencil. 19.7 x 12.4 cm (7¾ x 4⅞ in.). Paris, Musée National d'Art Moderne, Centre Georges Pompidou, gift of Louis Aragon to Georges Marchais for the Parti Communiste Français.

Fig. 78. Fra' Giovanni da Verona,
choirstall panel, c. 1500.
Wood intarsia. Monte Oliveto Maggiore, Abbey.

Fig. 79. Austrian, plate with *fond bois* decoration,
c. 1775–1800.
Glazed porcelain. Diameter: 23.8 cm (9⅜ in.).
London, Victoria and Albert Museum.

Fig. 80. Meret Oppenheim, *Breakfast in Fur*, 1936.
Porcelain, fur. Cup: 10.9 cm (4¼ in.) diameter; saucer:
23.7 cm (9⅜ in.) diameter; spoon: 20.2 cm (8 in.);
overall height: 7.3 cm (2⅞ in.).
New York, The Museum of Modern Art.

The intriguing appeal of these icons aside, there is certainly no shortage of appropriate targets in contemporary life at which artists may aim their creative arrows. Jeweler Bruce Metcalf, for one, directs his at political and social issues. In *Cactus Head in a Frame of Missiles* (cat. no. 183), his typically amoeboid character sets the stage for searing commentary on the arms race and smoking, two potentially lethal topics.

Illusion, with its ceaseless mysteries and compelling charms, has always proved irresistible, capturing our imagination and serving as a vehicle for our fantasies. From *trompe l'œil* to ersatz, we delight in experiencing something which pretends to be something else. Artists have tried—and succeeded—in fooling the eye since ancient times. Pompeian artists simulated revetments of costly marble, and these muralists delighted in painting away the walls with vistas of distant gardens and buildings. With the discovery of scientific perspective in the Renaissance, illusionistic deception abounded. The intarsia decoration of the choirstall panels at the Abbey of Monte Oliveto Maggiore (fig. 78), for example, gave depth and interest to flat surfaces. Veronese's frescoes in the Villa Barbaro (fig. 30) and Charles LeBrun's murals on the Staircase of the Ambassadors at Versailles exemplify the ongoing nature of this pictorial tradition. Likewise, furniture of the eighteenth century was often inlaid with architectural vistas in a continuation of the Renaissance tradition. A consummate twentieth-century example, which seems to be a cross between this tradition, the prints of Piranesi and, not least of all, Surrealism, is Piero Fornasetti's desk (fig. 81), with its moody architectural vistas. Japanese designer Kiyoshi Kanai's *Off-the-Wall Chair* (cat. no. 184) is yet another more recent link in this long chain.

Faux finishes and other forms of illusion were often employed during the Victorian period, when technical proficiency in imitating materials was an enchanting game. Industrial manufacturers gladly duplicated costly materials in crass, less expensive materials. Base metal was electroplated with a coating of silver; carved wood furniture was duplicated in pressed papier-maché. Moreover, it was not always an issue of creating cheaper substitutes; sometimes it was an issue of exalting skill at great expense—painting porcelain with convincing wood grain and veined stone, for example (fig. 79). The theorists of the British Reform Movement may have preached "truth to materials" and invoked a call to morality, but the populace rejoiced in these tours de force of simulation. Meret Oppenheim's fur-covered teacup (fig. 80) is an icon of twentieth-century art, but is it that different from nineteenth-century faux finishes, such as teacups gilded to look like precious metal, grained to look like wood, or shaped to resemble bamboo?

A group of late twentieth-century textiles produced at the Fabric Workshop, a Philadelphia institution where artists prominent in other media are invited to try their hand at designing fabrics, plays with the ideas of illusion and duplicity. Postmodern architects Robert Venturi and Denise Scott Brown's *Notebook* textile (cat. no. 186) is modeled after the pattern that covers American schoolchildren's composition books;[5] moreover, the ubiquitous pattern is itself an imitation of the veining of granite—reminding us in a forceful way that we are so accustomed to facsimiles that we take them for granted as part of the "natural" world. Ceramist Tony Costanzo's *Linoleum* textile (cat. no. 185) represents a similar deception. It mimics the synthetic floor covering which itself is patterned to look like marble, yet we no longer see the linoleum as imitation but, rather, as a "real" substance in and of itself. Sculptor Scott Burton's *Fabric for Window Curtains* (cat. no. 187) attempts to deceive our eyes by imitating the multipaned window it proposes to cover. In an equally disarming manner, Studio Tetrarch's plastic table, molded to

Fig. 81. Piero Fornasetti, desk, *Architecture*, 1951. Screen-printed wood. 219 x 81 x 39 cm (86¼ x 31⅞ x 15⅜ in.).

look as if it were draped with a flowing tablecloth (cat. no. 188), is a cunning visual pun — it replaces the table it conceals — and would be a natural component of a Jean-Michel Frank interior or a painting by Magritte.

Camouflage, inspired by Cubism and first employed during World War I, is the ultimate concealer.[6] Adelle Lutz's *Ivy Suit* (cat. no. 195), worn by David Byrne in the 1986 movie *True Stories,* explores the idea of camouflaging one's self to blend into a uniquely twentieth-century environment — the suburbs. The idea of transforming a person into an inanimate object, in this case a tree, recalls haunting imagery from earlier in the century, such as Magritte's 1928 painting *Discovery*, in which a woman's naked flesh turns into wood grain (fig. 82). Indeed, this type of imagery has been appropriated more and more, as in Robert Arneson's ceramic sculpture, *Kiln Man,* where his self-portrait and the kiln in which he fires become one and the same in a Kafkaesque metamorphosis. Our pleasure in such transformations compellingly attests to the delightfully antirational nature of our world.

Many of the objects that have become stars of the art world in the late twentieth century are absurd pretenders on a grand scale. The tradition can be seen in Surrealist paintings such as Magritte's *Personal Values* (fig. 83), in which the mammoth scale of everyday objects — a wineglass, a comb, a shaving brush — dwarf the tiny room they occupy. More recently, the beloved *Joe* sofa (cat. no. 192) offered seating in the form of a giant baseball glove. Named after American baseball hero Joe DiMaggio, this chair attests to the widespread influence of American culture and its "bigger the better" ethos. The design's absurdly grand size plays with scale much like the work of Pop artists such as Claes Oldenburg, whose sixty-six-inch-long *Giant Toothpaste Tube* sculpture heroicized the trivia of the commercial world. Underscaling can be equally humorous. Witness Beth Levine's Pop-era *Racing Car* shoes (cat. no. 191), which transform a most "pedestrian" form of transportation into high–speed vehicles.

Brash impersonators like Guido Drocco and Franco Mello's polyurethane coat and hat stand in the form of a giant cactus (cat. no. 197) and Piero Gilardi's polyurethane foam seating in the form of rocks (cat. no. 193) are irreverent aberrations in the domestic landscape. In one sense, these pretenders seem wholly representative of the late twentieth century — without precedence and without reverence. But, on the other hand, these similes are not that far removed from ideas of the early twentieth century. In a 1930s Surrealist fantasy, a chair in the form of a giant lobster endows the lowly crustacean with life-threateningly gargantuan proportions (fig. 86). Designers earlier in the century were perhaps more poetic in conception and their designs more intimate in scale, but they also created "unnatural" transformations of nature. Émile Gallé carved tables in the form of giant dragonflies (fig. 84), just as Tiffany created electric lamps in the form of graceful plants (cat. no. 199), their flowers fading in a Symbolist gesture as the lights dimmed. Similarly, Léon Kann modeled his elegant Sèvres coffee service (cat. no. 198) in the form of a fennel plant, injecting an unexpected touch of whimsy by ornamenting the lids with insects. In a certain sense these objects seem surreal, and it is little wonder, then, that Dalí was such an admirer of Art Nouveau.

Moreover, this type of fantasy was not merely the prerogative of the earliest part of the century. In the 1920s, especially in France, decorative arts of grand luxe delighted in this repertoire of exotic motifs. Armand-Albert Rateau created luxuriant suites of furniture such as his bedroom for Jeanne Lanvin, with tables and torchères supported by birds (fig. 85); not only were there references to nature, but also to the Near East, reminding us how these "novelties" really belonged to centuries-old traditions. Occasionally the choice of motif even had a symbolic function: Christofle's nut dish in the form of a squirrel (cat. no. 205) suggested

Fig. 82. René Magritte, *Discovery*, 1927.
Oil on canvas. 65 x 50 cm (25½ x 19¾ in.).
Brussels, private collection.

Fig. 83. René Magritte, *Personal Values*, 1952.
Oil on canvas. 81 x 100 cm (31⅞ x 39⅜ in.).
Private collection.

Fig. 84. Emile Gallé, table, *Dragonfly*, c. 1897. Walnut, wood veneer, marquetry.
74.8 x 81 x 57.5 cm (29⁷⁄₁₆ x 31⁷⁄₈ x 27⁵⁄₈ in.). Nancy, Musée de l'École de Nancy.

Fig. 85. Armand-Albert Rateau, coffee table,
c. 1920–22. Bronze, marble.
33.1 x 49.5 x 101.6 cm (13 x 19½ x 40 in.).
Private collection.

Fig. 86. Artist unknown, chair, *Lobster*, c. 1935.

this animal's diet, and a cocktail shaker in the form of a penguin (cat. no. 206) associated the icy habitat of the bird with the chilled temperature of the cocktail. These are sly jokes, but function is clearly superseded by the charm we experience in finding these animals in the domestic interior.

Despite the sane doctrines of Modernism, this delight in follies was evidenced throughout the century. Is Tom Dixon's *Cobra* lamp (cat. no. 211) at such a remove from Edgar Brandt's cobra lamp (cat. no. 212), even though they are separated by several decades and major changes in style and approach to materials? Likewise, there is a certain affinity between Ingo Maurer's birdlike *Bibibibi* (cat. no. 216) and the Chapelle and Muller lamp in the form of a stork (cat. no. 217). The earlier lamp was handcrafted with skill and expense, whereas the later was made from commercially crass, prefabricated parts (shoplifted from Woolworth's in an irreverent Dada act); they speak of different worlds and different ethics, but they are bound by a unity of human nature. So, too, we might link Tiffany's *Pond Lily* lamp of bronze and iridescent glass (cat. no. 199) with Masanori Umeda's lily-shaped chair of polyurethane foam and electric blue velvet (cat. no. 200); they approach the use of materials and the visual world of forms quite differently, yet the two designers speak with the same admiration of the natural world and the poetry of floral imagery.

Twentieth-century design was pregnant with Modernist theories that promised, at the very least, to transform our domestic environments into crisp, white spaces defined by functionalism and rationality. The ideal interior was impersonal, anonymous, capable of being found anywhere in the modern world and of being inhabited by any modern being. That ideal provided no couch for dreams, no shelf for fantasy. As it turns out, however, the Modernist canon was not an only child; it had other legitimate siblings who also wanted to be recognized and experienced.

**161. Salvador Dalí**
(born 1904, Figueras, Spain; died 1989, Figueras)
Brooch, *The Persistence of Memory*
Designed c. 1949-50. Gold, platinum, diamonds
6 x 6 x 1.9 cm (2⅜ x 2⅜ x ¾ in.)
Produced by Alemany & Ertman, Inc.
(New York, NY, USA), c. 1950-60
Engraved on front: *Dalí*; engraved on reverse on a
raised rectangular field: COP.ALEMANY/& ERTMAN INC.
D89.109.1, The Liliane and David M. Stewart Collection

*"Awareness of the colligation of time and space entered my con-sciousness in childhood. Yet my invention of the 'melted watch' — first in oil and later, in 1950, in gold and precious stones — evoked divided opinion; approval and understanding; skepticism and disbelief. Today, in American schools, my 'melted watch' is presented as a prophetic expression of the fluidity of time ... the indivisibility of time and space. The speed of modern travel — space travel — confirms this conviction. Time is fluid; not rigid."*
Salvador Dalí, 1959[7]

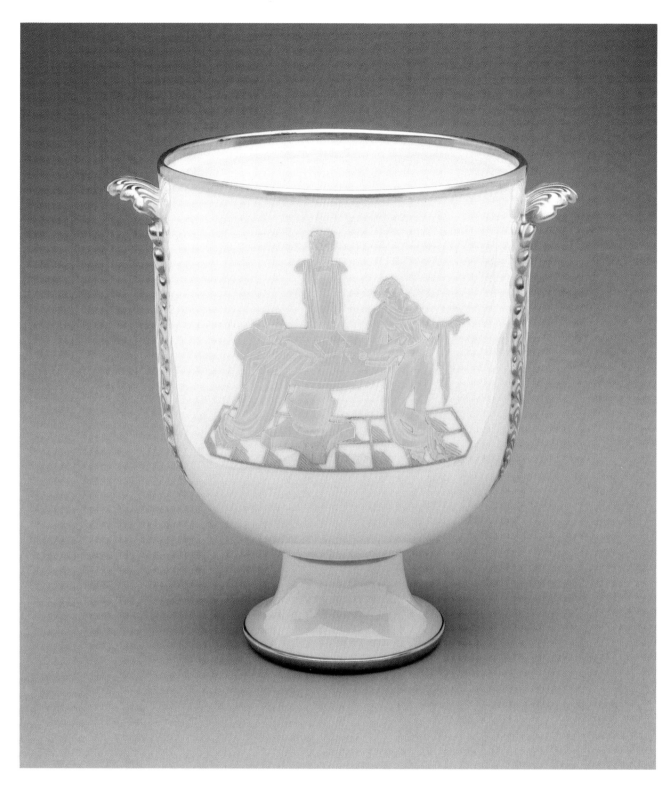

**162. Gio Ponti**
(born 1891, Milan, Italy; died 1979, Milan)
Vase, *The Classical Conversation*
*(La Conversazione Classica)*
Designed 1926 (form); c. 1927 (decoration)
Glazed and partially gilt porcelain
19.5 x 19.6 x 15.3 cm (7 11/16 x 7 11/16 x 6 in.)
Produced by Richard Ginori (Doccia), 1927-30
Printed in black on underside: MADE IN ITALY/RICHARD
GINORI/30=10; printed in black on gold paper label
affixed to underside: RICHARD-GINORI/PITTORIA/DI DOCCIA
The Montreal Museum of Fine Arts Collection,
purchase

*"Under [Ponti's] direction, a vast quantity of ceramics in the modern manner were produced, distinguished at the same time by an unusual individuality and by an evident appreciation of what had been done in the past. They were not serious in theme. Pottery, according to Ponti, should be amusing, giving the gay note of color in the home that was formerly supplied by the rubber plant. Classical forms and subjects were used, but not with that reverent spirit which inspired so many of our railroads to use Roman baths for stations."*
George Nelson, 1935[8]

"Peter Todd Mitchell is not about to put himself in the service of geometric abstraction. The play of light remains his greatest interest, as well as a feeling for distance.... Perspective rules and effects are so deliberately pursued by the artist that even the figures themselves are put to its exclusive service."
*Jardin des arts*, 1969[9]

**163. Peter Todd Mitchell**
(born 1924, New York, NY, USA;
died 1988, Barcelona, Spain)
Scarf, *Ballet: Scheherezade*
Designed c. 1955. Printed silk
82.4 x 73.7 cm (32 3/8 x 29 in.)
Produced by Wesley Simpson (New York), c. 1955-57
Silkscreened in pattern: *Peter/Todd/Mitchell*
D89.141.2, gift of the Peter Todd Mitchell Estate

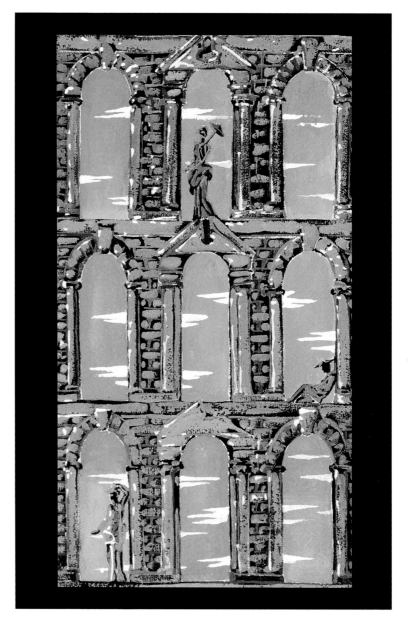

**164. Peter Todd Mitchell**
Textile design
Executed c. 1945. Gouache on paper
34.7 x 19.7 cm (13⅝ x 7¾ in.)
Unmarked
D89.144.19, gift of Priscilla Cunningham

*"... my best teachers have been the Greek vases at the Metro-*
*politan [Museum of Art], the mosaics at Ravenna; the patterns*
*of stairs and sidewalks, the tri-dimensional boiserie of the*
*Renaissance — wherever solid, pure and true design is to be*
*found.... You may not use them directly; they remain hidden in*
*your mind and emerge — later — perhaps when you are 'doodling'*
*with a paint brush."*
Peter Todd Mitchell, 1946[10]

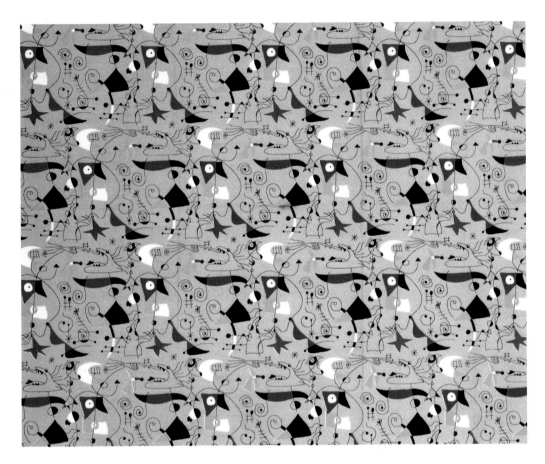

**165. After Joan Miró**
(born 1893, Montroig, Spain; died 1983, Palma de
Mallorca, Balearic Islands)
Textile, *Women and Birds*
Designed c. 1955. Printed cotton
92 x 100.3 cm (36¼ x 39½ in.)
Produced by Fuller Fabrics
(New York, NY, USA), c. 1955-56
Printed in black along one selvage: *Fuller Fabrics*
"WOMEN AND BRDS" BY MIRO  A MODERN MASTER ORIGINAL.
D.B. FULLER & CO.
D92.102.1, anonymous gift

*"It was about the time when the war broke out. I felt a deep
desire to escape. I closed myself within myself purposely.
The night, music, and the stars began to play a major role in
suggesting my paintings. Music had always appealed to me,
and now music in this period began to take the role poetry had
played in the early twenties."*
Joan Miró, 1948[11]

**166. Saul Steinberg**
(born 1914, Bucharest, Romania)
Textile, *Wedding Picture*
Designed c. 1950. Printed cotton
319 x 98.4 cm (125⁹⁄₁₆ x 38¾ in.)
Produced by Patterson Fabrics
(New York, NY, USA), c. 1950-60
Printed in dark brown along one selvage: WEDDING
PICTURE *by Steinberg* PATTERSON FABRICS *New York, N. Y.*
D93.225.1, anonymous gift

*"Humor is a very good trap. Laughter
disarms and opens the way for instinct.
It is like hiccups, yawns. When you try to
repress a yawn, it comes out of your ears.
Yawning is animal criticism – dogs yawn.
Laughter is mental or maybe mineral."*
Saul Steinberg, 1971[12]

**167. Edward Hald**
(born 1883, Stockholm, Sweden; died 1980, Stockholm)
Covered vase, *Lovers' Lane (Karleksstigen)*
Designed 1923. Glass
41.6 x 13.2 x 13.2 cm (16⅜ x 5³⁄₁₆ x 5³⁄₁₆ in.)
Produced by AB Orrefors Glasbruk (Orrefors), 1923–24
Engraved on rim of foot: Orrefors.Hald.312.27.R;
embossed in gold on off-white shield-shaped label
affixed to top of base: ORREFORS/SWEDEN/[device of
grouse within laurel wreath and three crowns]
The Montreal Museum of Fine Arts Collection, gift of
F. Cleveland Morgan

*"The more valuable engraved pieces appeal to a rather
limited public.... The material ... is transformed into
lacework by Hald's fantasy-filled 'embroideries.' This
of course does not prevent both artists from creating
unique, outstanding pieces. I will limit myself to
mentioning Hald's tall cup with the meandering path
of love (Hald loves to include fantastic novelettes in
the decor)."*
Erik Blomberg, 1923[13]

**168. Rudy Autio**
(born 1926, Butte, MT, USA)
Vase, *Lady with Dog*
Executed 1980. Slip-painted stoneware
44.4 x 50.2 x 31.1 cm (17½ x 19¾ x 12¼ in.)
Incised near base: *Autio/80*
D93.305.1, gift of Jean Boucher

*"My friend Hank Meloy, a great painter and draftsman, those were some of his themes — nudes, horses, landscapes — in the late '40s and early '50s. He was kind of a hero of mine.... Nudes have always been on pots, and animals as well. My first use of figures on shaped pots was actually quite early — 1960 or '61. Then I abandoned it. But the themes would reemerge again and again, beginning in the late '70s."*
Rudy Autio, 1994[14]

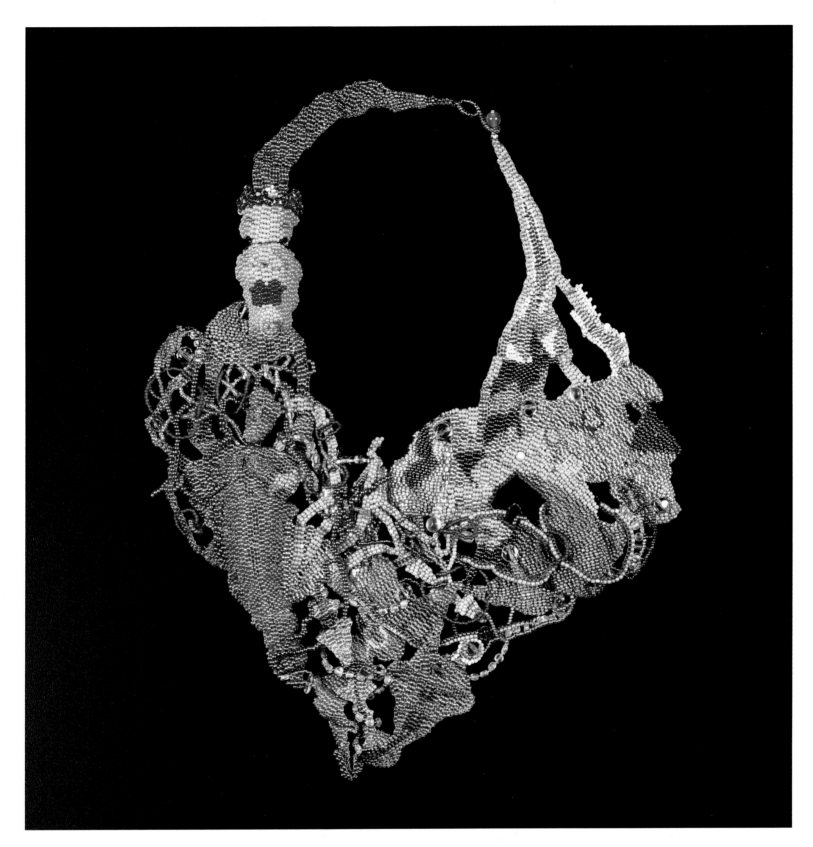

**169. Joyce Scott**
(born 1948, Baltimore, MD, USA)
Necklace, *Frosted*
Executed 1995. Glass beads, plastic beads
34.5 x 28.5 x 4 cm (13⁹⁄₁₆ x 11¼ x 1⁹⁄₁₆ in.)
Unmarked
D95.179.1, The Liliane and David M. Stewart Collection

*"Pink dreams, kind of light; frosty daylight, crystal. Lady sleeping but barely awake. Springtime, hazy colors of spring. When you're barely awake but barely asleep. Pink dreams from sunset, come and disappear."*
Joyce Scott, 1995[15]

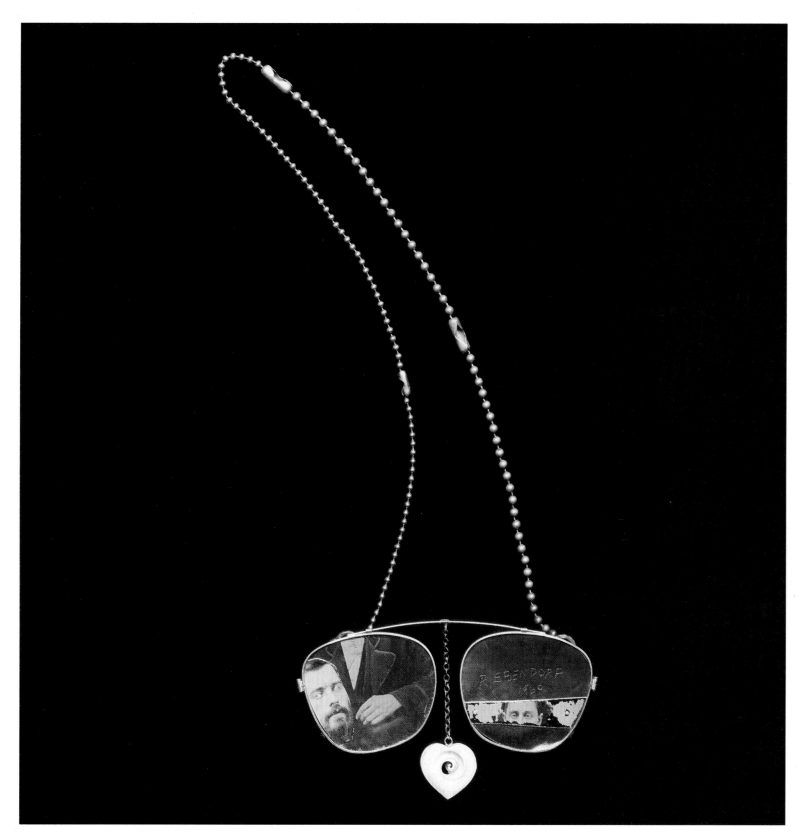

**170. Robert Ebendorf**
(born 1938, Topeka, KS, USA)
Necklace
Executed 1969. Ball-link chain, metal eyeglass frame,
tintype photographs, shell
Pendant: 5 x 10.7 x 1.5 cm (1¹⁵/₁₆ x 4³/₁₆ x ⁹/₁₆ in.);
extended: 55.2 cm (21¾ in.)
Incised into tintype: R. EBENDORF/1969
D94.108.1, gift of Doug Green and Marion Jambor*

*"Growing up in the Midwest, Kansas — also in a family that had
felt the hard times of the Depression — there was a thinking:
make do with what you have or make something of joy to play
with from what you find on the street, or cast-offs. So often
hours would be spent in total enjoyment making objects to play
with. The process of assembling things (materials) together
came with joy. The reassembling of bits and pieces brought
about very personal objects of joy."*
Robert Ebendorf, 1994[16]

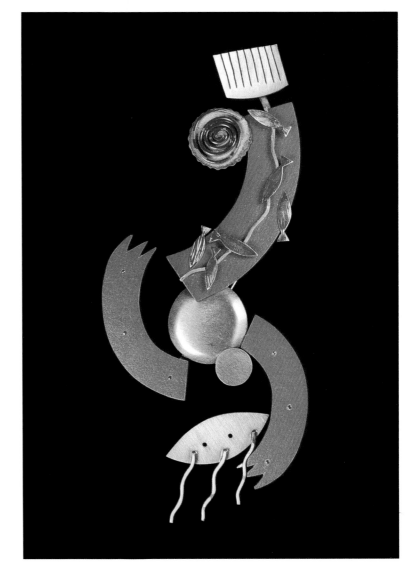

### 171. Form: Maurice Gensoli
(born 1892, Oran, Algeria; died 1973, Rouen, France)
### Decoration: Rabaey
(dates of birth and death unknown)
Pair of vases, *Winged Horses (Chevaux Ailés)*
Designed 1951–52. Glazed porcelain
29.6 x 10.3 x 10.3 cm (11⅝ x 4¹⁄₁₆ x 4¹⁄₁₆ in.) each
Produced by Manufacture Nationale de Sèvres
(Sèvres), 1952–c. 1958; decoration executed by
Gabriel Paul Sère (born 1923, Marignac)
Impressed on underside of each: 1-51-PN; printed in
green on underside of each: *Sevres* [within crossed
S's]/54/MANUFACTURE NATIONALE/DECORE/A/SEVRES/K
[within circle of dots]; painted in black on underside
of each: G.S. d'après RABAEY 127.50
D93.255.1-2, gift of Jean Boucher

### 172. Ramón Puig Cuyás
(born 1953, Mataró, Spain)
Brooch, *The Choral Mermaid*
Executed 1989. Silver, ColorCore, paint
15.5 x 7 x 1.5 cm (6⅛ x 2¾ x ⁹⁄₁₆ in.)
Unmarked
D90.116.1, The Liliane and David M. Stewart Collection

*"Between 1945 and 1966, the Manufacture Nationale de Sèvres was left practically to its own devices; the French government had too many problems to care about porcelain! The artists at the manufactory were thus free to develop an autonomous style.... The ceramists at Sèvres ... conceived objects admirably adapted to the possibilities of the art of clay, exploiting the graphic style that was then in vogue: the drawings of Jean Cocteau are the best known, but many artists used it, notably Jean Lurçat.*

*A decorative vocabulary was common to this group of artisans who were passionate about the revival of their techniques.... Others, whose culture was nourished with classical references, turned to motifs from Greek and Roman antiquity. All created a mythical world of happiness to escape the harsh realities of the times."*
Antoinette Faÿ-Hallé, 1996[17]

*"In The Choral Mermaid, there is a truly ironic game between the supposedly poetic title and the material actually used, ColorCore, an absolutely synthetic, practical and functional material. In reality, it is a joke that I have with myself.... Since my childhood, mythological figures, half-human, half-animal, have exercised a disturbing and seductive power on me. But nothing has awakened my fantasy with such power as the half-fish, half-woman figure — the Siren. I have always been fascinated by the image of Ulysses tied to the mast of his ship by force, enduring the irresistible song of the Sirens' voices."*
Ramón Puig Cuyás, 1994[18]

**173. Ettore Sottsass**
(born 1917, Innsbruck, Austria)
Armchair, *Flying Carpet (Tappeto Volante)*
Designed 1975. Wool carpet, wool and cotton velour
upholstery, wood, foam rubber
66 x 106.8 x 177.8 cm (26 x 42¹⁄₁₆ x 70 in.)
Produced by Bedding Brevetti (Milan, Italy), 1975
Unmarked
L96.100.1, extended loan from David M. Campbell

*"The general idea was to connect the chair with the surrounding
space and in some way make the chair disappear, as in Turkey
or Oriental places where you more or less sit on the ground....
[It's] a way of sitting on the ground while preserving the idea
that you are sitting up higher.... It's the Oriental idea of sitting,
slightly transformed for Western possibilities."*
Ettore Sottsass, 1994[19]

**174. Sue Thatcher Palmer**
(born 1947, Slough, England)
Textile, *Space Walk*
Designed 1969. Printed cotton
112.4 x 121 cm (44¼ x 47⅝ in.)
Produced by Warner & Sons Ltd (London), 1969–71;
printed by Stead McAlpin & Co. Ltd (Carlisle)
Printed in dark blue along both selvages:
SPACE WALK ⦂ DESIGNED FOR WARNER'S BY SUE THATCHER ⦂
D90.136.1, gift of Eddie Squires

**175. Eddie Squires**
(born 1940, Anlaby, England; died 1995, London)
Textile, *Lunar Rocket*
Designed 1969. Printed cotton
125.5 x 124.9 cm (49⅜ x 49⅛ in.)
Produced by Warner & Sons Ltd (London), 1969–71;
printed by Stead McAlpin & Co. Ltd (Carlisle)
Printed in dark blue along both selvages: ⋮ LUNAR
ROCKET ⋮ DESIGNED FOR WARNER'S BY EDDIE SQUIRES ⋮
D90.138.1, gift of Eddie Squires

"**Space Walk** *by Sue Palmer and* **Lunar Rocket** *by Eddie Squires were designed and produced to celebrate the hoped-for landing of a man on the moon.... * **Space Walk** *is influenced mainly by the space technology involved in attempting to place a man on the moon. Science fiction, also a strong influence during the 1960s, played its part as well. Sue Palmer used NASA photographs of rocket engines and boosters — the astronauts appear to be doing a space ballet over the moon's surface. The moon's gravitational pulse is indicated against the void of deep space. A huge amount of research was collected.*"
Eddie Squires, 1994[20]

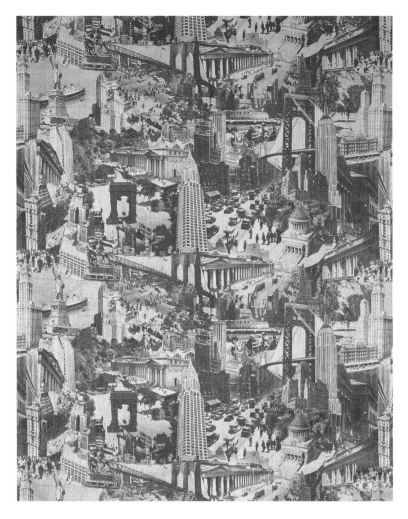

**176. Unknown designer**
Textile
Designed c. 1933–40. Printed cotton
89 x 127 cm (35 1/16 x 50 in.)
Produced by Springs Industries
(New York, NY, USA), c. 1933–40
Unmarked
D85.103.1, gift of Pauline Metcalf in memory
of David M. S. Pettigrew

*"Now design is taking to its own the skyscraper as the most interesting innovation in constructive design.... I see in the near future its influence upon all types of decorative art ... It is fascinating, inspiring and full of promise.... The new order ... involves the skyscraper, the aircraft, the radio and all the interesting interpretations of electric energy. The new view that looks down upon our world from the aircraft and up from the worm's view must of necessity be an inspiration resulting in new interpretations of decorative design."*
Edith M. Bushnell, 1928[21]

**177. Gaetano Pesce**
(born 1939, La Spezia, Italy)
Drawing, *Sunset in New York (Tramonto a New York)*
Executed 1980. Colored pencil and pastel on paper
149.6 x 72 cm (58 7/8 x 28 3/8 in.)
Signed in orange pastel at bottom right:
*Gaetano Pesce 1980*
D93.242.1, anonymous gift, by exchange

**178. Gaetano Pesce**
Sofa, *Sunset in New York (Tramonto a New York)*
Designed 1980. Polyurethane foam, Dacron, plywood
116.9 x 231.7 x 90.9 cm (46 x 91¼ x 35¹³/₁₆ in.)
Produced by Cassina S.p.A. (Milan),
1980 to the present
Unmarked
D91.415.1, The Liliane and David M. Stewart Collection

*"When I came to New York for the first time, I found it full of energy. But on a subsequent visit, I felt that vitality was less strong. I thought the lack of it was a sign of the city's decadence. Certainly New York was the capital of the twentieth century, but at the end of it, the force was draining elsewhere. As a result, New York today is a place of conservatism, the first sign of decadence. Like other cities in history — Constantinople, Athens, Rome, Florence, Venice, Amsterdam, London, Paris — that once have known a high tide of energy and its loss, New York is going through the same process. A good question is, which city will be the capital of the twenty-first century?"*
Gaetano Pesce, 1993[22]

**179. Maciej Jerzy Zdzieblan Urbaniec**
(born 1925, Zwierzyniec, Poland)
Poster, *Circus (Cyrk)*
Designed 1970. Offset lithograph
97.5 x 66.4 cm (38⅜ x 26⅛ in.)
Printed by PWPW [Panstwowa Wytwórnia Papierów
Wartosciowych] (Warsaw) for DESA Foreign Trade
Enterprise (Warsaw), 1972 (second edition)
Printed in black on bottom right: & URBANIEC; on
bottom left, in negative within black squares: KA/OW
D91.161.1, gift of Lucia and Miljenko Horvat

*"At the end of 1969, I received a commission for a poster
representing 'non-aerial acrobatics.' This ridiculously
formulated commission may have contained a provocation.
Among 'non-aerial acrobatics,' I chose the art of contortion,
which offers unending possibilities for configurations of the
human body. Unfortunately, there were no contortionists
whom I could see in performance, and there was no iconographic material to work with. I had to rely entirely on my
imagination. The question whether the position I had
imagined was realistic or not haunted me until the day when
on television I saw a famous Spanish contortionist. She was
in the identical position as the contortionist in my poster —
smoking a cigarette while holding it with her toes.*

*My attitude toward* La Gioconda *[Leonardo's* Mona Lisa*]
is not different from that toward other works of art. Comparing my poster with Duchamp's* Mona Lisa, *I can say that*
Gioconda *is the mustache of my contortionist. The subject
of Duchamp's work is* La Gioconda, *while the subject of my
poster is the contortionist. I would call my* Gioconda *a
splatter of the imagination, which I cannot explain."*
Maciej Urbaniec, 1994[23]

**180. Robert Arneson**
(born 1930, Benicia, CA, USA; died 1992, Benicia)
Charger, *Describing the Diameter*
Executed 1977. Glazed earthenware
3.8 x 47.6 x 47.6 cm (1½ x 18¾ x 18¾ in.)
Impressed on underside: *Arneson/1977*
D93.306.1, gift of Jean Boucher

*"The things that I'm really interested in as an artist are the things you can't do — and that's really to mix humor and fine art. I'm not being silly about it, I'm serious about the combination. Humor is generally considered low art but I think humor is very serious — it points out the fallacies of our existence."*
Robert Arneson, 1981[24]

*"Of the twenty-six letters of the alphabet, the letters 'B' and 'I'
are clearly the most graphic and the least subject to misinter-
pretation. The rebus is a mnemonic device, a kind of game
designed to engage the reader and, incidentally, lots of fun."*
Paul Rand, 1984[25]

**181. Paul Rand**
(born 1914, New York, NY, USA; died 1996,
Norwalk, CT)
Poster, *IBM*
Designed 1970. Offset lithograph
91.4 x 60.9 cm (36 x 24 in.)
Produced by IBM (New York), 1981;
printed by Mossberg & Co. (South Bend, IN)
Printed in white at bottom left: an Eye for perception,
insight, vision./a Bee for industriousness, dedication,
perserverance./an "M" for motivation, merit, moral
strength./A somewhat unusual perspective of the
familiar/IBM logotype, and a light reminder of some
of the funda-/mental qualities that have come to
characterize/the outstanding men and women who
have built, and who/continue to build, the success
of the IBM company; printed in brown at bottom
right: *Paul Rand*
D87.145.1, gift of Paul Rand

an Eye for perception, insight, vision.
a Bee for industriousness, dedication, perseverance.
an "M" for motivation, merit, moral strength.

A somewhat unusual perspective of the familiar IBM logotype, and a light reminder of some of the fundamental qualities that have come to characterize the outstanding men and women who have built, and who continue to build, the success of the IBM company.

**182. Richard Craig Meitner**
(born 1949, Philadelphia, PA, USA)
Vases, *Intention + Pretension = Invention*
*(Intentie + Pretentie = Inventie)*
Executed 1984. Glass, enamels
*Intention*: 44 x 19.6 x 9.8 cm (17⅜ x 6¾ x 3⅞ in.)
*+*: 41.6 x 18 x 9 cm (16⅜ x 7⅛ x 3⅝ in.)
*Pretension*: 42.1 x 18.6 x 9.5 cm (16⅝ x 7⅜ x 3¾ in.)
*=*: 38 x 19.4 x 10.4 cm (15 x 7⅝ x 4⅛ in.)
*Invention*: 40 x 18.6 x 10 cm (15¾ x 7⅜ x 4 in.)
Engraved on underside of each: *R Meitner 84*
D94.301.1, gift of Gérard Gaveau

*"[Meitner said] 'I am fascinated by the 'pre-verbal' experience.*
*In my work I search for combinations of materials, forms, colors,*
*and especially weights, whose individual meanings I only partly*
*understand. These are symbols in a language no one speaks but*
*we all understand.' ... 'To be and not to be, that is the answer,'*
*and for good measure (in Dutch this time): 'Intentie + pretentie =*
*inventie.' I like that piece, those five transparent bodies veiled*
*with white, turning their soft forms towards an uncertain future."*
Gérard Gaveau, 1991[26]

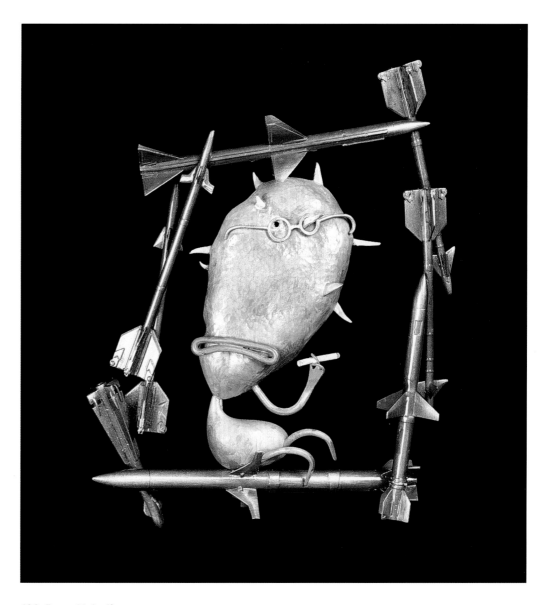

**183. Bruce Metcalf**
(born 1949, Amherst, MA, USA)
Brooch, *Cactus Head in a Frame of Missiles*
Executed 1989. Silver, brass, paint
12.1 x 9.5 x 2 cm (4¾ x 3¾ x ¹³⁄₁₆ in.)
Engraved on reverse of bottom missile: METCALF  89
D93.264.1, gift of Paul Leblanc

*"Cactus Head came about because I had the cactus head
and missiles available. The objects suggested the piece....
Cactus Head speaks of a maladjusted character, not totally
uncomfortable with violence, particularly socialized violence....
[It] is part of a series [that says] we are accomplices in
institutionalized warfare.... [It] is jarring in a funny way, but.
the context is quite serious."*
Bruce Metcalf, 1993[27]

**184. Kiyoshi Kanai**
(born 1938, Shinkyo, China)
Folding chair, *Off-the-Wall Chair*
Designed 1987. Screen-printed plastic laminate,
plywood
Folded: 165.5 x 86.4 x 3.1 cm (65³/₁₆ x 34 x 1¼ in.)
Unfolded: 113 x 86.4 x 63 cm (44½ x 34 x 24¹³/₁₆ in.)
Executed by Tony Koga (New York, NY, USA), 1987
Unmarked
D93.176.1, gift of Paul Leblanc

*"I designed this chair as a metamorphosis: [changing] the
dimensions from two to three and back fascinated me. The idea
was not so much to make a chair that functions well in the
routines of everyday life, but to have the user of this chair
involved in the making and unmaking of the chair/wall hanging.
Once the structure of the chair was solved, the image of our
old house came as spontaneously as the natural act of sitting
on its steps."*
Kiyoshi Kanai, 1994[28]

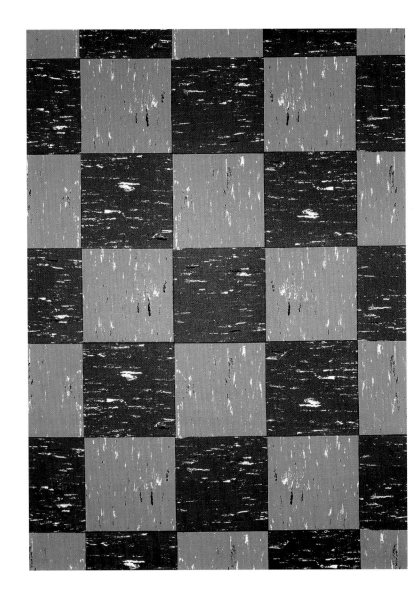

**185. Tony Costanzo**
(born 1949, Schenectady, NY, USA)
Textile, *Linoleum*
Designed 1980. Printed cotton
276.9 x 144.2 cm (109 x 56¾ in.)
Produced by The Fabric Workshop (Philadelphia, PA),
1980 to the present
Unmarked
D92.162.1, gift of Jody Kingrey, by exchange

*"I enjoy the way the marble of a cold, hard, shiny floor in a
great hall translates into the linoleum of a warm, beat-up, old
floor in a familiar kitchen. I pushed the irony further with
a third translation — into a soft, elegant fabric intended for
upholstery, draperies, table linens, even shower curtains —
anything but floors.*

*The ironic juxtaposition of the material (something seem-
ingly hard on something very soft like an armchair, something
seemingly mundane on something formal like draperies) allows
me better to notice and appreciate the formal qualities of the
design — the pattern, the color relationships, the vertical and
horizontal repetition.*

*Funny, pleases the eye, teases the brain. People seem to
like it."*
Tony Costanzo, 1994[29]

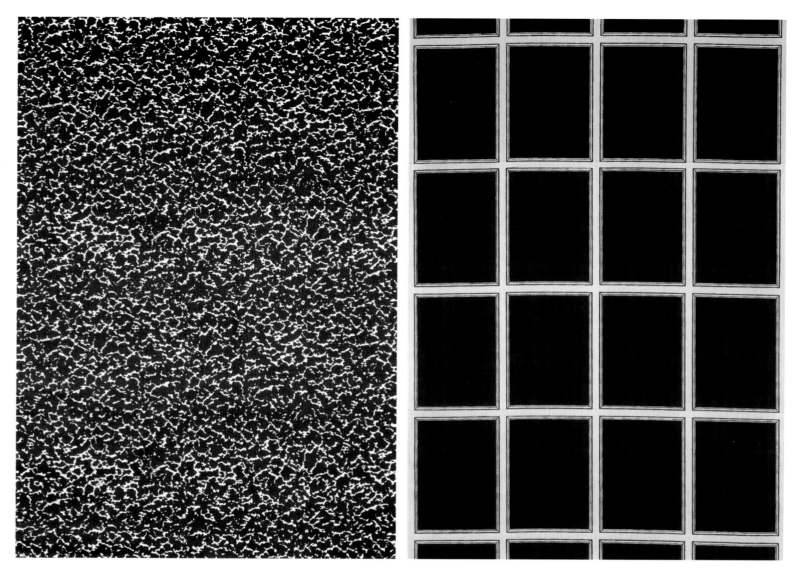

**186. Denise Scott Brown**
(born 1931, Nkana, Northern Rhodesia)
**Robert Venturi**
(born 1925, Philadelphia, PA, USA)
Textile, *Notebook*
Designed 1982. Printed cotton
291.5 x 132.8 cm (114¾ x 52⁵⁄₁₆ in.)
Produced by The Fabric Workshop (Philadelphia),
1982 to the present
Printed in black along one selvage: © *Robert Venturi*
1982 Hand printed at The Fabric Workshop,
Philadelphia
D85.106.1, The Liliane and David M. Stewart Collection


*"I found an old cardboard filing box — 3 x 5 card file — made of cardboard and covered with a black and white pattern which was the old convention for office pieces made from cardboard.... It was a nice pattern; but as we developed it, it changed somewhat from that cardboard file pattern. It lost some of the line quality and it became just the blops of the white and black and then it looked more like the conventional composition book cover that every kid uses in school. That is why it's called* Notebook. *Of course, we weren't terribly original in doing that. We were very much inspired by the Pop Art aesthetic of the moment."*
Denise Scott Brown, 1990[30]

**187. Scott Burton**
(born 1939, Greensboro, AL, USA;
died 1989, New York, NY)
Textile, *Fabric for Window Curtains*
Designed 1978. Printed cotton
297.2 x 127.7 cm (117 x 50¼ in.)
Produced by The Fabric Workshop
(Philadelphia, PA), 1978
Unmarked
D85.101.1, The Liliane and David M. Stewart Collection


*"Burton's* **Fabric for Window Curtains,** *described ... as 'the pattern of window mullions against the dark blue of the night's sky,' refers to what they conceal. Burton's intention that his curtains function as an antidote to claustrophobia is a light-hearted approach to issues of decoration."*
Carrie Rickey, 1979[31]

**188. Studio Tetrarch (Milan, Italy)**
Table, *Tablecloth (Tovaglia)*
Designed 1969. Fiberglass-reinforced polyester
38.4 x 111.1 x 111.1 cm (15⅛ x 43¼ x 43¼ in.)
Produced by Alberto Bazzani
(Bovisio Masciago), c. 1969-76
Unmarked
D94.135.1, gift of Eleanore and Charles Stendig in
memory of Eve Brustein and Rose Stendig*

"... the Tablecloth *table was created as a provocative answer
to the incapacity prevalent among the majority of designers of
that particular period to interpret correctly the use of a new
material like plastic.... In fact, with very few exceptions, this
new material and all its derivatives that were about to invade
the market came to be used, especially early on, in imitation of
other materials already widely used in design, such as wood,
iron, etc. In order to denounce such misuse, we wanted to give
a further twist to the argument by imitating a fabric tablecloth,
conferring on it the 'reality' of a table. Paradoxically, this was
meant to be a friendly admonition and a lighthearted reproach
to our fellow designers, almost as if we had wanted to tell them
to be careful, because by imitating the 'ways' of wood and iron,
one could end up not only confusing one material with another,
taking away their own semantic identity, but even mixing up form
and content, that is to say, in our case, tablecloth and table."*
Enrico De Munari, 1995[32]

**189. Marzio Cecchi**
(born 1940, Capalle, Italy; died 1990, New York, NY, USA)
Table lamp, *Bundle (Fagotto)*
Designed 1972
Cotton, polyester resin, iron
25.4 x 39.3 x 37.9 cm (10 x 15½ x 14¹⁵⁄₁₆ in.)
Produced by Studio Most (Florence), 1972 to the present
Signed in black ink at top: *Marzio Cecchi*
D94.332.1, gift of Eleanore and Charles Stendig in memory of Eve Brustein and Rose Stendig*

*"There are essentially two sources of inspiration for these objects: the 'transposition' of the animal world into design and the constant search for unusual materials. In fact, almost every piece was conceived from the relatively faithful transposition of themes and forms derived from the animal or vegetal kingdoms. Sometimes, there is a truly hyperrealistic effect. In other cases, the reference to nature is merely suggested and is achieved through the use of nontraditional materials (resins, steel, plexiglass).*

*Although the functional aspect of objects is always present, what undoubtedly prevails is the ironic spark, the intellectual provocation.... And maybe it is because of that very reason that, more than a quarter of a century later, we look at these objects with amazement and (why not) amusement: for luck, fantasy, and irony will never go out of style."*
Cesare Birignani, 1995[33]

**190. Peter Macchiarini**
(born 1909, Santa Rosa, CA, USA)
Necklace
Designed c. 1955. Silver, ebony, ivory
6.1 x 40 x 0.7 cm (2⅜ x 15¾ x ¼ in.)
Impressed on side of one silver element: MACCHIARINI
D94.250.1, gift of Paul Leblanc

*"I had bought some old, broken-down*
*ivory billiard balls. I cut up the billiard*
*balls and mounted some of the pieces*
*in rings, etc. Some of the ivory bits*
*suggested a piano to me. That is what*
*I was trying to state in a different sort*
*of a way. It was unconscious."*
Peter Macchiarini, 1994[34]

**191. Beth Levine**
(born 1914, Patchogue, NY, USA)
Shoes, *Racing Car*
Designed c. 1967. Vinyl, suede, patent leather, leather
D93.260.1: 11.5 x 22.8 x 7 cm (4½ x 9 x 2¾ in.)
D94.168.1: 11.3 x 22.4 x 7 cm (4⁷⁄₁₆ x 8¹³⁄₁₆ x 2¾ in.)
Produced by Herbert Levine (New York), 1967
Stitched in red on cloth label affixed to innersole of
each: *herbert levine*; written in black ink inside heel
of each: *Filly 4 1/2B*
D93.260.1, The Liliane and David M. Stewart
Collection; D94.168.1, gift of Beth Levine

*"Harper's Bazaar wanted to do something*
*about cars. So ... we did the first car*
*shoe ... [it became] a famous picture*
*and it really looked like a little car....*
*Look, shoes can be very serious, or very*
*funny.... I once said, 'These are shoes*
*that you don't need, but you want.' That's*
*about it.... Why not enjoy it? Why not?"*
Beth Levine, 1993[35]

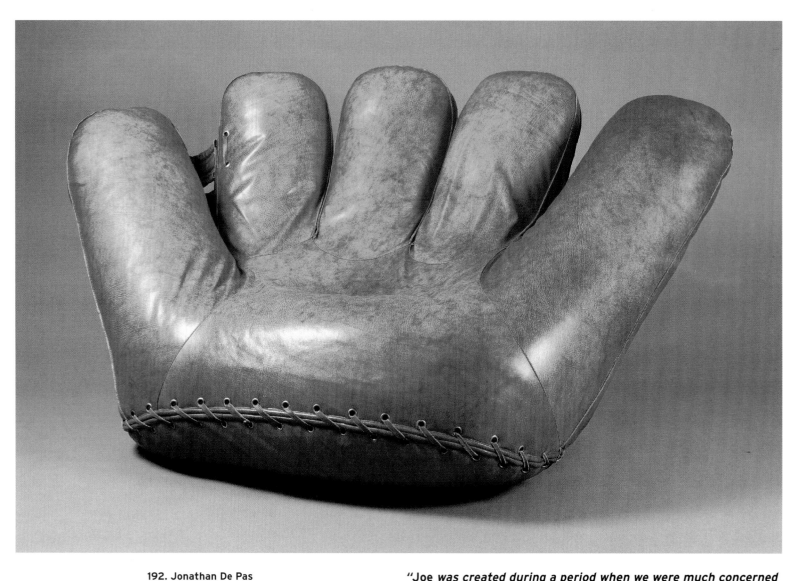

**192. Jonathan De Pas**
(born 1932, Milan, Italy; died 1991, Milan)
**Donato D'Urbino**
(born 1935, Milan)
**Paolo Lomazzi**
(born 1936, Milan)
Sofa, *Joe*
Designed 1970. Leather, polyurethane foam
94 x 191 x 120 cm (37⅛ x 75¾ x 47⅜ in.)
Produced by Poltronova S.p.A. (Pistoia),
1970 to the present
Embossed on bottom right corner:
DePas/D'Urbino/Lomazzi; on little finger:
[device of a star]
D95.163.1, gift of Eleanore and Charles Stendig in
memory of Eve Brustein and Rose Stendig*

"*Joe was created during a period when we were much concerned with getting off the beaten track and turning away from hackneyed methods.... We were spurred on by the technical possibilities arising from new materials which had just become available (poly-urethane foam and others) and which made feasible designs in forms hitherto impossible. We certainly had no desire to make inroads with the general public, preferring rather to reach a young clientele hoping to break with the 'bourgeois' interior design traditions of their parents....*

*The baseball glove has more ironic content than any real reference to any 'icon of American life.' We were obviously much preoccupied with and interested in works by Pop artists of the time to whom we felt a close affinity.*"
Donato D'Urbino, 1995[36]

**193. Piero Gilardi**
(born 1942, Turin, Italy)
Seating, *The Rocks (I Sassi)*
Designed 1967. Painted polyurethane foam,
mica flakes
1: 45.7 x 67.3 x 59.7 cm (18 x 26½ x 23½ in.)
2: 17.1 x 27.9 x 19 cm ( 6¾ x 8 x 7½ in.)
3: 14 x 20.3 x 14 cm (5½ x 11 x 5½ in.)
Produced by Gufram s.r.l. (Balangero), 1967–c. 1973
Impressed near underside of largest seat:
SEDISASSO/DESIGN/GILARDI/PER LA GUFRAM;
impressed on underside: 1
D94.154.1-3, gift of Eleanore and Charles Stendig in
memory of Eve Brustein and Rose Stendig*

*"My work is a kind of tactile art. I was trying to create a fantastic nature landscape for men living among all the modern city's concrete.... When I was in New York, I had a 160 square-foot nature fake displayed on the floor of Fischbach's gallery. Adults walked all around it and were amused and intrigued. Then a bunch of teenagers came in and in the most casual way sat and lay down on it and continued their talking. They were absolutely right and they got the message I wanted to express.*

*Maybe instead of nature fakes in man-made material I'll start making machine tool fakes in natural material. I don't know what will come out of my current research. And I don't want to know. Art today is nourished more by technology than tradition but it still keeps the magic of art ... it is a boundless happening."*
Piero Gilardi, 1968[37]

**194. Fulvio Bianconi**
(born 1915, Padua, Italy; died 1996, Milan)
Candlestick
Designed c. 1948. Glass
28.8 x 14 x 10.5 cm (11⁵⁄₁₆ x 5½ x 4⅛ in.)
Produced by Venini S.p.A. (Murano), c. 1948
Acid-stamped on underside: *venini*/MADE IN ITALY
D94.308.1, The Liliane and David M. Stewart
Collection

"He's an amusing boy, Fulvio. He has the
gift of life at his fingertips, takes a pencil
and produces 'living' drawings which are
incisive and cheeky.... Working at Venini,
Fulvio Bianconi is able to express his
sense of life in glass.... Bianconi animates
the glass as easily as a humorist works
with a pencil – the glass transforms into
characters, silhouettes or figurines,
masks or grotesques, all fundamentally
alive, ready to take on another form, to set
off into another life.... What is glass for
Bianconi? A way of expressing yourself
wittily; scintillating, lively, burlesque,
ironic – satirical behind the tomfoolery."
Marielle Ernould-Gandouet, 1986[38]

**195. Adelle Lutz**
(born 1948, Lakewood, OH, USA)
Jacket and pants, *Ivy Suit*
Designed 1986. Wool blend, polyester, cotton,
acrylic paint
Jacket: 77.5 x 44.5 cm (30½ x 17½ in.)
Pants: 109.5 x 38 cm (43⅛ x 15 in.)
Unmarked
D95.186.1-2, gift of David Byrne*

"The Urban Camouflage series was
designed as part of a fashion show for the
film True Stories.... Conceptually, the
first thought was that these outfits allow
one to blend into one's town rather than
stand out. Middle-class folks disappearing
into their suburban environment.
Secondly, it was important that the outfits be fantastic yet truly wearable; they
could be improbable but not preposterous
... although I never mass-produced any
of the pieces, fashion designers have
indeed incorporated the same motifs of
wood-paneling for their coats and created
clothing that looks like a brick wall going
for a stroll. It's not that inconceivable
anymore."
Adelle Lutz, 1995[39]

**196. Andrea Branzi**
(born 1938, Florence, Italy)
Floor lamp, *Sanremo*
Designed 1968. Enameled steel, enameled aluminum,
acrylic plastic
238.7 x 89 x 89 cm (94 x 34¹⁵⁄₁₆ x 34¹⁵⁄₁₆ in.)
Produced by Poltronova S.p.A. (Pistoia) for Archizoom
Associati (Florence), 1968-72
Printed on metallic paper label affixed to base:
L'altra casa Bruno Arosio Arredamenti s.a.s./
37100 Verona-stradone Scipione Mattei,
12/14/-tel. 27438/Centro Arredamenti Sormani/
37100 Verona via Carlo Cattaneo,
21-tel. 32246; typewritten on
paper sticker: MADE IN ITALY
D90.192.1, The Liliane and David M. Stewart Collection

*"This lamp belongs to the 'Islamic' period of Archizoom
Associati, referring to the theories of Malcolm X (to whom our
'Centro di Cospirazione Eclettica' at the Milan Triennale was
dedicated). This cultural position was meant to introduce some
Arabian elements, the 'kitsch,' and eclecticism (such as our
Afro-Tyrolian style) into modern design."*
Andrea Branzi, 1993[40]

**197. Guido Drocco**
(born 1942, San Benedetto Belbo, Italy)
**Franco Mello**
(born 1945, Genoa)
Coat/hat stand, *Cactus*
Designed 1972. Painted polyurethane foam, steel
168.4 x 71.8 x 63.2 cm (66⅜ x 28¼ x 24⅞ in.)
Produced by Gufram s.r.l. (Balangero),
1972 to the present
Unmarked
D91.371.1, anonymous gift

*"The attitude towards design during this period was closely linked to the Italian cultural experience of 1968, which was contesting rule-based attitudes. So it was that free rein was given to imagination, to transposing functions, to the 'idea' idea. In the case of the* Cactus *I think there is something else: irony. By irony I mean bracketing off and gazing unconvinced, yet amused, at what's being done and everything that arises from what's been done."*
Guido Drocco, 1995[41]

**198. Léon Kann**
(dates of birth and death unknown)
Coffee service, *Fennel (Fenouil)*
Designed c. 1898. Glazed porcelain
Coffeepot: 18.5 x 18 x 9 cm (7⁵/₁₆ x 7¹/₁₆ x 3⁹/₁₆ in.)
Produced by Manufacture Nationale de Sèvres
(Sèvres), 1898-1913
Coffeepot and sugar bowl, printed in black on
underside: s/1912 [in a triangle]; incised: RL-057PN
Each cup, printed in black on underside: s.98
[in a rectangle with rounded corners]; incised,
respectively: AD 1898 PN; AD 1298 PN
Each saucer, printed in black on underside: s/1902
[in a triangle]; incised: JC-011-01 AC/PN
Tray, printed in black on underside: s/1902
[in a triangle]; incised AD 1-02 PN
D94.300.1-7, The Liliane and David M. Stewart
Collection

*"... the humble plants of the forest and field, with their forms
clearly defined, furnish by far the largest part of the inspiration.
The attachment of the stems, the disposition of the leaves and
flowers upon their stems give the most characteristic elements
of the drawings. The elements of the flower, itself, its petals,
pistils, stamens and seeds will often give simpler motives of
ornament which are well-adapted to purposes of decoration."*
Paul Cret, 1904[42]

**199. Louis Comfort Tiffany**
(born 1848, New York, NY, USA; died 1933, New York)
Table lamp, *Pond Lily*
Designed c. 1900. Bronze, glass
54.5 x 28.5 x 28.5 cm (21½ x 11¼ x 11¼ in.)
Produced by Tiffany Studios (New York), c. 1900-20
Base impressed on underside: TIFFANY STUDIOS/NEW
YORK/382; shades engraved: *L.C.T. Favrile*
D94.177.1, The Liliane and David M. Stewart Collection

*"A visit to the Tiffany exhibit of electroliers ... will not only prove a delight but show the most surprising results in artistic and mechanical treatment. Metals and Favrile glass are the master-artist's favorite combinations. With these he produces forms of the greatest beauty, as well as wondrous colors.... To assist the designer's delicate fancy nature has been invoked through flowers, fruits, trees, shrubs, leaf, branch and vine, as well as many of the aquatic plants of Eastern lands.... What inspiration could excel that of using lily pad and stem as we see them in all their diversity and the admirable way they have been marked out in metal for the purpose."*
The Art Interchange, 1903[43]

*"A chair entitled Getsuen, meaning 'a moonlit garden,' has the image of the Kikyo flower [a Chinese bellflower] secretly blooming in such a garden. Kikyo is one of my favorite graceful flowers and I look forward to seeing it bloom in my little garden every summer.... [The] expression ka-cho-fu-getsu — meaning 'flowers, birds, the wind and the moon' — is often quoted to show the Japanese sense of beauty.... [The Japanese used to be] materially poor but spiritually rich. Japan's economic-growth-oriented progress since the Second World War, based on modern industrialization in the West, has given priority to function and efficiency, and has destroyed beautiful nature, historical heritage and peoples' minds.... This sad reality has made me try to love animals, plants and nature just like the good old Japanese used to do. That's why my design works are full of motifs of animals, plants, and nature. It also expresses my hope that people might remember to love creatures and nature in any way through my design."*
Masanori Umeda, 1994[44]

**200. Masanori Umeda**
(born 1941, Kanagawa, Japan)
Armchair, *Moonlit Garden (Getsuen)*
Designed 1990. Cotton velvet, polyurethane foam,
Dacron, polyethylene, lacquered iron, steel
83.2 x 100.4 x 92.1 cm (32¾ x 39½ x 36¼ in.)
Produced by Edra S.p.A. (Pisa, Italy),
1990 to the present
Unmarked
D93.259.1, gift of Maurice Forget

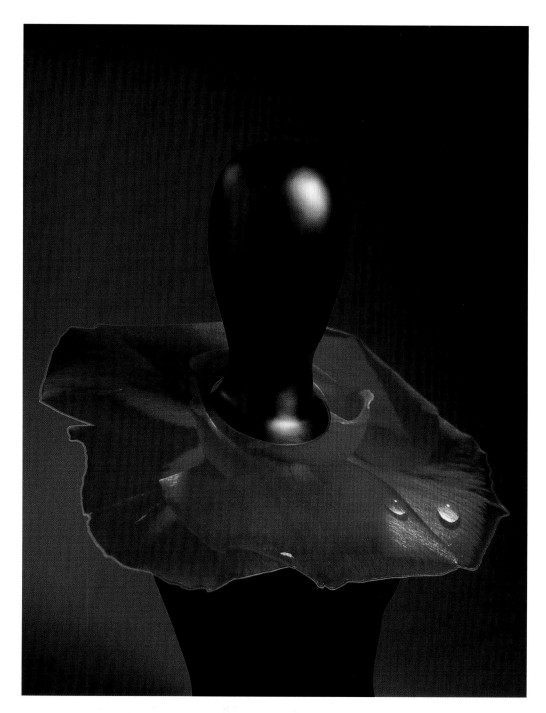

**201. Gijs Bakker**
(born 1942, Amersfoort, The Netherlands)
Neckpiece, *Dewdrop*
Executed 1982. PVC-laminated photograph
48.9 x 55.6 x 0.2 cm (19¼ x 21⅞ x ¹⁄₁₆ in.)
Signed in black ink on underside:
*"dew drop" 1982  nr 34/GBakk*
D90.100.1, The Liliane and David M. Stewart Collection

*"Throughout the history of jewelry, artists have always been influenced by nature; it is my preference, however, to use the natural images directly by incorporating actual photographs of flowers or by using the elements themselves (i.e., petals). We know that jewels can be, among other things, symbols of beauty; the rose is also a symbol of beauty and in Dewdrop I fuse them together to complement the person. By wearing this neckpiece, an individual becomes one with the flower and attains a state of natural beauty. I am intrigued also by the concept that this work appears as a visual metaphor for John the Baptist. One's head is offered on a red plate and the transferred value of a drop of blood appears in the form of a dewdrop. This work combines my interest in nature, illusion, design, and ornament."*
Gijs Bakker, 1994[45]

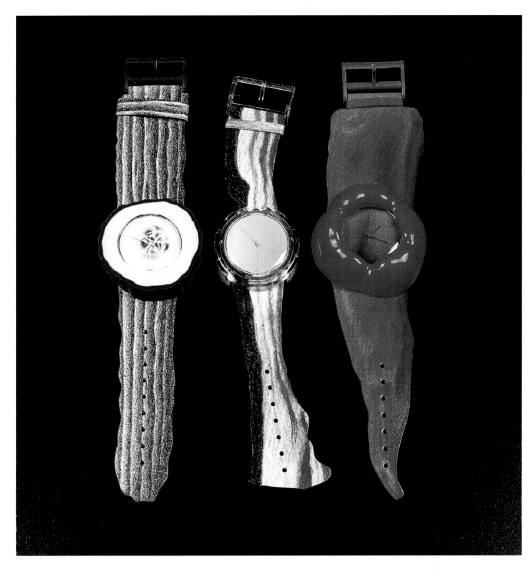

**202. Alfred Hofkunst**
(born 1942, Vienna, Austria)
Watch, *Swatchetable, One More Time: Guhrke*
Designed 1989. ABS plastic, silicone plastic, leather
25.5 x 5.6 x 1.5 cm (10¹⁄₁₆ x 2¹⁄₁₆ x ⁵⁄₈ in.)
Produced by Swatch AG (Biel, Switzerland), 1989
Printed in black on face: Swiss Quartz © SWATCH AG
1989/POP/swatch *Alfred Hofkunst*
D91.404.1, gift of Swatch AG

**203. Alfred Hofkunst**
Watch, *Swatchetable, One More Time: Bonjuhr*
Designed 1989. ABS plastic, silicone plastic, leather
23.7 x 5 x 1.3 cm (9⁵⁄₁₆ x 2¹⁄₄ x ¹⁄₂ in.)
Produced by Swatch AG (Biel), 1989
Printed in black on face: Swiss Quartz © SWATCH AG
1989/POP/swatch *Alfred Hofkunst*
D91.404.2, gift of Swatch AG

**204. Alfred Hofkunst**
Watch, *Swatchetable, One More Time: Verduhra*
Designed 1989. ABS plastic, silicone plastic, leather
25.2 x 6.6 x 2.2 cm (9⁷⁄₈ x 2⁹⁄₁₆ x ¹³⁄₁₆ in.)
Produced by Swatch AG (Biel), 1989
Printed in black on face: Swiss Quartz © SWATCH AG
1989/POP/swatch *Alfred Hofkunst*
D91.404.3, gift of Swatch AG

*"In studying the words* Swatchetable, Guhrke, Bonjuhr, *and* Verduhra, *I realized that they are, of course, a play on words — a* Wortspiel *in four languages:* Swatchetable=*English for vegetable;* Guhrke=*German for pickle;* Bonjuhr=*French for good morning; and* Verduhra=*Italian for vegetables.* Uhr *is German for watch, and three of the languages used are the languages of Switzerland. Furthermore, the imagery of each watch is a visual pun — a* Witz *based on the concept of language."*
Toni Greenbaum, 1995[46]

*"The titles of my watches represent a play on words, but at the same time the watches are a visualization of the interaction between vegetables, consumer GOODS, and the phenomenon of TIME. They symbolize the passage of time. Vegetables grow and VANISH. So does time — but we are not aware of this FACT. And therefore the ACT of measuring time with a watch is ULTIMATELY a strange way of closing our EYES to a natural PHENOMENON."*
Alfred Hofkunst, 1995[47]

**205. Antoinette Champetier de Ribes**
(born 1892, Paris, France; died 1972, Paris)
Nut dish, *Squirrel (Écureuil)*
Designed 1931. Silver-plated pewter alloy
19 x 18 x 11.2 cm (7½ x 7⅛ x 4⅜ in.)
Produced by Orfèvrerie Christofle (Paris), 1931–38
Impressed on underside: [device of a scale flanked
by two Cs within an oval, within a square]O.Gallia
[in rectangle]5989
D95.139.1, The Liliane and David M. Stewart Collection

*"This is the art which triumphed at the 1925 Exposition of Decorative Arts. Shapes have certainly become simplified and geometricized, although not necessarily always more functional; decoration is still based primarily on stylized floral and animal designs, but sinuous arabesques have given way to geometric simplifications in which some have wished to recognize Cubist influence."*
Tamara Préaud and Serge Gauthier, 1982[48]

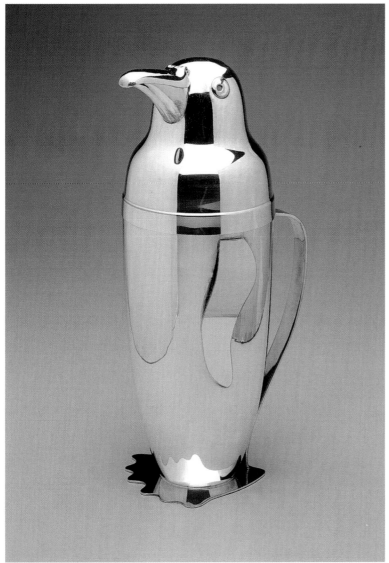

**206. Emile A. Schuelke**
(born 1901, Meriden, CT, USA;
died 1986, Wakefield, RI)
Cocktail shaker
Designed c. 1936. Silver-plated brass
31.7 x 10.4 x 15 cm (11¾ x 4⅛ x 5⅞ in.)
Produced by The Napier Co. (Meriden, CT),
c. 1936-38
Impressed on underside: NAPIER/PATENTS PEND./234
D95.107.1, The Liliane and David M. Stewart Collection

*"The perkiest shaker that ever poured a cocktail. And how
it pours ... right from the Penguin's beak with never a spill.
Holds 1½ quarts in his fat insides."*
Hammacher Schlemmer Advertisement, c. 1936[49]

**207. Leza Marie Sullivan McVey**
(born 1907, Cleveland, OH, USA;
died 1984, Mayfield Heights, OH)
Stoppered vessel
Executed c. 1955. Glazed earthenware
34.3 x 17.8 x 12.7 cm (13½ x 7 x 5 in.)
Incised on underside: *Leza*; painted in black on
underside: *Leza*
D82.127.1, gift of Mrs. Samuel Dushkin

*"Having been interested in sculpture before, I was just bored
with the regular forms.... I wanted things to be more interesting
and have more than one silhouette.... I like birds, I like animals,
I like movement, dancers. I like a sense of aliveness."*
Leza McVey, 1982[50]

**208. A. Douglas Nash**
(born 1885, Stourbridge, England;
died 1940, Pittsburgh, PA, USA)
Stemware, *Silhouette*
Designed c. 1933. Glass
Center bowl: 20.3 x 25.4 x 25.4 cm (8 x 10 x 10 in.)
Produced by Libbey Glass Company
(Toledo, OH), 1933-35
Unmarked
D94.303.1 and D94.304.1, The Liliane and
David M. Stewart Collection;
D95.113.1, gift of Geoffrey N. Bradfield*

*"To the invigorated huntsman, an amusing design called
Silhouette will go admirably on the hunt breakfast table. The
animals which form the stem are wonderfully molded, with
flat planes, in simple character. They may be had in black glass
with the pure glass tops, or in a fascinating, opalescent tone,
elusive but with great symmetry. The center bowl filled with
red crabapple branches would contrast strikingly with the ...
silhouetted animals and the sparkle of the crystal."*
Agnes Foster Wright, 1933[51]

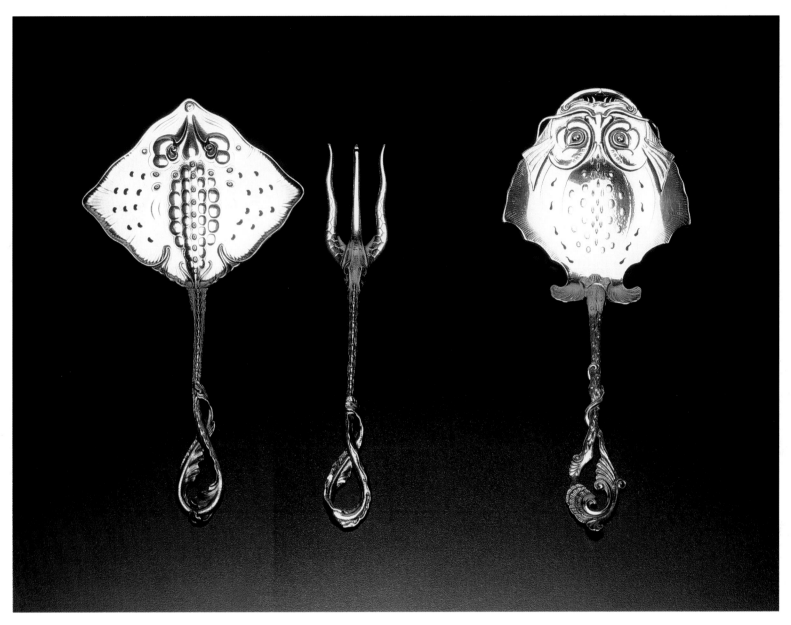

"What an inexhaustible source of beauty the sea is! If it contains wonders, its shores are of no less interest to us than its depths ...

   And from all these studies, the artist, and the decorative artist above all, easily brings forth numerous enticing styliz-ations, ornaments which might appear strange at first sight, but which are a new source of inspiration. They will help to renew the motifs of our ornamental art, which too often is content with forms, beautiful no doubt, but whose overly frequent and exclu-sive use has gradually made banal, and which it would be useful to abandon for a while."
Maurice P. Verneuil, 1924[52]

**209. Theodor Engebøe**
(born 1879, Bergen, Norway; died 1942, Bergen)
Fish service
Designed c. 1920. Silver
Server: 26.7 x 13.4 cm (10½ x 5¼ in.)
Fork: 24.5 x 4.2 cm (9⅝ x 1⅝ in.)
Produced by Theodor Olsen's Eftf.
(Bergen), c. 1920-30
Server: Impressed on underside of handle: 830s/NM
Fork: Unmarked
D94.184.1-2, The Liliane and David M. Stewart Collection

**210. Theodor Engebøe**
Fish server
Designed c. 1924. Silver
27.8 x 11.4 cm (10¹⁵⁄₁₆ x 4½ in.)
Produced by Kristian Hestenes (Bergen), c. 1924-32
Impressed on underside of handle: KH/830s
D94.203.1, The Liliane and David M. Stewart Collection

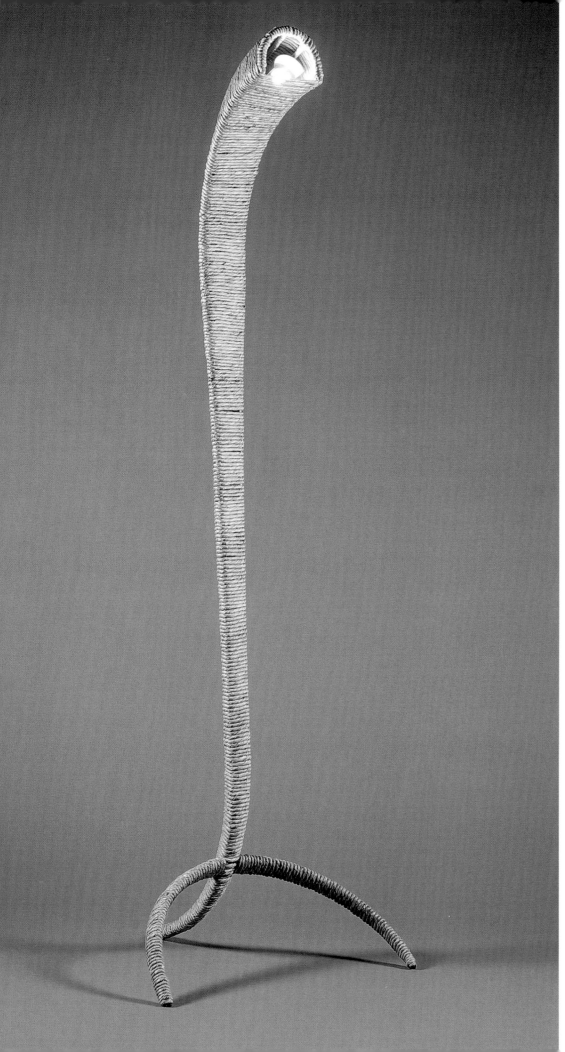

**211. Tom Dixon**
(born 1959, Sfax, Tunisia)
Floor lamp prototype, *Cobra*
Designed 1987. Steel, rush
214 x 75 x 61 cm (84¼ x 29½ x 24 in.)
Prototype produced by Dixon P.I.D. (London, England),
1987; produced by Cappellini International Interiors
(Arosio, Italy), 1990 to the present
Unmarked
D93.249.1, The Liliane and David M. Stewart Collection

*"The name of this lamp is incidental; it really did come after the object. I started working in a period in which people were using predominantly angular forms and applied finishes. Finding these unsatisfactory. I started my research into more natural and softer materials which could be used in a decorative way without having to add decoration as an end in itself.... I am always keen to encourage people to read meanings into work. I do, however, very rarely think about this type of thing when I am actually making the pieces. They evolve in an organic way and my main concerns have to do with elegance of lines and the nature of materials."*
Tom Dixon, 1993[53]

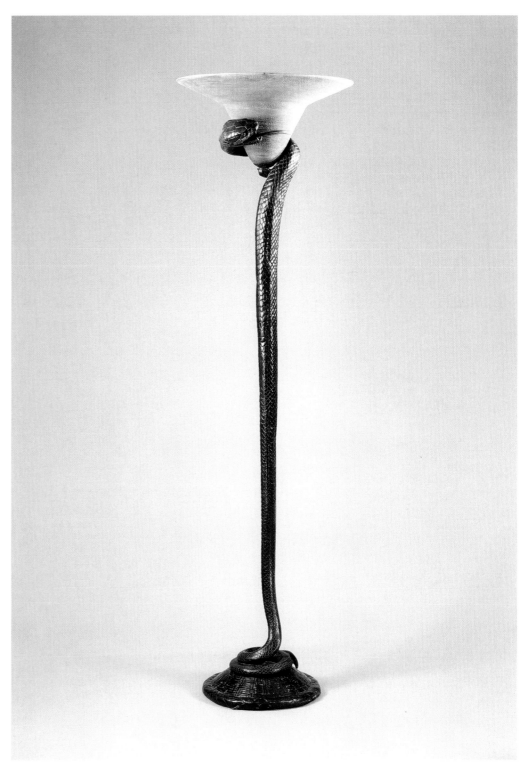

"The cobra appears repeatedly in the thematic language of Edgar Brandt, the **Snake Vase** of 1913 and this lamp, **The Temptation,** *being the two most famous examples. The exotic animal kingdom of the French colonies with its elephants, lions, and cobras had an influence on decorative arts in general and in particular on* animalier *sculpture (a category to which this artifact belongs as much as it belongs to Art Deco lighting)."*
Dan Klein, 1995[54]

**212. Edgar Brandt**
(born 1880, Paris, France;
died 1960, Geneva, Switzerland)
Floor lamp, *The Temptation (La Tentation)*
Designed c. 1925. Bronze, glass
161.3 x 47 x 47 cm (63½ x 18⅝ x 18⅝ in.)
Base produced by Edgar Brandt (Paris);
shade produced by Daum Frères, Verrerie de Nancy
(Nancy), c. 1925-30
Impressed near base: E BRANDT; incised on shade near
rim: DAUM [device of the cross of Lorraine] Nancy
D94.286.1, The Liliane and David M. Stewart Collection

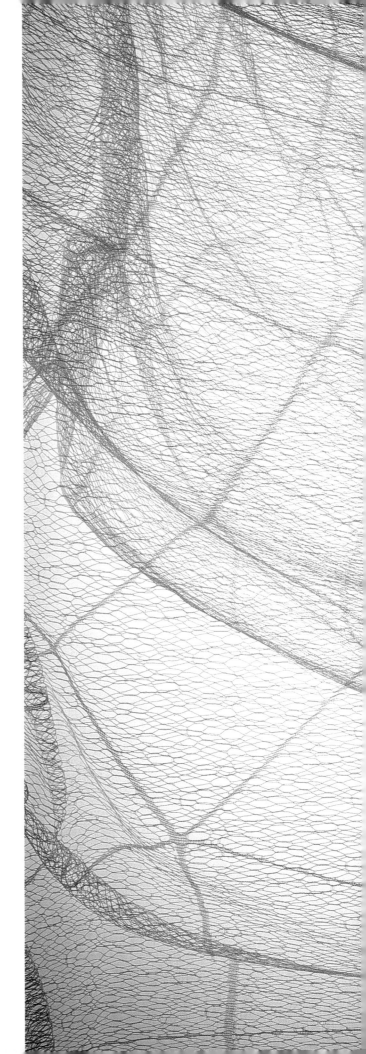

"It was twenty years ago that I saw the original Inca fabric. Concerning this, I found the following excerpt ... by Mr. Kasai, the director of Kawashima Fabric Research Institute, [which] moved me more than studying and analyzing the original art by myself: 'I have a dream. Lace was originally a handmade fabric, but nowadays almost all lace is made by machines....' His words struck me like lightning. After struggling with an old Raschel lace machine, I succeeded in producing the basic structure of Spider Web.... The drawing for Spider Web was done by my wife, Riko Arai. Very knowledgeable in Greek mythology, she drew dozens of spider webs. I selected two among them.... This one is the first of them."
Junichi Arai, 1995[55]

**213. Junichi Arai**
(born 1932, Kiryu, Japan)
**Riko Arai**
(born 1933, Kiryu)
Textile, *Spider Web*
Designed 1982. Silk
284 x 99.1 cm (111¹³⁄₁₆ x 39 in.)
Produced by Nuno Corporation (Tokyo),
1982 to the present
Unmarked
D92.147.1, The Liliane and David M. Stewart Collection

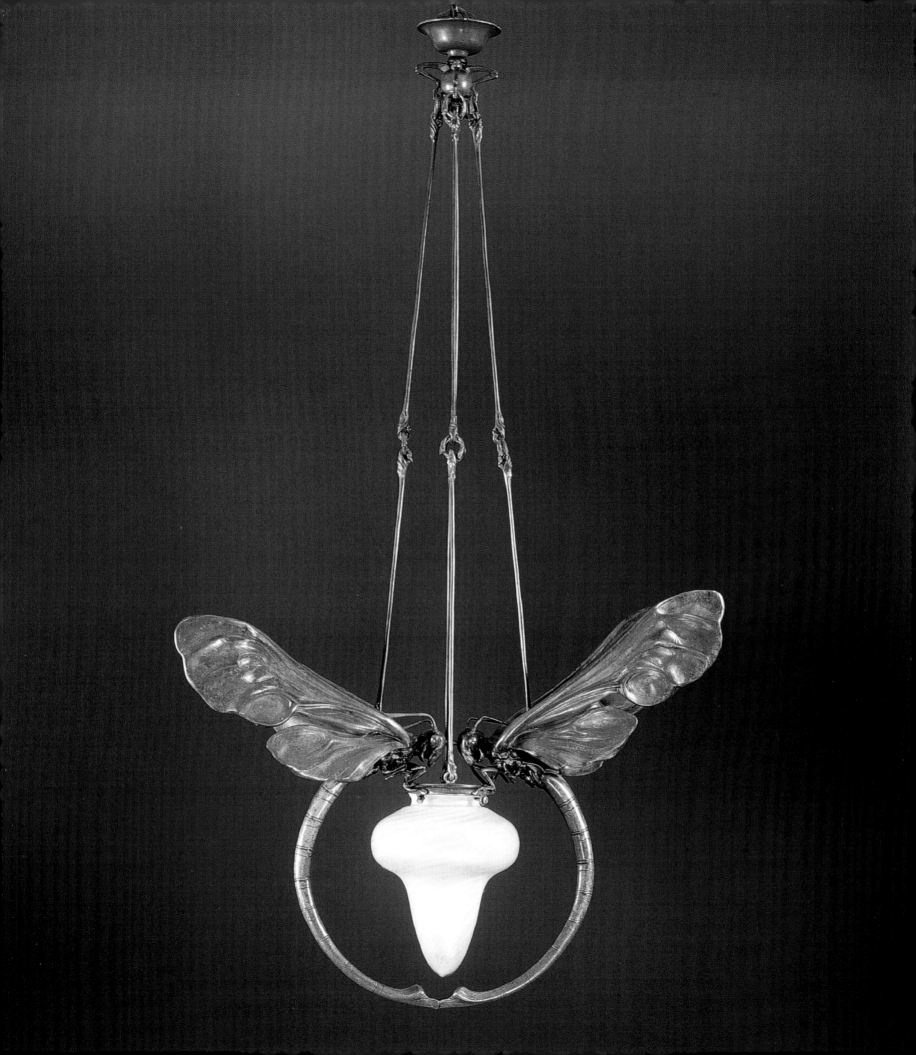

**214. Unknown designer
(France)**
Hanging lamp
Designed c. 1900. Bronze, glass
98.5 x 54 x 15 cm (38¾ x 21¼ x 5⅞ in.)
Unmarked
D95.142.1, The Liliane and David M. Stewart Collection

*"It is astonishing how little known are the
infinite resources that a well-organized
study of insects would bring to ornamental art. We were discussing those who
have already taken up this theme, and
you can see the happy result they have
been able to extract from several species:
the grasshopper, the dragonfly, and above
all, butterflies."*
Maurice P. Verneuil, 1904[56]

**215. Riccardo Dalisi**
(born 1931, Potenza, Italy)
Bench, *Mariposa*
Designed 1989. Steel, paint
88 x 102 x 59 cm (34⅝ x 40⅛ x 23¼ in.)
Produced by Zanotta (Nova Milanese), 1989;
painted by Dalisi
Impressed on seat back: 4;
signed in black ink: *2/9 Dalisi*
D95.164.1, The Liliane and David M. Stewart Collection

*"The* Mariposa *bench reminds us of a
butterfly. Many of the things we buy are
like sculptures, because we have everything
already.... We are working on a kind of
research design with free expression that
seems to have nothing to share with
design.... Knickknacks are back, new areas
now open to every kind of collector. Such
work coexists with art and creates
intermediary spaces for new art forms."*
Riccardo Dalisi, 1994[57]

**216. Ingo Maurer**
(born 1932, Reichenau, Germany)
Table lamp, *Bibibibi*
Designed 1982. Porcelain, steel, brass, aluminum, polyurethane, feathers
65.6 x 29.8 x 29.8 cm (25¹³/₁₆ x 11¾ x 11¾ in.)
Produced by Ingo Maurer GmbH (Munich), 1982 to the present
Printed in white on base:
400/500F/bibibibi/INGO/MAURER
D88.161.1, gift of Ingo Maurer GmbH

*"I went to Woolworth's just around the corner where they usually sell plastic things. I found the plastic flowers, and suddenly I saw a pair of bright red plastic feet, obviously belonging to a stork, but there was no body. I was electrified when I saw these feet. I grabbed them and immediately had a vision of what I would do with them: I would do a light. I asked the salesperson for the price but she was not prepared to sell the feet because of the missing body. There was no price tag for the feet only. So I had no option but to shoplift them.... The Milano Fair was coming up and I thought it would be nice to provoke the high priests of the design world. I showed it: shock and enthusiastic reactions."*
Ingo Maurer, 1994[58]

**217. Édouard-Eugène-Victor Chapelle**
(born 1897, Nancy, France; died 1968, Nancy)
Table lamp
Designed c. 1925. Wrought iron, glass, marble
39.4 x 31.8 x 17.2 cm (15½ x 12¾ x 6¾ in.)
Armature produced by Chapelle (Nancy); glass
produced by Muller Frères (Croismare), c. 1925
Incised on base: CHAPELLE = NANCY
D94.302.1, The Liliane and David M. Stewart
Collection

*"Members of the stork family (cranes, herons, and storks) have been no strangers to European decorative arts since their appearance as decorative symbols (imported from Japanese decorative art) in the mid-nineteenth century. They often make an appearance in French Art Deco furniture and lighting....*

*In this lamp ... a popular decorative theme has been subjected to a technical fad of the period for blowing coloured glass through a decorative wrought iron armature, a technique often also used by Daum and Majorelle working as a team to create coloured vases and bowls, sometimes with metallic inclusions in the glass."*
Dan Klein, 1996[59]

# Notes

MODERNISM'S ALTER EGO

1. Peter Behrens, quoted in W. Fred, "Artists' Colony at Darmstadt," *The Studio* 24 (October 1901): 29.

2. Irene Sargent, "The Wavy Line," *The Craftsman* 2 (June 1902): 131.

3. Sigmund Freud, *Civilization and its Discontents*, trans. James Strachey (1930; reprint, New York: W. W. Norton, 1961), 25–26.

4. Stig Lindberg, "Stig Lindberg," *Everyday Art Quarterly* 23 (Fall 1952): 15.

BODIES OF THOUGHT, BODIES OF EVIDENCE

1. Terence, *Heauton Timorumenos*, I, i, 25, "Humani nihil a me alienum puto."

2. See John Berger, *Ways of Seeing* (Harmondsworth, England: Penguin Books, 1972). The book derives from a BBC television series.

3. *New Observations* 70 (September 1989):14–15. The Guerrilla Girls typically produce broadsides that have become a familiar sight pasted onto buildings in lower Manhattan and which are gathered together in this issue of the magazine.

4. For Mammy's Cupboard, see John Margolies, *The End of the Road: Vanishing Highway Architecture in America* (New York: Penguin Books, 1981), fig. 61; Karal Ann Marling, *The Colossus of Roads: Myth and Symbol Along the American Highway* (Minneapolis: University of Minnesota Press, 1984), 77.

5. The design also recalls a central image in Günter Grass's *The Tin Drum* (1959) — that of seeking solace under a woman's skirt.

6. See Jeff Santori, "Not (in) These Parts," *New City* (Chicago), 14 May 1992.

7. See Peter Watrous, "Album Cover Change," *New York Times*, 21 August 1991; Liz Smith, "Hollywood Hari-Kari?" *New York Newsday*, 9 August 1991.

8. Bernth Lindfors, "'Hottentot Venus' and Other African Attractions in Nineteenth-century England," *Australasian Drama Studies* 1 (April 1983): 84, 86.

9. Lawrence W. Levine, *Highbrow/Lowbrow: The Emergence of Cultural Hierarchy in America* (Cambridge, Massachusetts: Harvard University Press, 1988), 208–12. People on display in "authentic" African villages, for example, were in actuality African-Americans, recruited locally; see Robert Bogdan, *Freak Show: Presenting Human Oddities for Amusement and Profit* (Chicago: University of Chicago Press, 1988), 47–51.

10. Quoted in Jane Clapp, *Art Censorship: A Chronology of Proscribed and Prescribed Art* (Metuchen, New Jersey: Scarecrow Press, 1972), 133.

11. Quoted in Nicola Beisel, "Morals Versus Art: Censorship, the Politics of Interpretation, and the Victorian Nude," *American Sociological Review* 58 (April 1993): 151.

12. See Anne Middleton Wagner, *Jean-Baptiste Carpeaux: Sculptor of the Second Empire* (New Haven, Connecticut: Yale University Press, 1986), 236–55.

13. Quoted in Charles C. Baldwin, *Stanford White* (1931; reprint New York: Da Capo Press, 1976), 209.

14. Ibid., 210. There were protests as well against nude statues displayed inside the Fine Arts Building at the exposition, protests orchestrated by Catholic leaders across the country; see "Object to the Nude," *Kansas City Star*, 20 February 1893. A stereopticon slide from the time shows part of the exhibit and declares — probably facetiously — "Go cover your Neckedness."

15. See Clapp, *Art Censorship*, 237.

16. I draw from my own previous account of this controversy: Steven C. Dubin, *Arresting Images: Impolitic Art and Uncivil Actions* (New York: Routledge, 1992), 48–49.

17. Clapp, *Art Censorship*, 218.

18. Richard Goldstein, "Doowutchyalike: In the Brave New World, Sex Sells," *Village Voice*, 6 November 1990.

19. Linda Nochlin, "Eroticism and Female Imagery in Nineteenth-Century Art," in *Women, Art, and Power and Other Essays* (New York: Harper & Row, 1988), 138, fig. 2.

20. Ibid., 141.

21. Sigmund Freud, "Humour," in *Collected Papers* (London: Hogarth, 1950), 218.

22. Chairs made by New Yorker Alan Siegel and by Londoner Anthony Redmile (reproducing a design from the 1930s) have also twisted the female form into furniture, their laps accommodating others' bodies.

23. A mid-twentieth-century British postcard shows two buddies golfing. One has just balanced his ball upon the nipple of a voluptuous naked woman, who appears to be passed out in the grass. The other says, "That's cheating Fred, you're not supposed to tee up in the rough!" In addition, a brand of golf tees manufactured in the United States in the 1920s was named "Nigger Head," the package featuring a grotesquely caricatured black man warily eyeing the golf tee sticking out from his own temple. There is also an abundance of American-made postcards that show women and blacks about to be eaten by hungry alligators. Presumably, neither group was intelligent enough to escape this danger. Taken together, these items and many

    others indicate that certain codes made disadvantaged groups interchangeable as the target of popular culture "gags."

24. Nochlin explains, "Created by the author with the sympathetic cooperation of the male model at Vassar College"; Linda Nochlin, *Women, Art, and Power*, 144, n. 5.

25. Eunice Lipton, *Alias Olympia: A Woman's Search for Manet's Notorious Model & Her Own Desire* (New York: Charles Scribner's Sons, 1993). In the Postmodernist spirit, Lipton also interweaves her findings with her own musings and autobiographical details.

26. Today we are much more sensitive to the role of models, their interaction with the artist, and what they contribute to the final product. When Australian designer and performance artist Leigh Bowery died in 1994, he was accorded an obituary in the *New Yorker* (16 January) that spilled over two pages. He was memorialized not as an artist, but in his better-known role as Lucian Freud's burly model, a presence that animated the painter's canvases in a signature manner.

27. Much more meaning can be squeezed from this work. For example, the fact that the artist/model is Asian raises questions regarding Western views of Asian sexuality. Furthermore, the type of mass-produced figurine substituted for the original black cat addresses questions of high and low culture.

28. See Margalit Fox, "A Portrait in Skin and Bone," *New York Times*, 21 November 1993; Roberta Smith, "Surgical Sculpture: The Body as Costume," *New York Times*, 17 December 1993. Mention should also be made of Cindy Jackson, a woman living in England whom you could call Orlan's low-culture counterpart: she has spent over $60,000 on more than twenty surgical procedures in order to make herself look like a Barbie doll.

## HOMO ORNARENS

1. John Summerson, *Heavenly Mansions and Other Essays on Architecture* (New York: W.W. Norton, 1963), 216.

2. Peter Nabokov and Robert Easton, *Native American Architecture* (New York: Oxford University Press, 1989), 255.

3. George Hersey, *The Lost Meaning of Classical Architecture* (Cambridge, Massachusetts: MIT Press, 1988), 31.

4. Mary McCarthy, *The Stones of Florence and Venice Observed* (New York: Penguin Books, 1985), 264–65.

## BODY LANGUAGE

1. Mario Botta, letter to the Montreal Museum of Decorative Arts [hereafter referred to as MMDA], 20 April 1995.

2. Niki de Saint-Phalle, as quoted in Roger Cohen, "At Home with Niki de Saint-Phalle," *New York Times*, 7 October 1993.

3. Riccardo Dalisi, "Pulcinella's Design," *Italian Quality* (Rome: Edisi, 1992), 52.

4. Richard Notkin, "Standing Alone," *Studio Potter* 16 (December 1987): 20.

5. Niki de Saint-Phalle, letter to MMDA, 28 April 1996.

6. Olivier Mourgue, "Une Histoire pour les architectes," *L'Architecture d'Aujourd'hui* 155 (April 1971): 46.

7. Mieczyslaw Górowski, letter to MMDA, 21 March 1994.

8. Red Grooms and Lysiane Luong, interview with MMDA, 12 October 1994.

9. Gaetano Pesce, interview with MMDA, 14 June 1993.

10. Ibid.

11. Riccardo Dalisi, letter to MMDA, 23 November 1994.

12. Jean Lorrain, as quoted in Philippe Jullian, *The Triumph of Art Nouveau: Paris Exhibition 1900* (New York: Larousse, 1974), 88–89.

13. Sam Kramer, "Gems in New Contexts," *Craft Horizons* 12 (October 1952): 34.

14. Franco Deboni, letter to MMDA, 8 October 1995.

15. "L'Art de la Rupture," press release, Jean-Paul Gaultier Haute Parfumerie, 1993.

16. Johan Møller Nielsen, *Wegner en dansk Møbelkunstner* (Copenhagen: Glydendal, 1965), 123.

17. Sam Kramer, "Creating Spontaneous Jewelry," *Design Magazine* 53 (May 1952): 179.

18. Roger Marx, "La Parure de la femme: Les Bijoux de Lalique," *Les Modes* 1 (June 1901): 10.

19. Hans Schliepmann, "Hans Christiansen," *Deutsche Kunst und Dekoration* 2 (June 1898): 298.

20. Ulysses Dietz, letter to MMDA, 30 May 1996.

21. Peter Selz, *Art Nouveau: Art and Design at the Turn of the Century*, exh. cat. (New York: The Museum of Modern Art, 1960), 16.

22. "Picasso as Potter," *Craft Horizons* 10 (Summer 1950): 13.

23. Vally Wieselthier, "Ceramics," *Design* 31 (November 1929): 101.

24. Dan Klein, letter to MMDA, 11 December 1995.

25. Sam Jornlin, letter to Michael McTwigan, 18 February 1994.

26. Martin Eidelberg, letter to MMDA, 3 April 1995.

27. Isamu Noguchi, *A Sculptor's World* (New York: Harper & Row, 1968), 24.

28. Barbara Lynn, letter to MMDA, 14 April 1994.

29. Andrea Branzi, letter to MMDA, 22 July 1993.

30. Ed Wiener, "Non-Objective Forms," in *Jewelry by Ed Wiener*, exh. cat. (New York: Fifty/50 Gallery, 1988), 25.

31. Sam Kramer, "Creating Spontaneous Jewelry," 198.

32. Andrea Branzi, letter to MMDA, 22 July 1993.

33. Brooks Adams, "Architects at Tea," *House and Garden* 156 (May 1984): 54.

34. Stephen Frykholm, "Twenty Picnics, Twenty Posters" (Address delivered at a retrospective of Frykholm's picnic posters, Herman Miller picnic, Zeeland, Michigan, 22 July 1989, Photocopy), 1–2.

35. Wendell Castle, interview with MMDA, 8 March 1996.

36. Bruno Martinazzi, "Autobiography of Bruno Martinazzi, Goldsmith and Sculptor, Professor at the Accademia di Belle Arti di Torino," *Goldsmiths' Journal* 4 (August 1978): 37.

37. David Palterer, letter to MMDA, July 1994.

38. Pedro Friedeberg, letter to MMDA, 24 August 1994.

39. Stephen Neil Greengard, *Piero Fornasetti: Furniture and Objects,* exh. cat. (New York: Gallery 280, 1989), n.p.

40. Richard Notkin, letter to MMDA, 3 December 1994.

41. Eugene M. Ettenberg, "Robert Brownjohn: A Young Designer Whose Work Is Marked with Wit and Intelligence," *American Artist* 23 (June 1959): 71.

42. Ettore Sottsass, "The Fornasetti World," in Patrick Mauriès, *Fornasetti: Designer of Dreams* (London: Thames and Hudson, 1991), 11.

43. Giò Pomodoro, letter to MMDA, 17 May 1995.

44. Gerd Rothmann, letter to Toni Greenbaum, 30 December 1993.

45. Ken Ferguson, letter to MMDA, February 1995.

## INVERSION AND TRANSFORMATION

1. Jasper Johns, "Sketchbook Notes," *Art and Literature* 4 (Spring 1965): 185–92.
2. Augustus Welby Northmore Pugin, as quoted in Christopher Dresser, *Principles of Decorative Design* (1873; reprint, London: Academy Editions, 1973), 20–21.
3. Edgar Kaufmann, jr., *What is Modern Design?* (New York: The Museum of Modern Art, 1950), 7.
4. Kirk Varnedoe, *Vienna 1900: Art, Architecture and Design*, exh. cat. (New York: The Museum of Modern Art, 1986), 87.
5. Gaetano Pesce, interview with MMDA, 11 March 1994.
6. Guido Niest, letter to MMDA, 23 July 1991.
7. Flavio, the son of Alfredo Barbini, is a designer and art director for his father's glassmaking firm. While this vase was previously attributed to the elder Barbini, Flavio was responsible for its design, as revealed by Alfredo and Flavio Barbini in an interview with MMDA, 16 June 1994.
8. John Ruskin, *The Seven Lamps of Architecture* (1880; reprint, New York: Dover Publications, 1989), 35.
9. Kaufmann, *What is Modern Design?*, 7.
10. Michael McTwigan, letter to MMDA, 9 March 1994.
11. Shiro Kuramata, as quoted in Chee Pearlman, "Shiro Kuramata," *International Design* 35 (September/October 1988): 31.
12. Martin Eidelberg, letter to MMDA, 18 October 1993.
13. Idem., 24 August 1994.
14. Masanori Umeda, letter to MMDA, 7 July 1995.
15. "New Forms That Are Not Bizarre," *House Beautiful* 101 (July 1959): 80.
16. Karel Wasch, *Glas en Kristal*, 1927, as quoted by Mecheld de Bois, *Chris Lebeau 1878–1945*, exh. cat. (Haarlem: Frans Halsmuseum, 1987), 172.
17. Gaetano Pesce, interview with MMDA, 11 March 1994.
18. David Palterer, interview with MMDA, 15 April 1994.
19. Claus Lorenz, director of the Friedrich Otto Schmidt Atelier für Antike Wohnungseinrichtung, Vienna, letter to MMDA, 23 August 1994.
20. Shigeru Uchida, letter to MMDA, 18 December 1995.
21. Dale Chihuly, letter to MMDA, 21 December 1994.
22. Chee Pearlman, "Shiro Kuramata," *International Design* 35 (September/October 1988): 31.
23. Ettore Sottsass, interview with MMDA, 13 April 1994.
24. Philippe Starck, letter to MMDA, 18 December 1995.
25. Edvard Lehmann, "Die Fabriek Rozenburg," in *Kunsthandwerk I: Jugendstil, Werkbund, Art Deco – Glas, Holz, Keramik*, exh. cat. (Berlin: Karl H. Bröhan, 1976), 1: 353.
26. Hans Tietze, "Josef Hoffmann zum Fünfzigsten Geburtstag am 15. Dezember," *Kunstchronik und Kunstmarkt* 32 (10 December 1920): 204.
27. Félix Marcilhac, letter to MMDA, 30 April 1996.
28. Ettore Sottsass, letter to MMDA, 9 July 1996.
29. Martin Eidelberg, letter to MMDA, 6 December 1994.
30. Alessandro Mendini, as quoted in Richard Horn, "Mystifyingly Familiar," *Metropolis* 6 (April 1987): 61.
31. Philippe Starck, letter to MMDA, 7 November 1995.
32. Philippe Garner, letter to MMDA, 4 April 1996.
33. Gianni Pettena, *Hans Hollein: Works 1960–1988* (Milan and New York: Idea Books Edizioni, 1988), 96.
34. *Rosenthal Verkaufsdienst* 63 (September 1955), n.p.
35. Masanori Umeda, letter to MMDA, 16 June 1994.
36. Toshiko Takaezu, letter to MMDA, 7 July 1995.
37. René Chavance, "Maurice Marinot, peintre et verrier," *L'Art et les artistes* 33 (January 1923): 154.

38. Franco Deboni, letter to MMDA, 8 October 1995.

39. Alfredo Barbini, interview with MMDA, 16 June 1994.

40. Matteo Thun, letter to MMDA, 22 December 1994.

41. Alessandro Mendini, letter to MMDA, 30 November 1995.

42. Andrea Branzi, letter to MMDA, 22 July 1993.

43. Gaetano Pesce, interview with MMDA, 11 March 1993.

44. Ron Arad, interview with MMDA, 15 April 1994.

45. Andrea Branzi, "Purple Shadows," *Terrazzo* 3 (Fall 1989): 84.

46. "Aus den Rosenthal-Ateliers," *Die Kunst und das schöne Heim* 50 (December 1951): 120.

47. Massimo Iosa Ghini, interview with MMDA, 14 April 1994.

48. Gianfranco Frattini, letter to MMDA, 25 January 1995.

49. Elizabeth Browning Jackson, letter to MMDA, 5 August 1994.

50. Guido Niest, letter to Toni Greenbaum, 10 January 1994.

51. Flavio Barbini, interview with MMDA, 16 June 1994.

52. Enzo Mari, letter to MMDA, 14 December 1993.

53. Alessandro Mendini, letter to MMDA, 30 November 1995.

54. Jane Fiske Mitarachi, "Kåge's Fractured Forms," *Interiors* 112 (June 1953): 81.

55. Stig Lindberg, in "Stig Lindberg," *Everyday Art Quarterly* 23 (Summer 1952): 15.

56. Andrea Branzi, letter to MMDA, 22 July 1993.

57. Astrid Sampe, letter to MMDA, 12 September 1994.

58. Junichi Arai, letter to MMDA, 27 January 1995.

59. William Warmus, "Foreword," *Venini and the Murano Renaissance: Italian Art Glass of the 1940s and 50s*, exh. cat. (New York: Fifty/50 Gallery, 1984), n.p.

60. Dale Chihuly, as quoted in Barbaralee Diamonstein-Spielvogel, "From a Seattle Boathouse Dale Chihuly Floats Ideas in Glass," *House and Garden* 165 (July 1993): 32.

61. Arnold Zimmerman, letter to Michael McTwigan, 9 February 1994.

62. Frank Gehry, interview with MMDA, 24 May 1991.

63. Ibid.

64. "Fashion: Paper Capers," *Time* 87 (18 March 1966): 71.

65. Issey Miyake, as quoted in Peter Popham, "The Emperor's Clothes," *Blueprint* 15 (March 1985): 16.

66. Janna Syvänoja, letter to MMDA, 27 January 1995.

67. Ron Arad, interview with MMDA, 15 April 1994.

68. Adele Freedman, "Breaking the Bonds," *Progressive Architecture* 9 (September 1988): 76.

69. Paco Rabanne, *Trajectoire: d'une vie à l'autre* (Paris: Édition° 1/Michel Lafon, 1991), 137–38.

70. Arline M. Fisch, letter to MMDA, 6 November 1995.

71. Reiko Sudo, letter to MMDA, 8 July 1994.

72. Oliver Lundquist, letter to MMDA, 10 May 1994.

73. Junichi Arai, letter to MMDA, 26 January 1995.

## Is Ornament a Crime?

1. Adolf Loos, "Ornament und Verbrechen," in *Trotzdem 1900–1930* (Innsbruck: Brenner-Verlag, 1931), 79–92.

2. See the exhibition catalogue *Die Form ohne Ornament* (Stuttgart: Deutsche Verlags Anstalt, 1924). The exhibition encompassed a wide range of examples, from Ancient Rome and China to modern Europe.

3. Alfred H. Barr, Jr., foreword, in Philip Johnson, *Machine Art*, exh. cat. (New York: The Museum of Modern Art and W.W. Norton, 1934), n.p.

4. Edgar Kaufmann, jr., *What is Modern Design?*, exh. cat. (New York: The Museum of Modern Art, 1950), 7.

5. Christopher Dresser, *The Art of Decorative Design* (London: Day and Son, 1862), 179.

6. John Ruskin, *The Stones of Venice*, 3 vols. (London: 1851–53), 1: 14.

7. Charles F. A. Voysey, as quoted in "An Interview with C.F.A. Voysey," *The Studio* 1 (April

1893): 236.

8. "For the decoration, take up once again the motif[s] which did not change from the Renaissance until Louis Philippe. Give them renewed life." André Mare, letter to Maurice Marinot, 20 February 1912, as quoted in Nancy J. Troy, *Modernism and the Decorative Arts in France: Art Nouveau to Le Corbusier* (New Haven: Yale University Press, 1991), 72.

9. Robert Venturi, "Process and Symbol in the Design of Furniture for Knoll" (Venturi, Scott Brown and Associates, Inc., Philadelphia, 1983).

10. "We wanted to use ordinary and conventional patterns in a relatively not ordinary and unconventional way ... to juxtapose hard and soft — pretty and geometric ... contrasting the geometric kind of dark double-stick pattern on the kind of sentimental floral." Robert Venturi, interview with Marion Boulton Stroud of the Fabric Workshop, Philadelphia, March 1990.

11. Owen Jones, "Proposition 8," in *The Grammar of Ornament* (London: 1850), 5.

12. Armin Friedmann, "Sezessionistische Tafelfreuden," *Neues Wiener Tagblatt* (16 October 1906).

13. Jack Lenor Larsen, letter to MMDA, 2 June 1995.

14. Walter Dorwin Teague, "Industrial Art and its Future," *Art and Industry* 22 (May 1937): 194.

15. Frank Lloyd Wright, "Organic Architecture," *Architects' Journal* (August 1936); reprinted in Frederick Gutheim, ed., *Frank Lloyd Wright on Architecture: Selected Writings 1894–1940* (New York: Duell, Sloan and Pearce, 1941), 188.

16. Siegfried Giedion, *Mechanization Takes Command* (New York: Oxford University Press, 1948), 344.

17. Eugène Grasset, "Introduction," in *La Plante et ses applications ornementales*, 2 vols. (Paris: E. Lévy. 1899) 1: n.p.

18. Berta Zuckerkandl, *Wiener Allgemeine Zeitung* (3 December 1905), as quoted in Werner J. Schweiger, *Wiener Werkstätte: Design in Vienna 1903–1932* (New York: Abbeville, 1984), 47.

19. Helmut Ricke, ed., *Lötz: Böhmisches Glas 1880–1940*, 2 vols. (Munich: Prestel–Verlag, 1989), 1:268.

20. W. Fred, "Austrian Jewellery," in Charles Holme, ed., *Modern Design in Jewellery and Fans* (London: The Studio, 1901), n.p.

21. Hartwig Fischel, "Neue Serapis-Fayencen," *Dekorative Kunst* 21 (December 1912): 149–50.

22. Arthur Roessler, "Emanuel Margold Architekt Wien," *Deutsche Kunst und Dekoration* 28 (April 1911): 53.

23. *Italian Ceramics* (Rome: Italian Institute for Foreign Trade, n.d.), 16.

24. André Véra, "Le Nouveau style," *L'Art décoratif* 27 (January 1912): 32.

25. Léon Moussinac, "Quelques interprétations nouvelles de la flore," *Art et décoration* 39 (January 1921): 3–4.

26. Nicole Maritch-Haviland, letter to MMDA, 30 January 1996.

27. David Revere McFadden, ed., *Scandinavian Modern Design 1880–1980* (New York: Harry N. Abrams, 1982), 192.

28. Peter Max, interview with MMDA, 9 August 1994.

29. Emilio Pucci, as quoted in Susan Smith, "Pucci's Survival Plan: Hold the Italian Line," *Women's Wear Daily*, 23 April 1976.

30. Denise Scott Brown, interview with Marion Boulton Stroud of the Fabric Workshop, Philadelphia, 10 March 1990.

31. Ettore Sottsass, letter to MMDA, 4 July 1995.

32. J. Alastair Duncan, letter to MMDA, 26 February 1996.

33. Colin McDowell, *McDowell's Directory of Twentieth-Century Fashion* (Englewood Cliffs, New Jersey: Prentice-Hall, 1985), 224.

34. Berta Zuckerkandl, "Ludwig Heinrich Jungnickel — Frankfurt," *Deutsche Kunst und Dekoration* 32 (August 1913): 360.

35. Floris Meydam, letter to MMDA, 16 June 1995.

36. P.-M. Grand, "Verrerie," *Art et décoration* 24 (September/October 1951): 2.

37. Massimo Vignelli, letter to MMDA, 18 October 1995.

38. Gunnar Cyrén, letter to MMDA, 10 June 1995.

39. Mario Botta, letter to MMDA, 20 April 1995.

40. Roseline Delisle, letters to MMDA, 26 and 27 June 1995.

41. Dorothy Hafner, interview with MMDA, 15 December 1994.

42. Sergio Asti, letter to MMDA, 20 October 1994.

43. Josef Folnesics, "Wiener Kunstgewerbeverein," *Dekorative Kunst* 9 (January 1902): 138.

44. Jack Lenor Larsen, letter to MMDA, 2 June 1995.

45. Earl Pardon, "A Wall of Rugged Elegance," *Skidmore Alumnae Bulletin* 39 (December 1960): 3.

46. Jeanne Anne Vincent, "A New Northern Light," *Interiors* 112 (April 1953): 96.

47. Léon Werth, "Le XVIIe Salon des Artistes Décorateurs," *Art et décoration* 51 (June 1927): 162.

48. Ibid., 163.

49. Walter Dorwin Teague, *Design This Day* (New York: Harcourt Brace, 1940), 91, 141.

50. Edna L. Nicoll, *A travers l'exposition coloniale* (Paris: E. L. Nicoll, 1931), 61.

51. Blanche Naylor, "Textiles Derived from Paintings," *Design* 33 (February 1933): 219.

52. Rolph Scarlett, interview by Harriet Tannin, 1979, as quoted in *Rolph Scarlett: Early Master of the Non-Objective*, exh. cat. (Woodstock, New York: Woodstock Artists Association, 1993), n.p.

53. Ruth Adler Schnee, letter to MMDA, 17 September 1994.

54. Ross Littell, letter to MMDA, 24 August 1995.

55. Eva Rudberg, *Sven Markelius, Architect* (Stockholm: Arkitektur Förlag, 1989), 123.

56. Ralph Bacerra, letter to Michael McTwigan, 2 March 1994.

57. Fujiwo Ishimoto, letter to MMDA, 3 May 1994.

58. Alessandro Mendini, letter to MMDA, 30 November 1995.

59. Nathalie Du Pasquier, letter to MMDA, 24 November 1995.

60. Alessandro Mendini, letter to MMDA, 30 November 1995.

61. Peter Chang, letter to Helen W. Drutt English, 17 July 1995.

62. Eddie Squires, letter to MMDA, 27 June 1994.

**FLIGHTS OF FANTASY**

1. Le Corbusier, *L'Art décoratif d'aujourd'hui*, 1925, as quoted in Renato De Fusco, *Le Corbusier, Designer: Furniture, 1929* (Woodbury, NY: Barron's, 1977), 17.

2. Franz Kafka, *Tagebücher, 1910–23* (Frankfurt: 1951), 552, as quoted in Stephen Kern, *The Culture of Time and Space 1880–1918* (Cambridge, Massachusetts: Harvard University Press, 1983), 17.

3. Gio Ponti, "The Teaching of Others and the Fantasy of the Italians," *Domus* 259 (June 1951): 11.

4. Matthew Kangas, "Rudy Autio: Massive Narrations," *American Craft* (October/November 1980): 13.

5. Two decades earlier, Roy Lichtenstein was inspired by the same type of commonplace composition book, as seen in his painting *Composition I* (1964), now in the Museum für Moderne Kunst, Frankfurt.

6. Guirand de Scévola, the inventor of camouflage, acknowledged his debt to Cubism, noting: "In order to totally deform objects, I employed the means Cubists used to represent them." See André Ducasse, Jacques Meyer, Gabriel Perreux, *Vie et mort des Français, 1914–1918* (Paris: 1962), 510–11, as cited in Kern, *The Culture of Time and Space*, 302–03.

7. Salvador Dalí, as quoted in Lida Livingston, ed., *Dalí: A Study of his Art-in-Jewels: The Collection of The Owen Cheatham Foundation* (Greenwich, Connecticut: The New York Graphic Society, 1959), 12.

8. George Nelson, "Architects of Europe Today, 4: Gio Ponti, Italy," *Pencil Points* 16 (May 1935): 215–16.

9. "Peter Todd Mitchell," *Jardin des arts*, no. 172 (March 1969), 85.

10. Peter Todd Mitchell, "Textile Design as a Career," 1946, 2, Peter Todd Mitchell Papers, New

York, private collection.

11. Joan Miró, as quoted in James Johnson Sweeney, "Joan Miró: Comment and Interview," *Partisan Review 15* (February 1948): 200.

12. Saul Steinberg, as quoted in Pierre Schneider, *Louvre Dialogues* (New York: Atheneum, 1971), 83–84.

13. Erik Blomberg, "Swedish Practical Art at the Göteborg Exhibition," *Stockholmstidningen* (June 1923), as cited in Arthur Hald, *Simon Gate, Edward Hald* (Stockholm: Svenska Slöjdföreningen, 1948), 76–77.

14. Rudy Autio, interview with Michael McTwigan, 10 February 1994.

15. Joyce Scott, interview with MMDA, 31 October 1995.

16. Robert Ebendorf, letter to Toni Greenbaum, 5 June 1994.

17. Antoinette Faÿ-Hallé, letter to MMDA, 22 February 1996.

18. Ramón Puig Cuyás, letter to Toni Greenbaum, 10 January 1994.

19. Ettore Sottsass, interview with MMDA, 13 April 1994.

20. Eddie Squires, letter to MMDA, 27 June 1994.

21. Edith M. Bushnell, "Skyscraper in Design," *Design* 30 (May 1928): 23.

22. Gaetano Pesce, interview with MMDA, 11 March 1993.

23. Maciej Urbaniec, letter to MMDA, 13 June 1994.

24. Robert Arneson, as quoted in Neal Benezra, *Robert Arneson: A Retrospective*, exh. cat. (Des Moines, Iowa: Des Moines Art Center, 1985), 67.

25. Paul Rand, "The Rebus," *Design Quarterly* 123 (1984): 24.

26. Gérard Gaveau, "Richard Craig Meitner," *Richard Meitner: Le Verre, le contraire et l'autre*, exh. cat. (Paris: Musée des Arts Décoratifs, 1991), 27–28.

27. Bruce Metcalf, interview with Toni Greenbaum, 11 October 1993.

28. Kiyoshi Kanai, letter to MMDA, 6 July 1994.

29. Tony Costanzo, letter to MMDA, 25 August 1994.

30. Denise Scott Brown, interview with Marion Boulton Stroud of The Fabric Workshop, Philadelphia, 10 March 1990.

31. Carrie Rickey, "Art of Whole Cloth," *Art in America* 67 (November 1979): 79.

32. Enrico De Munari, letter to MMDA, 19 January 1995.

33. Cesare Birignani, ed., *Marzio Cecchi: Fancy Designs 1969–1979* (Florence: Studio Most, 1995), n.p.

34. Peter Macchiarini, interview with Toni Greenbaum, 6 May 1994.

35. Beth Levine, interview with MMDA, 14 October 1993.

36. Donato D'Urbino, letter to MMDA, 3 November 1995.

37. Piero Gilardi, as quoted in Elisa V. Massai, "Youth Power," *Home Furnishings Daily*, 17 May 1968.

38. Marielle Ernould-Gandouet, "Galeries: Paris: Fulvio Bianconi," *L'Oeil* 371 (June 1986): 85.

39. Adelle Lutz, letter to MMDA, 5 October 1995.

40. Andrea Branzi, letter to MMDA, 22 July 1993.

41. Guido Drocco, letter to MMDA, 3 June 1995.

42. Paul Cret, "A Comparative Study of Sèvres Methods," *The Craftsman* 6 (July 1904): 363.

43. "Electroliers," *The Art Interchange* 51 (July 1903): 10.

44. Masanori Umeda, letter to MMDA, 15 June 1994.

45. Gijs Bakker, interview with Helen W. Drutt English, 29 March 1994.

46. Toni Greenbaum, letter to Alfred Hofkunst, 31 March 1995.

47. Alfred Hofkunst, letter to Toni Greenbaum, 3 April 1995.

48. Tamara Préaud and Serge Gauthier, *Ceramics of the 20th Century* (New York: Rizzoli, 1982), 58.

49. Undated (c. 1936) advertisement by Hammacher Schlemmer, New York, in the Napier Co. Archives, Meriden, Connecticut.

50. Leza McVey, interview with Martin Eidelberg, 24 June 1982.

51. Agnes Foster Wright, *The Hostess Through the Day* (Toledo, Ohio: Libbey Glass Company,

1933), n.p.

52. Mathurin Meheut and Maurice Pillard Verneuil, *Étude de la mer: faune et flore de la Manche et de l'océan*, 2 vols. (Paris: Éditions Albert Lévy, 1924), 1:10–12.

53. Tom Dixon, letter to MMDA, 18 October 1993.

54. Dan Klein, letter to MMDA, 11 December 1995.

55. Junichi Arai, letter to MMDA, 27 January 1995.

56. Maurice P. Verneuil, "Insecte," *Art et décoration* 15 (January 1904): 1, 12–13.

57. Riccardo Dalisi, letter to MMDA, 23 November 1994.

58. Ingo Maurer, letter to MMDA, 13 July 1994.

59. Dan Klein, letter to MMDA, 7 February 1996.

# Index

A selective index of names of artists, historical personages, institutions of learning, museums, professional associations, and exhibitions.

## Colophon

Typeset in Sabon and Interstate by Richard Hunt,
Archetype, Toronto

Printed on R-400, 150 g/m$^2$
Printed and bound by Milanostampa, Farigliano